Eusèbe Salverte, Anthony Todd Thomson

The Occult Sciences

The philosophy of magic, prodigies, and apparent miracles - From the French of

Eusèbe Saverte

Eusèbe Salverte, Anthony Todd Thomson

The Occult Sciences
The philosophy of magic, prodigies, and apparent miracles - From the French of Eusèbe Saverte

ISBN/EAN: 9783337314521

Printed in Europe, USA, Canada, Australia, Japan

Cover: Foto ©Lupo / pixelio.de

More available books at **www.hansebooks.com**

THE OCCULT SCIENCES.

THE

PHILOSOPHY OF MAGIC,

PRODIGIES, AND APPARENT MIRACLES.

FROM THE FRENCH OF

EUSEBE SALVERTE.

WITH NOTES ILLUSTRATIVE, EXPLANATORY,
AND CRITICAL,

BY ANTHONY TODD THOMSON, M.D., F.L.S., &c.

" Non igitur oportet nos magicis illusionibus uti, cum potestas philoso-
phica doceat operari quod sufficit."—ROG. BACON, *De secr. Oper. Art. et
Nat.*, c. v.

IN TWO VOLUMES.

VOL. II.

NEW YORK:

HARPER & BROTHERS, PUBLISHERS,
FRANKLIN SQUARE.

1862.

CONTENTS

OF

THE SECOND VOLUME.

CHAPTER IV.

CHAPTER V.

CHAPTER VI.

CHAPTER VII.

CHAPTER VIII.

CHAPTER IX.

CHAPTER X.

CHAPTER XI.

CHAPTER XII.

THE PHILOSOPHY

OF

MAGIC, PRODIGIES,

AND

APPARENT MIRACLES.

CHAPTER I.

Preparations of Drugs and Beverages, some Soporific, others for producing temporary Imbecility.—Circe.—Nepenthes.—Delightful Illusions; fearful Illusions; involuntary Revelations.—Invincible Courage, produced by Meats and Potions.—The Old Man of the Mountain deceived his Disciples by Illusions: he probably fortified them against Torture by stupefying Drugs.—The Use of them becomes habitual, and conduces to bodily Insensibility and Imbecility.

TRIUMPHANT over the obstacles which debarred him from attaining perfection, the initiated beheld all the hidden treasures of science laid open to him. It was no difficult task for him to unravel the secret of the wonders that, in the scenes of his first reception, penetrated him with religious admiration; but destined, thenceforth, to lay open to the profane the path of light, it was time he should learn to what operations he himself had been submitted; how his whole moral being had been subjected to their influences, and how he must employ the same means that had been used in his initiation, in order to obtain dominion over the minds of those who might aim at attaining to the same point at which he had arrived, and by what means he should display himself all-powerful, by his works, before those who were not permitted to participate in the divine dignity of the priesthood.

The aspirants to initiation, and those who came to request prophetic dreams of the gods, were prepared by a fast, more or less prolonged, after which they partook of meals expressly prepared; and also of mysterious drinks, such as the water of *Lethe** and the water of *Mnemosyne* in the grotto of Trophonius, or of the *Ciceion* in the mysteries of the Eleusinia. Different drugs were easily mixed up with the meats, or introduced into the drinks, according to the state of mind or body into which it was necessary to throw the recipient, and the nature of the visions he was desirous of procuring.

We know what accusations had been raised against some of the early sects of Christianity—charges which were unjustly reflected upon all Christian assemblies. They would scarcely be considered as unfounded, had many heresiarchs adopted the criminal practices imputed by popular rumor to the high-priests of the Markesians.† It is said that in their religious ceremonies aphrodisiac beverages were administered to women. Without

---

* The river which yielded the water of Lethe, and the fountain Mnemosyne, were both near the Trophonian grotto, which was in Bœotia. The waters of both were drunk by whoever consulted the oracle : the Lethian draught was intended to make him forget all his former thoughts; the Mnemosynian, to strengthen his memory, that he might remember the visions which he was about to see in the grotto. The latter seemed essential, as the consulter was obliged, after emerging from the grotto and recovering from his alarm, to write down his vision on a small tablet which was preserved in the temple.—Ed.

† The Markesians were a sect named from their chief, the heresiarch Mark, who was guilty of so many superstitions and impostures. Among others, St. Irenæus informs us, that in consecrating chalices filled with water and wine, according to the Christian rite, he filled the chalices with a certain red liquor which he called blood. He also permitted women to consecrate the holy mysteries.—Butler, *Lives of the Fathers, Martyrs, &c.,* vol. v., chap. xxviii

judging in this particular case, we believe that powerful aphrodisiacs* were occasionally used in the mysterious orgies of Polytheism; and it is only by admitting such a supposition, that we can explain the monstrous debaucheries to which the votaries of Bacchus gave themselves up in the Bacchanalian festivals, denounced and punished at Rome, in the year 186 B.C. A scene in a romance by Petronius† shows that they were used much later in the nocturnal reunions where superstitious rites were employed as a veil and an excuse for the excesses of libertinism. But such an expedient was extremely limited in its power : it disordered the senses ; yet it did not act on the imagination, though it delivered up the physical man to the power of the guilty Thaumaturgist; it did not destroy the moral faculty. The substances destined to produce, in secret ceremonies, the most important effects, were the simplest and most common opiates. We may readily conceive of what service they were to the Thaumaturgist; whether intended to close eyes too observing, and too quick to scrutinize the causes of the apparent miracles ; or to produce the alternatives of an unconquerable sleep, and a sudden awakening: effects well adapted to persuade the man who experiences them, that a supernatural power is sporting with his existence, and changing at his pleasure every circumstance that troubles or that amuses it. Their methods were various; a collection that we possess, and from which we shall

---

* St. Epiphan., *contr. Haereses*, lib. i., tome iii. ; *contr.* Marcosios, *Haeres.*, 24.

† Arbiter Petronius is supposed to have been a fictitious name bestowed upon the romance alluded to in the text ; while others assert that the romance was the production of Caius Petronius, a favorite of Nero, and a minister to his vicious pleasures. The work is a picture of the profligate manners of the period it describes, totally unfit for general perusal.—ED.

quote, furnishes us with two examples. In one case we are informed that a young prince was sent to sleep every evening by the juice of a plant, and every morning recovered from his torpor by the scent of a perfume.* Again—a sponge, steeped in vinegar and passed under the nose of Aben Hassan, provoked sneezing and a slight vomiting, which suddenly destroyed the effects of the soporific powder which rendered him insensible. In another instance, the same symptoms and results were produced, when a young princess, who had been sent into a deep sleep by a narcotic, was exposed to the open air.†

In a spot, far removed from the scenes of the Thousand and one Nights, we find the employment of a similar secret. Among the Nadoessis‡ in South America, there existed a religious society of men devoted to the Great Spirit. Carver witnessed the admission of a new member into it. The priests threw into the mouth of the candidate something that resembled a bean : almost immediately he fell down, immovable, insensible, and apparently dead. They gave him violent blows on the the back, but these did not restore sensibility, nor, for some minutes, bring him as it were to life again. When he did revive, he was agitated with convulsions, that did not cease until he had thrown up what they had made him swallow.§

Plutarch has preserved to us a description of the mysteries of Trophonius, related by a man who

* *The Arabian Nights*, 26th night, vol. i, p. 221.
† *Ibid.*, 295th night, vol. iv., pp. 97–149.
‡ Carver, *Travels in South America*, pp. 200, 201.
§ It is probable that the seed employed was the fruit of a species of strychnos, the effect of which is to produce paralysis, with convulsions. That it did not cause death might depend on the entire seed having been swallowed ; its influence in that state being considerably less than if it had been administered in pow der.—Ed.

had passed two nights and a day in the grotto.*
They appear to be rather the dreams of a person
intoxicated by a powerful narcotic than the description of a real spectacle. Timarches, the name of
the initiate, experienced a violent headache when
the apparitions commenced—that is to say, when
the drugs began to affect his senses; and when the
apparitions vanished and he awoke from this delirious slumber, the same pain was as keenly felt.
Timarches died three months after his visit to the
grotto; the priests, no doubt, having made use of
very powerful drugs. It is said that those who
had once consulted the oracle acquired a melancholy which lasted all their lives;† the natural consequence, no doubt, of the serious shock to their
health from the potions administered to them.

The consulters of the oracle, were, I believe,
carried to the gate of the grotto, when their forced
sleep began to be dissipated. The visions that occupied this slumber most probaby formed (as has
been also suspected by Clavier)‡ all the incidents
of the miraculous spectacle they believed to have
been exhibited by the gods. On awakening also,
after having been presented with a drink, probably
intended to restore entirely the use of their senses,
they were ordered to relate every thing they had
seen and heard; the priest requiring to know what
they had dreamed.

Powerful soporifics often possess the property
of deranging the intellect: the berries of the belladonna,§ when eaten, produce furious madness,

* Plutarch, *De Dæmonio Socratis.*
† Suidas.... Clavier, *Mémoire sur les Oracles, &c.*, pp. 159,
160.
‡ Clavier, *Mémoire sur les Oracles, &c.*, pp. 158, 159.
§ Atropa *belladonna,* deadly nightshade. has fruit resembling a
black cherry, seated within a large, green, persistent flower-cup
or calyx. The fruit is of a deep-black purple color, and contains

followed by a sleep that lasts twenty-four hours.
Still more frequently than bodily sleep, the sleep
of the soul, temporary imbecility, delivers up man
to the power of those who could reduce him to
this humiliating state. The juice of the datura*
seed is employed by the Portuguese women of
Goa : they mix it, says Linschott,† in the liquor
drank by their husbands, who fall, for twenty-four
hours at least, into a stupor, accompanied by continued laughing ; but so deep is the sleep, that nothing
passing before them affects them ; and when they
recover their senses, they have no recollection of
what has taken place. The men, says Pyrard,‡
make use of the same secret in order to submit to
their desires women who would consent by no
other means. Francis Martin,§ after having de-

many seeds, enveloped in a sweetish juice. Every part of the
plant is poisonous, and when eaten causes symptoms resembling
those of intoxication, with fits of laughter and violent gesticulations, followed by dilatation of the pupils of the eyes, delirium
and death. Buchanan, the Scottish historian, states that the victory of Macbeth over the Danes was obtained chiefly by mixing
the juice of this plant with wine, which was sent as a donation
from the Scots to Sweno during a truce. He adds, " Vis fructui,
radici, ae maxime semini somnifera, et quæ in amentium, si lar
gius sumantur, agat."—*Rerum Scot. Hist.*, lib. viii., § vi.—Ed.

* Datura *feros*, in doses sufficiently large to affect the brain,
causes indistinctness of vision, with a disposition to restless
sleep, accompanied with delirium, in which the most ridiculous
actions and absurd positions are exhibited. All the daturas,
namely, *fastuosa, metel, tatula*, and even *stramonium*, which is
employed as a medicine in this country, possess nearly simila.
poisonous properties. The species *metel* and *tatula* are employed
in the East Indies to cause intoxication for licentious and criminal purposes.—Ed.

† Linschott, *Narrative of a Voyage to the East Indies, with the
notes of Paludanus*, 3d edit., folio, pp. 63, 64, 111. The thorn-
apple, stramonium, a plant of the same family as the datura, produces similar effects ; it has sometimes been criminally employed
in Europe.

‡ *Voyage of Francis Pyrard* (2 vols. in 4to., Paris, 1679), tome
ii., pp. 68, 69.

§ Francis Martin, *Description of the first Voyage made by the
French to the East Indies*, pp. 163, 164.

tailed all the injurious effects of the daturas, adds, that the delirium may be arrested by placing the feet of the patient in hot water; the remedy causes vomiting, a circumstance which reminds us of the manner in which the sleeper and the young princess in the Arabian Nights, and the initiated Nadoessis, were delivered from their stupor.

A secret so effectual having fallen into the hands of the ignorant, must, there is reason to believe, have belonged to the Thaumaturgists, to whom it was much more important. Among the aborigines of Virginia, the aspirant to the priesthood was made to drink, during the course of his painful initiation, a liquor* which threw him into a state of imbecility. If, as we may suppose, the object of this practice was to render him docile, we may believe also, that the custom did not commence in the New World.† Magicians have, in all ages, made use of similar secrets.

The Oriental tales frequently present to us stories of powerful magicians changing men into animals. Varro, quoted by St. Augustin,‡ relates that the magicians of Italy, attracting near them the unsuspecting traveler, administered to him, in cheese, a drug which changed him into a beast of burden. They loaded him then with their baggage, and at the end of the journey restored him to his own form. Under these figurative expressions, quoted from Varro, who probably quoted from some prior work, we perceive that the traveler, being intoxicated by the drug he had taken,

* This liquor was procured by decoction from certain roots called *vissocan*; and the initiation was termed *Husca nawar*.

† In consulting most of the Grecian oracles, it was the custom either for the officiating priest, or the consulting person, to drink of some secret well, the water of which, most probably, contained some narcotic infusion.—ED.

‡ St. Augustin, *De civit. Dei*, lib. xviii., cap. xvii. et xviii.

blindly submitted himself to this singular degradation until the magician released him by giving him
an appropriate antidote. This tradition has, no
doubt, the same origin as that of Circe.*

Wearied by the amorous pursuit of Calchus,
King of the Daunians, Circe, if we may believe
Parthenius, invited him to a banquet, in all the
viands of which she had infused narcotic drugs.
Hardly had he eaten of them, when he fell into
such imbecility that Circe shut him up with the
swine. She afterward cured him, and restored
him to the Daunians, binding them, however, by a
vow, never to allow him to return to the island she
inhabited.

The cup of Circe, says Homer, contained a poison
that transformed men into beasts; implying that,
when plunged by it into a state of stupid inebriety,
they believed themselves reduced to this shameful
degradation. This explanation, the only one admissible, agrees with the relation of Parthenius.
In spite of the decision of some commentators, I
venture to affirm, that the poet did not intend this
narration as an allegorical lesson against voluptu-
ousness. Such an explanation would not accord
with the rest of the narrative, which terminates by
the wise Ulysses throwing himself into the arms
of the enchantress, who kept him there a whole
year. In many other passages also of his poem,
Homer has noticed purely physical facts. This is
so true that he mentions a natural preservative
against the effect of poison; a root which he describes with that minuteness, which, better than
any other poet, he knew how to unite with the

---

* This does not contradict the assertion of Solinus, that Circe
deceived the eyes by phantasmagorial illusions. She might make
use of these to strengthen the established belief, that the drugs
which rendered men imbecile metamorphosed them into beasts.

brilliancy of poetry and the elegance of versification.

Neither can we take, in a figurative sense, the account given by the prince of poets respecting the nepenthes which, bestowed by Helen on Telemachus, had the effect of suspending all feelings of grief in the heart of the hero.* Whatever might have been the substance thus designated, it is certain that in Homer's time there was a belief in the existence of certain liquors, which were not less stupefying than wine, and more efficacious than the juice of the grape, in diffusing a delicious calm over the mind. It is probable that Homer was acquainted with these beverages, and those also that Circe poured out for her guests, either from having witnessed the exhibition of their effects, or

* Many opinions have been advanced respecting nepenthes; but the most probable is, that which refers it to the hemp, *caunabis satira*, from which the Hindoos make their bang, which is narcotic, and produces delightful dreams.

The native plant, after it has flowered, is dried, and sold in the bazars of Calcutta, for smoking, under the name of *ganjah*. The large leaves and capsules, employed also for smoking, are called *bang*, or *subjee*. In both of these forms the smoking of the hemp causes a species of intoxication of a most agreeable description, and consequently the plant has acquired many epithets, which may be translated "assuager of sorrow," "increaser of pleasure," "cementer of friendship," "laughter-mover," and several others of the same description.

In Nepaul, the resin only is used, under the name of *churrus*. It is collected in some places by naked coolies walking through the fields of hemp at the time when the plant exudes the resin, which sticks to their skin, from which it is scraped off, and kneaded into balls. In whatever manner it is collected, when it is taken in doses of from a grain to two grains, it causes not only the most delightful delirium, but, when repeated, it is followed by catalepsy, or that condition of insensibility to all external impressions which enables the body to be, as it were, molded into any position, like a Dutch jointed doll, in which the limbs remain in the position in which they are placed, however contrary to the natural influence of gravity; and this state will continue for many hours. Such an instrument could not fail to prove a most powerful agent in working apparent miracles in the hands of a Thaumaturgist.—ED.

from tradition only; it always appears from his narrative, that the ancients possessed the means of making them. Wherefore should we, then, doubt that such a secret was practiced in the temples, whence the Greek poet derived the greatest part of his knowledge, and where all the secrets of experimental philosophy were concentrated?

Roman and Greek historians, and also modern naturalists, in speaking of the properties of different beverages, mention facts, which prove that they were known to the ancient Thaumaturgists, and that their powers have not been exaggerated.

A. Laguna, in his Commentary on Dioscorides, mentions a species of *solanum*, the root of which, taken in wine in a dose of a drachm weight, fills the imagination with the most delicious illusions. It is well known that opium, when administered in certain quantities, produces sleep accompanied with dreams so distinct and so agreeable that no reality can equal the charm of them.* In recapit-

---

* The magical influence of opium is well described, allowing for some degree of exaggeration, in M. de Quincy's extraordinary work entitled *The Confessions of an English Opium-Eater*, to which the Editor refers the reader. It is necessary to mention here only a few facts descriptive of its influence on the inhabitants of Turkey and India.

In the Teriakana, or opium shops of Constantinople, and throughout the Ottoman Empire, opium is usually mixed with aromatics, and made into small cakes or losenges, which are stamped with the words " *Mash Allah*,"—gift of God. After a certain number of these have been swallowed, the first effect is a degree of vivacity, which is even followed by delirium and hallucinations, that vary in their character according to the natural disposition of the individual. Is the opium-eater ambitious—he beholds his sublime ideas realized, monarchs at his feet, and slaves in chains following his triumphant chariot. Is he timid—he feels himself either endowed with courage to which he is naturally a stranger, or scenes of horror and dismay arise before him, the brain of the lover heaves with tenderness and rapture; that of the vindictive man swells with a ferocious delight, in feeling his victim within his power, and his dagger already in his heart. High-flown compliments are uttered, and the most ridiculous actions performed, until sleep overpowers the senses, and leaves

ulating all the speculations that have been made respecting nepenthes, M. Virey supposes that he has discovered it to be the hyosciamus *datura* of Forskhal,* which is still employed for the same purpose in Egypt, and throughout the East. Many other substances, capable of producing effects not less marvelous, are mentioned by the same learned person.

The potamantis, or thalassegle, says Pliny,† grows on the banks of the Indus, and gelatophyllis near to Bactria. The juices extracted from both these plants produce delirium; the one causing extraordinary visions, the other exciting continual laughter. The one acts in a similar manner as the beverage made with the hyosciamus of Forskhal; the other like that expressed from the seeds of the datura.‡ Other compositions concealed virtues still more useful to the workers of miracles.

In Ethiopia, says Diodorus,§ was a square lake of a hundred and sixty feet in circumference and

the person on awaking pensive, melancholy, and exhausted, until recourse is again had to the regular daily supply.

In China, Siam, Borneo, and Sumatra, opium prepared in a peculiar manner, and called *chandoo*, is both eaten and smoked with nearly the same effects as the Turks experience; but it renders the Malays almost frantic. When misfortune, therefore, or a desire of desperate revenge influences a Malay, he makes himself delirious with opium; then sallies forth armed, and running forward, calling out "Amok! amok!" he attempts to stab, indiscriminately, every one he meets, until he himself is killed for the preservation of others.

Such is the apparent supernatural felicity in some, and the demoniacal frenzy and wretchedness in others, which the juice of the poppy occasions; and there can be little doubt that it was administered in some form to the aspirants during their initiation into the mysteries of Polytheism.—ED.

* *Bulletin de Pharmacie*, tome v. (Février, 1813), pp. 49–60.

† Plin., *Hist. Nat.*, lib. xxiv., cap. xvii.

‡ All the daturas are narcotic; but, from its native place, that species mentioned by Pliny under the name *gelatophyllis*, was either datura *ferox* or datura *metel.*—ED.

§ Diod. Sic., lib. ii., cap., xii., p. 12.

forty feet broad, the waters of which were of the
color of vermillion, and exhaled an agreeable odor.
Those who drank these waters became so delirious,
that they confessed all their crimes, and even those
that time had permitted them to forget. Ctesias*
mentions a fountain in India, the waters of which
became, when newly drawn, like cheese. This
coagulum, when dissolved in water, possessed virtues like those mentioned by Diodorus. In the
first example the name of lake, particularly after
the dimensions specified, reminds us of the sea of
brass in the Temple of Jerusalem, which signified
only a large basin hollowed by the hand of man,†
such as is seen in every village of Hindostan.‡
The word fountain as employed by Ctesias is
equally applied to the spring whence water flows,
and to a reservoir from which water is drawn.
When we reflect on the color and scent of the
water contained in the lake of Ethiopia, the property of the Indian liquid of coagulating like cheese,
and call to remembrance also the fluid drugs employed by the magicians of Egypt—do they not all
announce pharmaceutical preparations?

Democritus had, before Ctesias and Diodorus,
mentioned plants that were endowed with such
virtues, that they caused the guilty to confess what
the most rigorous tortures would not have constrained them to avow. According to Pliny,§ there
is an Indian plant called *achœmenis*, the root of

---

* Ctesias, *Indic. apud. Photium. Biblioth.*, cod. lxxii.

† Lacus, in Latin, often takes the same signification. Pliny
applies this name to the basin of a fountain situated near Man-
durium, in the country of Salente. Vitruvius also applies it to
a basin for receiving lime.

‡ Some of these basins (tanks) are more than twenty-three
thousand two hundred and thirty-nine yards in circumference.
Haafner, *Travels in the Western Peninsula of India, &c., passim*,
tome ii., p. 299.

§ Plin. *Hist. Nat.*, lib. xxiv., cap. xvii.

which, when made into lozenges and swallowed in wine during the day, torments the guilty all night. They suppose that they are pursued by the gods, who appear to them under many forms ; and they confess their crimes. The juice of the *ophiusa*, a plant of Ethiopia, when taken internally, creates a belief of being attacked by serpents : the terror that it produces is so violent, that it leads to suicide ; therefore the sacrilegious were compelled to drink this liquor.

These wonders seem fabulous ; they may be repeated, however, every day under the eye of the observer. The extract of belladonna is given to children affected with the hooping-cough ; if the quantity exceeds ever so little the proper dose, this remedy occasions the most painful dreams, that fill the little patients with fear. In Kamtschatka they distill from a sweet herb* "a spirit which easily intoxicates in a very violent manner. Those who drink it, although even in very small quantities, yet are tormented during the night with fearful dreams ; and the following day they are afflicted by inquietudes and agitations as great as if they had committed some crime."

The *muchamore* is a fungus common to Kamtschatka and Siberia.† If it be eaten dry, or infused in liquor and drunk, it sometimes produces death, and always profound delirium, which is sometimes gay, sometimes full of sorrow and fear. Those who partake of it believe themselves subject to the irresistible power of the spirit that inhabits the poisonous fungus. In a fit of this stupor, a Cossack imagined that the spirit ordered him to con-

---

* *Pastinaca.*—Gmelin.

† Krachenninikof, *Description du Kamtschatka*, 1st part, chap. xiv. Beniowski relates that a Siberian Schaman whom he consulted made use of an infusion of *muchamore ;* the beverage first plunged him into raving delirium, and then into deep sleep.

fess his sins; he made, therefore, a general confession before all his comrades.*

Other beverages have a different influence, but are equally capable of creating the marvelous. The Caliph Abdallah, son of Zobeir, when besieged in Mecca, decided on making a sally, and thus finding either deliverance or death. He received from the hands of his mother a beverage containing musk,† to sustain his courage; and he only yielded after prodigies of valor, which made the victory, for a long time, uncertain.‡ When the Turks go to battle, a strong drink, named *maslach*, mixed with opium, is distributed among the soldiers, and excites and renders them almost frantic.§ The intoxication produced by the *muchamore* often brings on an increase of strength, inspires fearless boldness, and excites a desire of committing criminal actions, which are then re-

* The muchamore, the plant here referred to, is the fly amanita, amanita *muscaria*, found in Kamtschatka, and also abundantly in the Highlands of Scotland, and in woods in England, in the autumn. It is a beautiful plant, rising like a mushroom, upon a white stalk four to eight inches high, bulbous at the base: the pileus, or top, is from three to six inches broad, of an orange-brown color, with white warty spots regularly scattered over its surface. It is the most splendid of the agaricoid tribe. "In the Highlands of Scotland," says Dr. Greville (*Scottish Cryptogamic Flora*, vol. i., p. 54), "it is impossible not to admire it, as seen in long perspective between the trunks of the straight fir-trees; and should a sunbeam penetrate through the dark and dense foliage, and rest on its vivid surface, an effect is produced by this chief of a humble race which might lower the pride of many a patrician vegetable." It is always deleterious, and often fatal when eaten. In Kamtschatka its juice, mixed with that of the great bilberry, or the runners of the *willow-herb*, is drunk to cause intoxication. It acts most powerfully when dried, and swallowed after mastication: it then causes delirium, and occasionally convulsions.—ED.

† Musk is a powerful stimulant; it raises the pulse without elevating the heat of the body; and increases, in a remarkable degree, the energy of the brain and nerves.—ED.

‡ Hegira, 73; Ockley, *Histoire des Sarrasins*, tome ii., pp. 4, 5.

§ *Considérations sur la Guerre présente entre les Russes et les Turcs*, 1769, p. 173.

garded as imperiously inspired by the Spirit of the muchamore. The savage inhabitant of Kamtschatka and the fierce Cossacks have recourse to this intoxication to dissipate their fears when they project assassinations.*

The extract of hemp, mixed with opium, has, even in the eighteenth century, been used in the armies of the Hindoo princes, by the Ammoqui, fanatic warriors, whom it makes fiercely delirious. They dart off, striking without distinction every thing they meet before them, until, overwhelmed with blows, they fall on the bodies of their victims.† Neither fear nor humanity arrests their course of crime. Those fanatics, also, who have been named Assassins, were intoxicated by a preparation of hemp, called *hashiché*, given to them by the Old Man of the Mountain.‡

All the historians of the Crusades have spoken of the enchanted abode of the Old Man of the Mountain,§ who gave to his credulous neophytes

* Krachenninikof, *Description du Kamtschatka*, part i., chap. xiv.

† Paulin de St. Barthélemi, *Voyage aux Indes Orientales*, tome ii., pp. 426, 427.

‡ J. Hammer, *Mines of the East.—Nouvelles Annales des Voyages*, tome xxv., pp. 337–379.

§ This is an absurd translation of the title of Seydna, and Sheikh-al-Jebal, literally, *Elder Mountain Chief*, which was assumed by Hassan Sabah, a chief of a sect of Eastern Ismailites, who made himself master of Alamoot, one of the strong hill-fortresses which cover the mountainous region that divides Persian Irak and the northernly provinces of Dilem and Taberistan. The followers of Hassan were bound to the most rigid obedience to the precepts of Islam, or Abdallah Maimom, the projector of the sect. It is unnecessary here to describe the rules which were requisite to be practiced by the aspirants, proselytes to the faith of the society. Assassination was an obligation on the Ismailite Fedavee, one of the divisions of the sect, any one of whom, ordered by a superior to assassinate a stranger, was obliged to obey; and, in the peformance of the order, the wretched Fedavee firmly believed he was promoting the cause of truth. It has been supposed that the name *Assassins*, given to the society, originated in this obligation; but the appellation is derived, according to M.

such a foretaste of paradise, that the hope of one
day returning to this place of delights made them
consent to the commission of every crime, brave

De Sacy, from the Oriental term *Hashisheen*, corrupted by the
Crusaders into assassin. This term implies takers of hashiché,
a species of hemp, from which an intoxicating drug was compounded, which the Fedavee took previously to their engaging
in their daring enterprises; and which procured for them the
delicious visions of paradise, promised to all the followers of the
Sheikh-el-Jebal. This paradise was typified on earth, according
to Marco Paulo, who traveled over the East in the thirteenth
century, by gardens of the most luxurious description, stored
with the most delicious fruit and flagrant flowers and shrubs,
and containing palaces inhabited by exquisitely beautiful and
highly accomplished damsels, clothed in the richest dresses, and
educated to display every grace and fascination that could capti-
vate the senses.

The chief, in discoursing of paradise to his followers, persuaded
them that he had the power of granting admission to it; and to
prove the truth of his assertion, he caused a potion of a soporific
kind to be administered to ten or twelve of them at a time, and
when they were sound asleep, he had them conveyed to the
palaces in the garden. On awaking from their sleep, their senses
were struck with the beauty and splendor of every object upon
which their eyes rested; their ears were ravished with the most
harmonious voices; and their fond glances at the lovely damsels
were returned with the most alluring caresses; until, truly intoxicated with the excess of enjoyment, they believed themselves
actually in paradise. After a time they were again thrown into
sleep, and carried out of the garden. They were questioned before the whole court as to where they had been and what they
had seen; and having detailed all the pleasures they enjoyed, the
chief assured them that those who yielded implicit obedience to
him should inherit such a paradise forever.

The effects of such an imposture display, most strikingly, the
lengths to which credulity and superstition will conduct mortals.
The following anecdote powerfully elucidates this remark. " An
ambassador from the Sultan Malek Schah having come to Alamoot to demand submission and obedience of the sheikh, Hassan
received him in a hall in which he had assembled several of his
followers. Making a sign to one youth, he said, ' Kill thyself!'
Instantly the young man's dagger was plunged into his own
bosom. To another he said, ' Fling yourself down from the
wall!' In an instant his shattered limbs were lying in the castle
ditch. Then turning to the terrified envoy, he exclaimed—' I
have seventy thousand followers who obey me after this fashion.
This is my answer to your master!' "* These victims died in

* Marinus Sanatus, lib. III.—*Secret Societies, Library of Entertaining
Knowledge*, p. 81.

the most cruel tortures, and undaunted meet certain death. At a much earlier period, Shedadbenad, King of Arabia, desiring to be worshiped as a god, collected in a garden, the name of which was proverbial in the East, all the delights of paradise; and allowed them to be enjoyed by the faithful whom he deigned to admit into it.* In both cases, we think that these gardens of pleasure only existed in dreams, caused among young men habituated to a simple and austere diet by the use of potions to which they were unaccustomed, and which exalted their weak reasons, and filled their heated imaginations.† Under the name of *bendjé*, a preparation of *hyosciamus* (henbane),‡ the same plant, no doubt, as the *hyosciamus datura*, served to intoxicate them so completely, that they believed themselves in paradise, of which glowing descriptions had been previously given to them; they experienced also a violent desire to be transported

the full conviction that they were immediately to pass into that sensual paradise, of which they had received a foretaste in the gardens of the sheikh.

It is out of place to trace here the history of a people whose chief object was evil; and who—for Providence provides retribution for crime even in this world—have ceased to live politically for nearly six centuries. The sect still exists in Persia, and scattered over great part of Asia. They regard their imam as an incarnate ray of the Divinity; they hold him in the highest veneration; and they make pilgrimages from the most distant places to the village of Khekh, in the district of Koom, where he resides, to obtain his blessing.—ED.

* D'Herbelot, *Bibliothèque Orientale*, art. *Iram*.

† The foregoing note has proved that the opinion of this author is erroneous as far as regards the followers of Hassan Sabah. —ED.

‡ M. J. Hammer (loc. cit.) appears to think that the *bendjé* was the same thing as the *hashiché;* but in a fragment of an Arabian romance, for the translation of which we are indebted to him, it is positively stated that the *bendjé* was a preparation of henbane.—p. 380.

I am disposed to differ from the opinion of our author respecting bendjé, which I have been informed is a preparation of hemp, cannabis *indica.*—ED.

to it, even through death; while, in order to incite
them to some desperate act, the hashiché, or extract of hemp, was administered to them—and is
still employed in the East for the same purpose.

The real existence of the gardens of the Old Man
of the Mountain, has, nevertheless, been acknowledged by enlightened men.* In opposition to them,
however, we may be permitted to mention the basis
upon which we had established our opinion to the
contrary,† even before it acquired another degree
of probability by the assent of M. Virey.‡ This is
no deviation from our subject; the wonders employed for operating upon the credulity of men by
beings who pretended to be endowed with supernatural powers form a part of our inquiry.

The Old Man of the Mountain, whose history
is obscured by so many fables, surrounded himself
by a troop of fanatics, ready to dare every thing at
his first signal. It is said, that their unbounded
devotion was produced by a narcotic, during the
effect of which they were transported into the
most delicious gardens, where, when they awoke,
every luxury was collected to make them believe
that for some hours they tasted the pleasures of
heaven. The exactitude of this recital may be
questioned. How many indiscretions might every
day compromise the existence of a fictitious paradise? How would it be possible to assemble and
bind to inviolable secrecy so many agents, exempted
from the fanaticism which their artifices produced
in others, and who, not regarding silence as a duty,

* MM. Malthe-Brun et J. Hammer.—*Mines de l'Orient.*—*Nouvelles Annales des Voyages*, tome xxv., pp. 376–382.

† *Bulletin de Pharmacie*, tome v., pp. 55–66 (Février, 1812).

‡ Eusèbe Salverte, *Des Rapports de la Médicine avec la Politique*
(in 12mo., 1806). We transcribe this passage, with the correc-
tions that have been prepared for another edition. The whole
work was read in 1804 to the *Société Médicale d'Emulation de Paris*

would, on the contrary, doubt the blind obedience
which they labored to inspire, since, at the least
caprice of the tyrant, they might become the first
victims of it ? The slaves of both sexes, who figured before the initiated as angels and houris, could
not be supposed to prove always discreet. What
would become of them, at last, when the progress
of years did not permit them to appear in the same
parts ? Death alone could insure future silence ;
and would not the prospect of such a reward untie
their tongues on the first favorable occasion, or lead
them to kill their tormentor when, wandering alone
among them, he came to confirm the neophyte in
his false persuasion ? How, also, would this tribe
of actors support themselves ? Could their master
every day administer to their wants without its being perceptible abroad ? In addition, the number
of precautions to be taken—the provisions to be
renewed—the frequent necessity of getting rid of
these agents, from whose indiscretion there was
every thing to be feared—are all difficulties in the
way of our belief in this abominable mystery, much
less that it could be maintained for even three
years.

"Beside, it is certain that bodily enjoyment,
with whatever ingenuity they may be varied or
arrested, have intervals too marked—contrasts too
sensible of void and reality—to permit the creation,
or the long endurance, of such an illusion. How
much more simply is every thing explained, by
ascribing the illusions to physical intoxication, combined with the intoxication of the soul! Among
credulous men, previously prepared by the most
flattering pictures of paradise and promises of future felicity, the narcotic potion would easily produce the most pleasurable and desirable sensations,
and the magical continuation of them would render

them doubly valuable. 'To speak plainly, they can only be regarded as a vision,' says Pasquier,* who, after having examined every thing related by cotemporary authors on the subject of the Assassins, arrives at that conclusion. Ask a man, in whom a dose of opium has lulled an excruciating pain, to display a picture of the enchanting illusion which he experienced, and the state of ecstasy into which he was plunged for more than twenty-four hours, and they will be found exactly those of the supernatural delights heaped by the chief of the Assassins upon his future Seïdes. We know with what avidity the Easterns, who are accustomed to take opium, give themselves up to its delights, in spite of the ever growing infirmities which it heaps upon their wretched existence. This eagerness may afford some idea of the pleasures that accompany this species of intoxication, and enable us to comprehend that uncontrollable desire which may urge an ignorant and superstitious youth to dare every thing in order to possess, for eternity, such ineffable delights."

The remembrance of the devotion of the disciples of the Old Man of the Mountain to their master, is naturally united to that of the constancy with which they endured the most cruel tortures. The intoxication of fanaticism would arm them with this invincible constancy: the noble pride of courage, the obstinacy even of a trifling point of honor, would often be sufficient to inspire it. It was, however, much too important to their chief, to be certain that none of them should fail him, to allow him to rely solely on the power of the recollection of the delights that they experienced: especially when time and distance might reasonably

* E. Pasquier, *Les Recherches de la France*, liv. viii., chap. xx. (2 vols. in fol.), Amsterdam, 1723, tome i., p. 798.

be supposed to weaken their influence. If he was acquainted with the means of allaying bodily feelings, he doubtless took care, also, to provide for the ministers of his vengeance the same means, in order that they might employ it in a critical moment. The promise of sustaining his followers when under the empire of pain, exalted still more their fanaticism; and the accomplishment of this promise became a new miracle: an additional proof of the certain power of him they regarded as the governor of nature. In advancing this conjecture, we must acknowledge that we can not support it by any historical proofs.* But is it likely that the Thaumaturgists would be unacquainted

---

* The reasoning of our author is ingenious, and very plausible; but it is not sufficient to overthrow the testimony of Marco Paulo, Hammer, and others, respecting the existence of the gardens of the Ismailite chief at Alamoot. What, we may ask, would the followers of the Sheikh-el-Jebal, to whom were intrusted his secrets, not suffer rather than divulge them, when we see them laying down their lives in his service every time that he demanded the sacrifice? These were not acts of obligation, but of a persuasion that obedience to their chief was to gain them eternal felicity in paradise after death. Beside, the pains that are taken by all Oriental nations, to confirm the truth of their creeds, can not be denied; and the secrecy in which their impostures are veiled and preserved is almost incredible. Thus, in a late communication made to the Royal Asiatic Society, by Sir Claude Wade, on the geography of the Punjaub, we are informed that, in a small but deep lake seven coss from Soohait, named Rawalsir, are seven floating islands, which are objects of worship to Hindoo pilgrims. These votaries proceed to the shores of the lake, address the islands, and present their offerings; upon which, it is stated, the islands approach the shores, receive the offerings upon their surface, and then retire. " As this tale," adds Sir Claude, "is invariably accredited among the natives, it is not improbable that artificial means are taken to cause the islands to traverse the yielding surface."* What the nature of this cause is, however, remains an inviolable secret; although many persons must be employed in working it, and successive changes of workmen must be required. This fact, therefore, gives the coloring of truth to all that has been related respecting the gardens at Alamoot.—ED.

* *Literary Gazette*, No. 1524 p. 317.

with a secret known to all antiquity, and especially
in Palestine? The Rabbins* inform us, that a
drink of wine and strong liquors was given to the
unhappy ones condemned to death, and powders
were mixed in the liquor, in order to render it
stronger and to deaden the senses. The object of
this custom was, no doubt, to reconcile with humanity the intention of exciting alarm by the sight
of executions. In the second century of our era,
it is related by Apuleius, that a man fortified himself against the violence of blows by a potion containing myrrh.† If, as we think, myrrh could only
be drunk in the form of a tincture, the effect of the
alcohol must have increased the efficacy of the stupefying drug. We observe everywhere, that this
property attributed to the myrrh is not among
those for which it is employed in the present day
as a medicine. The name of myrrh, however,
might serve to disguise a preparation, the ingredients of which were intended to be kept secret.
But in either case, the Old Man of the Mountain
could not certainly have been ignorant of a secret
which had for so long a time prevailed in Palestine, and which he might also have borrowed from
Egypt. The stone of Memphis (*lapis memphiticus*)
was a round body, sparkling, and about the size
of a small pebble; it was regarded as a natural
body. I consider it to have been a work of art.
It was ground into powder and laid as an ointment
on the parts to which the surgeon was about to
apply the knife or the fire.‡ It preserved the person, without danger, from the pains of the operation; if taken in a mixture of wine and water, it
deadened all feelings of suffering.§

---

* *Tract. Sanhedr.*—D. Calmet, *Commentaire sur le Livre des Pro-
verbes*, chap. **xxi.**, v. 6.   † *Evang. sec. Marc*, cap. **xv.**, v. 25.
‡ Dioscorid., lib. v., cap. clviii.
§ Plin., *Hist. Nat.*, lib. **xxxviii.**, cap. vii.

A similar secret has existed in all ages in Hindostan. It is probably by such means that the widows* are preserved from shrinking from the dread of the blazing pile upon which they place themselves with the dead bodies of their husbands. The eye-witness of one of these sacrifices that took place in July, 1822, saw the victim arrive in a complete state of bodily insensibility, the effect, no doubt, of the drugs which had been administered to her. Her eyes were open, but she did not appear to see; and, in a weak voice, and as if mechanically, she answered the legal questions that were put to her regarding the full liberty of her sacrifice. When she was laid on the pile, she was absolutely insensible.† The Christians carried

* Le P. Paulin de St. Barthélemi, *Voyage aux Indes Orientales*, tome i., p. 358.

† *The Asiatic Journal*, vol. xv., 1823, pp. 292, 293. The custom of drugging the Indian widows previous to gaining their consent to this monstrous concremation, is stated to be not unusual, when their relations have any advantage to gain by their decease; but as many of those who submit to it are of the lower order of women, vanity, and the force of a prevailing superstition, are the chief inducements. There can be no doubt that this, one of the dominant passions of the sex, frequently impels them to the sacrifice; for women who commit this suicide are canonized after death, and crowds of votaries frequent their shrines, to implore their protection, and to pray for their aid and deliverance from evil.

When this self-sacrifice is by concremation, it is termed *Sahamarana*; but occasionally, although rarely, it is performed when the husband is at a distance; it is then solitary, or *Anamarana*. The name given to these immolations, by the English in India, is *Suttee*, a corruption of the word *Sati*, or *pure*, the appellation bestowed not upon the sacrifice, but upon the female after she has been purified by the fire. The woman is not, say the Bramins, destroyed, but only *consumed*; not annihilated, but merely *changed*. The tradition of the origin of the custom relates, that the father-in-law of SIVA having omitted to invite her to a wedding, his wife PARAVATI felt so offended at this neglect, that in the paroxysm of her rage she flung herself into the fire, and was consumed. She thence became *Sati* (*transcendent purity*), which is also one of her names.

These shameful immolations have been attempted to be put down by the Indian government, but ineffectually; and, so late as

this secret from the East into Europe, on the return of the Crusaders.   It was probably known to the subaltern magicians, as well as that of braving the action of fire, from which, I imagine, arose the rule of jurisprudence according to which physical

1825, the number in one year amounted to one hundred and four. When once a woman declares her intention of submitting to concremation with the dead body of her husband, she can not revoke.   The interest of the whole community is at stake as well as her own character; for, if she refuse, it is a prevailing belief that the whole country would be visited with some awful calamity.   Every effort is therefore employed to inspire her with sacred heroism, and to exalt her imagination to the highest pitch that fanaticism and superstition can impart; and when these are likely to fail, she is rendered nearly insensible by some narcotic beverage.   The sacrifice is preceded by a procession, in which the wretched victim appears decorated with jewels and flowers of the tulse, or holy ocymum plant (ocymum *sanctum*, Linn.) is borne on a rich palanquin, following a kind of triumphal car, on which the dead body of her husband is seated, also decorated with jewels and costly vestments.   When the procession has reached the pile, and the dead body has been laid upon it, the widow is bathed without removing her clothes and jewels, and then reconducted to the pile, around which she is walked three times, supported by some of her nearest relations.   These ceremonies being concluded, she is cast upon the dead body of her husband; and gee, a species of semi-fluid butter, being poured upon the dry wood, it is instantly fired, and she quickly dies of suffocation before the fire reaches her body.

In examining the accounts of the composure and almost philosophical indifference with which these women sacrifice their lives to the prevailing superstition, there is no necessity for believing that it is the sole result of the narcotics administered to them. Woman, in every country and in every age, displays more the character of the sincere devotee than man.   Convinced of the truth of the doctrine she embraces, it absorbs her whole mind; her contemplation rests firmly upon it; and when an hour of trial arrives, she reposes upon its promises in undisturbed tranquillity; all the ties of relationship and of country are forgotten; every act of memory and consciousness is suppressed; and under the circumstances, such as have been described as taking place in these concremations, her whole mind turned upon the beatitude she is about to attain, the frailties of our nature are surmounted, and the mortal seems almost already invested with supernatural powers.   To the operation of this state of mind, in the opinion of the writer of this note, may we attribute some, at least, of the extraordinary displays of heroism occasionally exhibited in these self immolations.—Ed.

insensibility, whether partial or general, was a certain sign of sorcery. Many authors quoted by Fromann[*] speak of the unhappy sorcerers who have laughed or slept through the agonies of torture; and they have not failed to add that they were sent to sleep by the power of the devil.

It is also said that the same advantage was enjoyed by pretended sorcerers about the middle of the fifteenth century. Nicholas Eymeric, Grand Inquisitor of Arragon, author of the famous *Directoire des Inquisiteurs*, loudly complained of the sorceries practiced by accused persons, through the aid of which, when put to the torture, they appeared absolutely insensible.[†] Fr. Pegna, who wrote a commentary on Eymeric's work, in 1578, believed also the reality and efficacy of the sorceries.[‡] He strengthens himself by the evidence of the inquisitor Grillandus, and Hippolytus de Marsilies. The latter, who was Professor of Jurisprudence at Bologna in 1524, positively declares, in his "Pratique Criminelle," that he has seen the effect of the philters upon the accused persons, who suffered no pain, but appeared to be asleep in the midst of the tortures. The expressions he makes use of are remarkable; they describe the insensible man, as if plunged into a torpor more like the effect produced by an opiate, than the proud bearing which is the result of a perseverance superior to every pain.

To many instances of this temporary insensibility, Wierius adds an important observation: he saw a woman thus inaccessible to the power of torture—her face was black, and her eyes were

* Fromann, *Tract. de Fasc.*, &c., pp. 593, 594, et 810, 811.
† *Aliqui sunt maleficiati et in quæstionibus malefictis utuntur—efficiuntur enim insensibles.* — *Direct. Inquisit.*, cum adnot. Fr Pegna (Romæ, folio), part iii., p. 481.
‡ *Direct. Inquis.*, &c., p. 183.

starting out as if she had been strangled; her exemption from suffering was due to a species of apoplexy.* A physician† who witnessed a similar state of insensibility compares it to fits, epileptic or apoplectic.

A humorous writer, a cotemporary of Francis Pegna and of J. Wierius, whose name inspires us with little confidence, but who, on this occasion, speaks of what he had seen, and whose place in a tribunal enabled him to know with certainty what occurred,‡ has also described, with Taboureau, the soporific state which preserved the accused from the sufferings of torture. According to him it was almost useless to put the question. All the jailers were acquainted with the stupefying recipe, and they did not fail to communicate it to the prisoners; nothing could be easier than to practice it elsewhere, if confidence was reposed in its influence. The secret consisted in swallowing soap dissolved in water.

Common soap does not, certainly, possess the virtues ascribed to it by Taboureau; but does it therefore follow that the principal incident, namely, the administration of some potion, is false? I consider it does not; for this author is not the only person who has stated this fact. On this occasion only did the possessors of the secret impose on mankind, less to insure to themselves the exclusive possession of it, than to preserve the power of employing it. This becomes credible, if there are substances capable of realizing it; and how many may we not number that stupefy, that suspend,

* J. Wierius, *De Præstig.*, lib. iv., cap. x., p. 520 et seq.
† Fromann, *Tract. de Fasc.*, pp. 810, 811.
‡ Et. Taboureau, *Des faux sorciers et leurs impostures* (1595). Discourse inserted in the fourth Book of the *Bigarrures du Sieur des Accords*. Et. Taboureau was the king's counsel at the bailiwick of Dijon.

and destroy nervous sensibility. *Opium, henbane, belladonna, aconite, solanum, stramonium,* have been used to deaden pain in surgical operations; and if they are not now so much prescribed, it is because the stupor they induce endangers the cure, and sometimes the life, of the patient. Such a fear would not, however, prevent them from being used by the Bramins, who conducted the Hindoo widows to the funereal piles of their husbands. It had, however, we perceive, little hold on the disciples of the Old Man of the Mountain, or on the accused who were menaced with torture. Among the substances mentioned, we may distinguish some that were no doubt made use of by the Eastern Thaumaturgist; and others so common in Europe, that they might easily have been furnished, as Taboureau states, to the prisoners by the jailers when they were required. .

Such there are, and from the number of these substances, and the facility of procuring them, we may be permitted to suppose that, known in all ages, they have been, at all times, employed to work apparent miracles. It is not the moderns alone who have witnessed the atrocious cruelties, almost above human strength to bear, which before the eyes of a whole nation have been endured by the Hindoo penitents; the historians of Greece and Rome have spoken of them,[*] and national traditions state their practice to have existed from the commencement of religious civilization. The patience of man in submitting to them, most probably, has resulted from the cause we have pointed out, namely, the actual use of stupefying drugs: they repeat it often, and this practice, thus prolonged, ends in a perpetual torpor, and renders these fanatics capable of supporting tortures that

[*] Solinus, cap. lv.

II. C

last their lifetime.   The almost entire destruction of bodily feeling can not be effected without injuring the mind, and plunging the soul into complete imbecility—which is in fact the ruling feature of nearly all these miraculous penitents.

It is also in this state of imbecility that Diodorus represents the Ethiopian savages, whom he describes as being quite insensible to blows, wounds, and the most extraordinary tortures.*   A learned man of the seventeenth century† supposes that the traveler Simmias, from whom Diodorus copied his narration, had taken as the general character of a nation the temporary state of some individuals intoxicated by a potion similar to the nepenthes which Homer mentions.   It is more probable that Simmias‡ met, on the shores of Ethiopia, penitents such as those that exist at the present day in Hindostan; and the state in which he saw them§ had

* Diod. Sicul., lib. iii., cap. viii.
† Pierre Petit. D. M., *Dissertation sur le Népenthès*, 8vo. Utrecht.
‡ Simmias was a philosopher of Thebes, but neither he nor Diodorus is high authority: both were extremely credulous, and both equally ambitious of recording wonders.—ED.
§ Hasselquist (*Voyage dans le Levant*, 1st part, p. 257), observes, that opium, habitually taken in excess by the dervises, conduces to complete stupidity.
The torments which the *Yogis*, or Indian penitents, impose upon themselves, are not borne by the individual becoming insensible through the influence of stupefying drugs, but they are truly the result, either of an ambition to become worthy of eternal bliss, or a slavish obedience to vanity, that they may enjoy in this world the respect of the noble and the great, and the admiration of the unthinking multitude.   A Yogis will stand in a certain position for years: sometimes with his hands above his head, until the arms wither, and become incapable of action; others keep the hands closed until the nails pierce through their palms; some double themselves up like a hedgehog, and thus are rolled along from the Indus to the banks of the Ganges; or suspend themselves by the heels over the fiercest fires, or sit in the center of many fires, throwing combustibles into them to increase the flames.   These, and a thousand other tortures which they brave, are not all the result of trick, aided by stupefying drugs, as our author asserts, but the effects of an absurd, super

become permanent by the continual use of drugs competent to produce it.

CHAPTER II.

Effect of Perfumes on the Moral Nature of Man.—Action of Liniments; the Magic Ointment frequently operated by occasioning Dreams, which the Predisposition to Credulity converted into Realities.—Such Dreams may explain the whole History of Sorcery.—The principal Causes which multiplied the Number of Sorcerers were the Employment of Mysterious Secrets. —The Crimes which these pretended Mysteries served to conceal; and the rigorous Laws absurdly directed against the Crime of Sorcery.

THE impression of the marvelous increases upon us in proportion to the distance which seems to

stitious credulity, that those acts are to gain for them eternal felicity. That many of them are sincere is demonstrated in their belief that even tigers will respect them—will come voluntarily to them—and lie down, and fondle, and lick their hands: a belief which sometimes costs them their lives. Upon what other plea can we account for the suicides that are perpetrated at the temple of Juggernaut, and at the sacred spot where the Ganges and the Jumna mingle their waters; and the disgusting abominations that nothing but a sincere belief in their efficacy could have admitted into several of their religious ceremonies. That many penitents perish by tigers every year, but nevertheless that numbers of these penitents are impostors, there is little doubt. Their putting to death and resuscitating a human victim, or what is termed *pahvadam*, is undoubtedly a mere counterfeit rite to impose upon the ignorant and extort charity from the rich; and many others of their exhibitions are intended for the same purpose. This does not, however, weaken our argument in favor of the extreme length to which a desire to confirm extraordinary doctrines will carry enthusiasts. Without going to Hindostan, we may find in Europe sufficient evidence of this fact; but the mention of one only will suffice to demonstrate the temper of the period when such proofs could be demanded or believed. When Antioch was taken by the Christians, in the eleventh century, the identity of the lance which was reputed to have pierced the side of our Savior was disputed. The monk who had recently made the discovery, by the suggestion of a vision, offered to undergo the ordeal of fire to establish the truth of what he said. His offer was accepted, and he passed through the terrible proof. He died, however, within a few days, and the fact of the supposed discovery became problematical.*—ED.

---

* Berrington, *Literary History of the Middle Ages*, 4to., 1814, p. 265.

separate the cause from the effect. Draughts and drugs could not be administered without the concurrence of the individual on whom they were intended to operate; but persons might involuntarily become intoxicated by the perfumes shed around the altar and the incense lavishly used in magical ceremonies, even without a suspicion of their powers. This fact afforded many advantages to the Thaumaturgist, especially when it was his interest to produce visions and ecstasy. The choice and the combination of these perfumes were scrupulously studied.

It may be remembered that, in order to give children a capability of receiving revelations in dreams, the use of fumigations with certain ingredients was recommended by Porphyrus.[*] Proclus, who frequently, in common with his philosophic cotemporary, transmitted mere medicinal prescriptious under the form of an allegory, relates[†] that the founders of the ancient priesthood, after collecting various odors, combined them according to the process of divine art; by which means a singular perfume was compounded, in which the energy of the numerous odors was brought to a climax by this union, and became necessarily weakened by separation.

In the hymns ascribed to Orpheus, and which evidently belong to the ritual of some very ancient worship, a separate perfume is assigned to accompany the invocation of each divinity. These diverse rites had not, invariably, an actual meaning in their application; but general rules being thus established, they were more easily taken advantage of on necessary occasions, the priest having the power of directing

---

[*] Proclus, *De Sacrificis et Magiâ*.   .   [†] *Ibid.* ·

the perfume to be used in addressing any particular divinity.*

The physical and moral action of odors has not perhaps, in this view, been so much studied by modern philosophers as by the ancient Thaumaturgists. Herodotus, however, informs us, that the Scythians became intoxicated by inhaling the vapor arising from the seeds of a species of hemp, thrown upon heated stones.† We learn also from modern science, that a disposition to anger and to strife is produced by the mere odor of the seeds of henbane, when its strength is augmented by heat. Three examples, related in *Le Dictionnaire de Médecine*‡ and in *L'Encyclopédie Méthodique*, go

* The ancients were particularly fond of perfumes. In Athens, when the guests invited to a feast entered the house of their host, their beards " were perfumed over with censers of frankincense, as ladies have their tresses on visiting a Turkish harem. The hands, too, after each lavation, were scented." . It was usual, also, " after supper to perfume the guests."* The influence of odors on the organs of smelling depends more on the condition of the nervous tissue of that organ, than upon the nature of the odors; and much also is due to the healthy or the diseased condition of the system. Odors delightful to one person are intolerable to another: mignionette possessed nothing agreeable in its odor to the celebrated Blumenbach; and the distinguished Baron Haller declared that no odor was so agreeable to him as that of a dissecting-room. The impression made upon the olfactory nerves is generally transitory, the sensation vanishing when the odorous substance is withdrawn; but the sensations of some odors continue after the impression of the odorous matter has ceased. In some persons odors do not operate as merely topical stimulants, but affect the whole system: thus, in some ipecacuanha causes an asthmatic fever; in others, the odor of the African geranium, *pelargonium*, causes faintings; the odor of the rose has produced epilepsy; while a few nervous people either lose the power of smelling, or have a constant consciousness of a bad odor, or of something which is not present. Many odors excite powerfully the brain; some animals, as, for example, cats, are intoxicated by valerian; while other animals, and man himself, are sickened by the odor of tobacco.—ED.

† Herodot., lib. iv., cap. lxxv.
‡ Tome vii., art. *Jusquiame*.

* St. John, *Manners and Customs of Ancient Greece*, vol. i., pp. 175–184.

to prove this effect.   The most striking is the case
of a married couple, who, although everywhere
else they lived in perfect harmony, could not, without coming to blows, remain a few hours in their
ordinary workroom.   The room got credit for
being bewitched, until the cause of these daily
quarrels, over which the unfortunate pair were
seriously concerned, was discovered ; a considerable quantity of seeds of henbane were found near
the stove, and with the removal of the substance
which emitted this unfortunate odor all tendency
to quarrel vanished.

This class of agents was so much the more valuable to the Thaumaturgist, that it not only eludes
the eye, but it does not even affect the olfactory
nerves in proportion to the violence of its effects.

There are substances still more energetic than
perfumes, which affect our nature by acting on the
exterior of the body.·   The extract·or the juice of
belladonna, when applied to a wound, produces
delirium accompanied by visions : one drop of this
juice, if it touch the eye, will also cause delirium,
but preceded by *ambliopia*, or double images.*   A
man under its influence sees every object doubled;†
and when subjected to its influence by the vengeance of the Thaumaturgist, he would exclaim,
like a new Pentheus, " that he beheld two suns,
and two cities of Thebes."‡

* This observation was made by Dr. Hymli.   See also Pinel,
Nosographie Philosophique (5th edition), tome iii., p. 46, et Giraudy,
" *Sur le délire causé par la Belladone*," &c.   A thesis sustained in
1818.
† No extract, or expressed juice of deadly nightshade, atropa
belladonna, known at present, will produce the effect described in
the text when the eye is touched with it ; but when it is taken
in full doses into the stomach, it causes dilatation of the pupils,
visual illusions, confusion of the head, and delirium resembling
that of intoxication.—ED.
‡ Virgil, *Æneid*, lib. iv., v. 469.   Pentheus was King of Thebes,

Experiments have decidedly proved, that several medicaments, administered in the form of liniments, are taken in by the absorbent system, and act upon the habit in the same manner as when they are directly introduced into the stomach. This property of liniments was not unknown to the ancients. In the romance of Achilles Tatius, an Egyptian doctor, in order to cure Leucippus of an attack of frenzy, applied to his head a liniment composed of oil, in which some particular medicament was dissolved; the patient fell into a deep sleep, shortly after the anointing. What the physician was acquainted with, the Thaumaturgist could scarcely be ignorant of; and this secret knowledge endowed him with the power of performing many apparent miracles, some merciful, some marvelous and fatal in their tendency. It can not be disputed that the customary and frequent anointing, which formed part of the ancient ceremonials, must have offered opportunities and given facility for turning this knowledge to advantage. Before consulting the oracle of Trophonius, the body was rubbed with oil;* this preparation undoubtedly concurred in

in Bœotia. In his efforts to put down in his kingdom the Bacchanalian rites, on account of the gross sensualities which attended them, and his refusal to acknowledge the divinity of Bacchus, he was allured into a wood on Mount Cithæron, with the view of witnessing the ceremonies unnoticed, and was attacked by the Bacchanals and murdered. It is said that his mother was the first who attacked him, and she was followed by his two sisters—Ino, who afterward committed suicide, and was deified by the gods, and Antihoe. His body was hung upon a tree, which was afterward cut down by order of the oracle, and made into two statues of the Dyonesian god, which were placed on Mount Cithæron. The priests, no doubt, could have given a satisfactory explanation of the whole transaction.—ED.

⁓* Pausanias, lib. ix., cap. xxxix. Pausanias was initiated into these mysteries. The priests first made him drink from the well of *Oblivion*, to banish his past thoughts; and then from the well of *Recollection*, that he might remember the vision he was about to behold. He was then shown a mysterious representation of

producing the desired vision. Before being admitted to the mysteries of the Indian sages, Apollonius and his companions were anointed with an oil, the strength of which made them imagine *that they were bathed with fire.*[*]

The disciples of the men who established, in the heart of America, religious doctrines and rites, evidently borrowed some of them from the Asiatics. The priests of Mexico, preparatory to their conversing with their divinity, anointed their bodies with a fetid pomatum. The base of it was tobacco, and a bruised seed called *ololuchqui*, the effect of which was to deprive man of his judgment, as that of the tobacco was to benumb his senses. After this, they felt themselves very intrepid and not less cruel;[†] and, no doubt, predisposed to have visions, since the intention of this practice was to bring them into connection with the objects of their fantastical worship.

But, quitting the temples for a while, let us trace the effects of this secret when divulged, and after it had fallen into the hands of ordinary magicians.

Trophonius, and forced to worship it. He was next dressed in linen vestments, with girdles around his body, and led into the sanctuary, where was the cave into which he descended by a ladder; at its bottom, in the side of the cave, there was an opening, and having placed his foot in it internally, his whole body was drawn into it by some invisible power. He returned through the same opening at which he had entered ; and being placed on the throne of Mnemosyne, the priests inquired what he had seen, and finally led him back to the sanctuary of the Good Spirit. As soon as he recovered his self-command, he was obliged to write the vision he had seen on a little tablet, which was hung up in the temple.—ED.

[*] Philostrat., *De vit. Apol.*, lib. iii., cap. v.

[†] Acosta, *Histoire des Indes Occidentales*, liv. v., chap. xxvi., French translation (in 8vo., 1616), pp. 256, 257. The Mexican priests introduced into this ointment the ashes of the bodies of insects that were esteemed venomous, undoubtedly to distract the attention from the nature of the drugs that were to prove efficacious.

It is difficult to conceive that all is imposture in the imaginings of poets and writers of romance respecting the effects of magical ointments. The ingredients of which they were composed had, undoubtedly, some efficacy. We have suggested that sensual dreams were mingled with the sleep which they induced; a supposition whose probability rests on the fact, that those who sought their aid were generally those whose love had been disappointed or betrayed.*

The demands of passion or curiosity for enchantments were generally answered by means of dreams produced by these magical ointments, and so vivid were the illusions that they could not fail to pass for reality: a circumstance demonstrated in the history of prosecutions for sorcery, the number of which almost surpasses belief.

It was in the night, and during sleep, that the sorcerers were transported to the *Sabbat.* In order to obtain this privilege, they were obliged to rub themselves in the evening with pomatum,† the

* As these ointments seem to have operated upon the nervous system nearly in the same manner as the philters of the Greeks and Romans, it is probable that cantharides was one of the ingredients. Its active principle, *canthariden,* is very soluble in oils and fatty matters, and in this solution it is readily absorbed and carried into the system. It is this principle that causes stranguary after the application of a blister. The ancient love-philters were administered in the form of potions, which often acted so violently as to produce dangerous delirium. The madness of Caligula was attributed to one which was given to him by his wife Cæsarina. Juvenal* speaks of the Messalian philter as one of the most powerful.—ED.

† The confessions made by the sorcerers, at the Inquisition of Spain, in 1610, speak of the necessity, in order to be present at the Sabbat, to rub the palms of the hands, the soles of the feet, &c., with the water of a frightened or irritated toad (Llorente, *Histoire de l'Inquisition*, chap. xxxvii., art. 2, tome iii., p. 431, et suivantes): a puerile receipt, only intended to conceal the composition of the real ointment, even from the initiated.

composition of which was unknown to them, but its effects were precisely such as we have mentioned.

A woman accused of sorcery was brought before a magistrate of Florence, a man whose knowledge was greatly in advance of his age and country. She declared herself to be a sorceress, and asserted that she would be present at the *Sabbat* that very night, if allowed to return to her house and make use of the magic ointment. The judge assented. After being rubbed with fetid drugs, the pretended sorceress lay down and immediately fell asleep; she was tied to the bed, while blows, pricking, and scorching failed to break her slumber. Roused at length, with much trouble, she related the next day that she went to the *Sabbat*, and she detailed the painful sensations which she had really experienced in her sleep, and to which the judge limited her punishment.*

From three anecdotes precisely similar, which we might quote from Porta and Fromann,† we shall only extract a physiological remark. Two of the reputed sorcerers sent to sleep by the magic ointment had given out that they should go to the Sabbat, and return from it flying with wings. Both believed that this really happened, and were greatly astonished when assured of the contrary. One in his sleep even performed some movements, and struck out as though he were on the wing. It is well known that, from the blood flowing toward the brain during sleep, it is not uncommon to dream of flying and rising into the air.‡

* Paolo Minucci, a Florentine jurisconsult, who died in the sixteenth century, has transmitted this interesting fact, in his commentary on the *Malmantile Racquistato*, cant. iv., ott. 76.

† J. B. Porta, *Magia Natur.*, lib. ii., cap. xxvi.—Fromann, *Tract. de Fascin.*, pp. 562, 568, 569.

‡ When sleep is not very profound, the senses, in a certain de-

While they acknowledge that they used a magical ointment in order to be present at the Sabbat, these ignorant creatures could give no recipe for making it; but medicine will readily furnish one. Porta and Cardanus* have mentioned two : the solanum *somniferum* forms the base of one, while henbane and opium predominate in the other. The learned Gassendi endeavored to discover and

gree, are excitable, and the conception of ideas by the mind does not entirely cease: consequently dreams occur. If a light is suddenly brought into a room where a person is in this kind of sleep, he will either dream of being under the equator, or in a tropical landscape ; or of wandering in the fields in a clear summer's day ; or of fire. If a door is slammed, but not so loud as to awake the sleeper, he will dream of thunder ; and if his palm be gently tickled, his dream will be one of ecstatic pleasure. If some particular idea completely occupies the mind during the waking state, it will recur in dreams during sleep ; hence the minds of these unfortu nate people mentioned in the text, being strongly impressed with the idea of being present at the *Sabbat*, the dreams would apparently realize that event. If a person in sleep folds his arms closely over his breast, he is likely to dream of being held down by force, and the images of the persons employed in holding him down will be also present to his mind. The predominant emotions of the mind influence greatly the character of dreams. When the influence is depressing, the dreams are generally terrible or distressing ; when the exhilarating occupy it, the dreams are delightful and joyous. In dreams, circumstances may present to the mind forebodings ; and it is not impossible that these may really come to pass, without any thing wonderful in the occurrence ; yet it appears wonderful, although, when the circumstances are analyzed, it will be seen to be merely the result of some leading thought fixed upon the mind, and cherished during the hours of waking. In sleep, a certain degree of voluntary motion may be exerted, and the person may talk, and appear to hear and understand those who speak to him in return : such a state constitutes somnambulism. In such a condition, the functions of the brain are always more or less disturbed. The oily frictions said to have been employed by the sorcerers must have had narcotic properties ; but, independent of these, whatever gently stimulates the skin operates sympathetically on the sensorium, and favors sleep and dreaming.—ED.

* J. Wierius, *De Præstig.*, lib. ii., cap. xxxvi., p. 4.—J. B. Porta, *Magia Natur.*, lib. ii.—Cardan., *De Subtilitate*, lib. xviii. Wierius says that the ointment mentioned by Cardanus consisted of the fat of boys, mixed with the juice of parsley, aconite, solanum, pentaphylum, and soot.—ED.

to imitate this secret, in order to undeceive the
miserable beings who imagined themselves to be
sorcerers.   He anointed some peasants, whom he
had fully persuaded that they should attend the
Sabbat, with an ointment containing opium.   After
a long sleep, they awoke, satisfied that the magic
process had produced its effect; and they gave a
detailed account of all they had seen at the *Sabbat*,
and the pleasures they had enjoyed; in the particulars of which, and the mention of voluptuous sensations, we may trace the action of opium.*

In 1545, a pomatum composed of opiates was
found in the house of a sorcerer.   André Laguna,
physician to Pope Julius III., made use of it to
anoint a woman laboring under frenzy and loss of
rest.   She slept thirty-six hours consecutively; and
when they succeeded in awaking her, she com-

* The most absurd stories were told and believed respecting
this assembly of demons and sorcerers. Among others, we are
told that a husband having suspected his wife of being a sorceress,
and desirous to know whether she attended the *Sabbat*, and how
she transported herself there, watched her, and, one evening,
found her occupied in anointing her body. She then took the
form of a bird, and flew away; but, in the morning, he found her
in bed at his side. He questioned her respecting her absence;
but she would make no confession until she was severely beaten,
when she acknowledged that she had been at the *Sabbat*. He
pardoned her, on the condition that she would convey him thither,
and she assented to his wish. On arriving at the place, he was
placed at table with the assembled magicians and demons; but
finding the food very insipid, he asked for salt, which was not
brought.   Perceiving, however, a salt-cellar near him, he exclaimed,—" God be praised, the salt is come at last!"   In an instant, the whole assemblage and the repast vanished, and he found
himself in the midst of barren mountains, more than thirty leagues
from his house.   On returning, he related the whole affair to the
inquisitors, who immediately ordered the arrest of his wife, and
many of her accomplices; all of whom, accordingly, were found
guilty, and unmercifully condemned to the stake.

In such a period, it was unnecessary to poison or to murder a
wife who had lost her husband's affection, or incurred his suspi
cion; the law was willing and ready to perform the office of executioner for him.—ED.

plained of being taken from a most extraordinary situation.* We may, with the judicious and unfortunate Llorente, compare this illusion to those experienced by the women devoted to the worship of the mother of the gods, when they heard continually the sound of flutes and of tamborines, saw the joyous dances of the fauns and satyrs, and tasted inexpressible pleasures: similar medicaments were the cause among them of a similar kind of intoxication.

To this cause we may, likewise, refer the success of the magicians in their amours, such as those which Lucian and Apuleius have rendered so famous. This gives new grounds for the probability that the same secret, with slight variations, was obtained by the wretched sorcerers of the West from the inferior magicians, who made a merchandise of love-philters in Greece and in Italy.

In all ages the number of sorceresses has surpassed that of sorcerers; which is accounted for by women possessing a warmer imagination and a more sensitive organization than men. In the same way we may explain why, in the fables so often -repeated, where the demons or Magi were magically united to mortals, the greater number of instances are referable to nightmare. They were real dreams, heightened by a disposition to hysteria; and this was the only reality they possessed.

In short, we do not scruple to say that, in order to explain the principal facts registered in the bloody archives of civil and religious tribunals, and in the voluminous records of demonology; in order to explain the confessions of the multitude of credulous or imbecile persons of both sexes who

---

* A. Laguna, *Commentaire sur Dioscoride*, lib. lxxvi., cap. iv., cité par Llorente, *Histoire de l'Inquisition*, tome iii., p. 428.

firmly believed themselves to be sorcerers, and were convinced that they had attended the *Sabbat*, it is only necessary to connect, with the use of the magical ointment, the deep impression on the imagination produced by previous descriptions regarding the *Sabbat*, with the ceremonies that were witnessed there, and the joys in which those who joined such abominations were to participate.

These presumed assemblies, indeed, and their guilty purposes, had been notorious from the commencement of the fifth century, and awakened at an early period the increasing severity of the clergy and the magistrates. They are described as of frequent occurrence and long duration; yet all this time the sorcerers were never once detected at any of these meetings. It was not that fear prevented it; the same records and trials mention certain proceedings by which either the legal agents or ministers of religion, far from having any thing to fear from the spirits of darkness, obtained an ascendency over them, and had power to apprehend the miserable creatures, in spite of the evil spirit by whom they were misled. But in reality these assemblies had no existence, otherwise they must have survived the wrecks of Polytheism. Solitary initiations were substituted for them, and these were soon reduced to a mere confiding of secrets; all that remained then was a mutilated tradition of ceremonies borrowed from various pagan mysteries, and a description of the joys promised to the initiated. Conformably to the declarations of the sorcerers themselves, we can not fail to perceive that they believed the ointment with which they rubbed their bodies to be magical; and the facts quoted prove that its effect was so powerful as to leave them no more in doubt as to the reality of the fanciful impressions it occasioned,

than of those sensations received by them in their
waking hours.   Thus they had the full persuasion
of having partaken of rich feasts, while they acknowledged before the judges that at these ban-
quets neither hunger nor thirst were appeased ;*
the impression of reality was so great, that they
could not believe they had merely dreamed of eating and drinking. With their dreams, however, as is
usually the case, were mingled various reminiscen-
ces.   On one hand, memory presented to them a
confused succession of absurd scenes, which they
had been led to expect; and, on the other, in the
midst of magical ceremonies they saw introduced,
as actors, persons of their own acquaintance, whom
they actually denounced, swearing they had seen
them at the Sabbat ; yet this homicidal oath was
no perjury !   They made it with the same conviction that led them to confessions and revelations,
and which devoted them to frightful punishments.
Fromann relates† that the confessions of sorcerers
condemned to be burnt at Ingolstadt were publicly
read ; they confessed to having cut off the lives of
several persons by their witchcraft : these persons
lived, were present at the trial, thus refuting the
absurd confession; and, nevertheless, the judges
continued to institute suits against sorcery.   In
1750, at Wurtzburg, a nun was accused of this
crime, and carried before a tribunal, where she
firmly maintained that she was a sorceress : like
the accused at Ingolstadt, she named the victims
to her sorceries ; and although these persons were
then alive, yet the unfortunate creature perished
at the stake.‡

* Fromann, *Tract. de Fasc.*, p. 613.
† *Ibid*, p. 850.
‡ Voltaire, *Prix de la Justice et de l'Humanité*, art. x.
In 1515 not less than five hundred persons were tried at Ge-
neva, on charges of witchcraft, and executed ; and in Scotland,

The opinion which these revelations tend to establish is not new; J. Wierius had already honored himself by establishing it. A Spanish theologian* addressed a treatise to the Inquisition, in which, representing the opinion of many of his cotemporaries, he maintained that the greater number of the crimes imputed to the sorcerers have existed only in dreams; and that for the production of these dreams it was only necessary to anoint the body with drugs, and to establish a firm faith in the individual that he should really be transported to the *Sabbat.*†

in 1599, scarcely a year after the publication of the "Demonologie" of King James, not less than six hundred human beings were destroyed at once for this imaginary crime.* The sufferers in England, also, were very numerous. The statute of James, which adjudged those convicted of witchcraft to suffer death, was not repealed until the year 1736, the ninth of George II.

In every country, it may be asked, who were the assumed witches? We may reply, in the words of Reginald Scott, in his "Discoverie of Witchcraft,"† they were " women which be commonly old, lame, bleare-eied, pale, fowle, and full of wrinkles; poore, sullen, superstitious, and papists; or such as know no religion; in whose drousie minds the divell hath gotten a fine seat; so as, what mischafe, mischance, calamitie, or slaughter is brought to passe, they are easilie persuaded the same is doone by themselves, imprinting in their minds an earnest and constant imagination thereof. They are lean and deformed, shewing melancholie in their faces, to the horror of all that see them. They are doting, scolds, mad, divelish, and not much differing from them that are thought to be possessed with spirits; so firm and stedfast in their opinions, as whosoever shall onlie have respect to the constancie of their words uttered, would easilie believe they were true indeed." No comment could throw any additional light upon the cruel nature of these persecutions, and the description of their miserable victims.—Ed.

* Llorente, *Histoire de l'Inquisition*, tome iii., pp. 454, 455.

† It has been, with some degree of probability, supposed, that the idea of the Sabbat arose from the secrecy with which the meetings of the Waldenses were compelled to be held, and the accusations of indulging in unhallowed rites which were brought against them. At a very early period, these persecuted people

---

* Nashe's *Lenten Stuff*, 1599.—*Shakspeare*, vol. ii., p. 477.
† See Book i., chap. iii., p. 7.

We do not say that particular causes, in subordination to this general one, may not have had a very sensible influence in producing the accusations of witchcraft among a very ignorant population; for example, the possession of superior science has brought upon a man the reputation of being a sorcerer. The opportunity afforded for observation was the source of the accusation of sorcery against shepherds. In their frequent iso-

had separated and kept themselves distinct from the Church of Rome. In 1332, Pope John XXII. issued a bull against them, and another was sent forth, in 1487, by Innocent VIII., enjoining the nuncio, Alberto Capitaneis, " to extirpate the pernicious sect of malignant men called the poor people of Lyon, or the Waldenses, who have long endeavored in Piedmont, and other neighboring parts, to ensnare the sheep belonging unto God, under a feigned picture of holiness." Many persecutions followed ; but the Waldenses defended their opinions with the most determined resolution, and even with the sword. In some of the defeats which they suffered, both women and children were put to death ; and the prisoners were, in several instances, burned alive. These excesses drove the wretched Waldenses, thus suffering for conscience' sake, to take refuge in the fastnesses of the mountains, a step which brought upon them the accusations already noticed, and originated the supposition that the *Sabbat*, which the wretches suspected of witchcraft were stated to attend, was a real meeting. The Waldenses were also sometimes called *Scobases*, from the belief that, like the witches, they proceeded through the air to their meetings, riding upon broomsticks. Credulity regarded the *Sabbat* as real; for Reginald Scott informs us, that it was generally believed that the witches met together " at certaine assemblies, at the time prefixed, and doo not onlie see the divell in visible forme, but coufer and talke familiarlie with him ;" and he adds that, on the introduction of a novice, the arch-demon, " chargeth hir to procure men, women, and children also, as she can, to enter into this societie . . . . . At these magical assemblies, the witches never fail to danse, and whiles they sing and danse everie one hath a broome in hir hand, and holdeth it up aloft."* Such was the extraordinary length to which credulity extended respecting this imaginary assembly; and one of the chief features of the monstrous and gross superstition which existed, at the period alluded to, was the melancholy fact that it was the creed of all ranks, from the monarch to the beggar. Happily, since the light of education has penetrated into the cottage, it remains merely as a matter of fanciful tradition.—ED.

---

* *Discoverie of Witchcraft*, book i., chap. iii.

II.   **D**

lations from society, necessity has forced these men to be the physicians and surgeons of their flocks; and, favored by chance and guided by analogy, they were sometimes enabled to perform cures on their own race. The sick man was healed; and the question was put, whence did the uninstructed individual derive so marvelous a faculty if not from magic? Several shepherds, it is well known, also became, in a short time, so intimate with the individual physiognomy of their sheep, as readily to distinguish any one of his own flock mingled with the flock of another shepherd.* The man who could thus select his own from a thousand animals, apparently similar, could not easily avoid being deemed a sorcerer; particularly if vanity or interest should lead him to favor the error which gains him the reputation of superior power and knowledge. What must be the consequence, then, if the center whence light ought to emanate; if the authority, which rules the destiny of every citizen, is governed by the common opinion? Even in our own day, the French legislation has treated shepherds as accused, or, at least, as suspected of sorcery; for we find that simple menaces from them are punished by tortures, reserved, in other cases, for assaults and murders. Does not this arise from the supposition, that there is a power of evil in their mere words? This law, enacted in 1751,† although fallen into disuse, has not yet been formally abrogated.

* M. Desgranges, *Mémoire sur les Usages d'un Canton de la Beauce.*—*Mémoires de la Société des Antiquaires de France,* tome i., pp. 242, 243.

† A similar law forbids all shepherds to menace, ill treat, or do any wrong to the farmers or laborers whom they serve, or who are served by them, as well as their families, shepherds, or domestics, under penalty, for the said shepherds, of five years at the galleys for simple menaces, and for ill treatment nine years.—*Préambule du Conseil-d'Etat du Roi, du* 15 *Septembre,* 1751.

The severity exercised toward sorcerers, although altogether absurd in principle, yet was not always unjust in its application, since sorcery served frequently as the mask or instrument for the perpetration of criminal actions. Thus the use of drugs, by which the fish in a preserve are rendered so stupefied that they can be taken by the hand, although considered now a delinquency, provided against and punished by law, was formerly regarded as the effect of sorcery. The tricks of sharpers, with whose delinquencies our small courts are daily filled, and which consist of selling the imaginary aid of supernatural power at a high rate, were acts of sorcery. Sorcery, indeed, was a cover for many atrocities, and crimes, sometimes arising from the mere desire to impose; sometimes from transports of cruelty or refinements of revenge, and the wish to transfer their load of guilt to those whom they initiated.*

But it can not be denied, that poison alone has too often constituted the real efficacy of sorcery: this is a fact of which the ancients were not ignorant, a proof of which exists in the passage in the

* "Commodus . . . . . sacra Mithriaca homicidio vero polluit; cum illic aliquid, ad speciem timoris, vel dici, vel fingi soleat."— (Æl. Lamprid. in *Commod. Anton.*) This phrase is obscure; and shows us the extreme reserve of ancient writers on all that concerned the initiations. We may, nevertheless, deduce from it, that the novice in the mysteries of Mythra believed himself obliged to obey the command of the initiating to kill a man. These mysteries, which penetrated into Rome, and afterward into Gaul, toward the commencement of our era, belonged, in Asia, to the remotest antiquity, since Zoroaster was thus initiated before setting out on his religious mission. Now this prophet was much earlier than Ninus; the religion which he founded was general and powerful in the Empire of Assyria, in the time of Ninus and Semiramis. The trial which the priests of Mythra, in order to assure themselves, made use of to determine the resolution and docility of an aspirant, is still practiced by one of the superior lodges of Freemasons. Similar trials necessarily passed into the schools of magic from the ancient temples; and that which was only used as a pretense in general, might easily on occasion become reality

second eclogue of Theocritus,* which we have just
quoted. It is a curious fact, confirmed by judicial
trials in modern times,† that the victim persisting
in ascribing his sufferings to supernatural agency
has thus aided in shielding the real crime of the
guilty from the investigation of the law.

In such a case, had the magistrates been enlightened as well as severe, they would have acquired
great claims to public gratitude, by giving some
attention to the real nature of the crime as well as
to the punishment of it.   They might, by unveiling
and giving publicity to pretended magical operations, have exposed the impotency of the magicians, when prevented by circumstances from having recourse to their detestable practices : and by
such revelations, many disordered imaginations
might eventually have been cured.

But far from doing so, the judges, for a long
period, reasoned like the inquisitors who, when
obliged, by formal depositions, to admit that the
secret of the sorcerers consisted in the composition
of poisons, punished nevertheless the imaginary
rather than the real crime.‡   Legislators had no
clearer discernment than the populace : they issued

---

* See chap. ix.

† In 1689, some shepherds of Brien destroyed the cattle of
their neighbors, by administering to them drugs on which they
had thrown holy water, and over which they recited magical incantations. Prosecuted as sorcerers, they were condemned as
poisoners. It was discovered that the basis of these drugs was
arsenic.

It is curious to observe the similarity of customs in very distant
countries. In Shetland, the religious charmer imbued water
with magical powers for a very opposite purpose, namely, to preserve from mischance ; to combat an evil eye or an evil tongue.
The charmer muttered some words over water, in imitation of
Catholic priests consecrating holy water, and the fluid was
named "forespoken water." Boats were sprinkled with it ; and
diseased limbs washed with it, for the purpose of *telling out* pains.
—Ed.

‡ Llorente, *Histoire de l'Inquisition*, tome iii., pp. 440, 441.

terrible decrees against sorcerers, and even by these means doubled, nay, tenfold increased their number. To doubt, in this case, the effect of persecution, were to betray great ignorance of mankind. Opening a vast field for all the calumny and tale-bearing that might be dictated by folly, by fear, by hatred, or vengeance, in preparing instruments of torture and erecting stakes in every market-place, they multiplied absurd or false accusations and still more absurd confessions.* In giving

* No portion of the history of witchcraft is more extraordinary than the confessions occasionally made by the wretched beings who were brought to trial as sorcerers. Although many of them were extorted under torture, and afterward revoked during moments of mental and bodily resuscitation, yet some of those recorded were voluntary. What condition of mind, it may be asked, could lead to the latter, if we can believe that the accused could ever fancy that they were really actors in such supernatural transactions? In reply, we may venture to suggest, that vanity, one of the most powerful agents in the female character, in raising an idea of importance at being thought possessors of the extraordinary powers which they assumed, must have had a considerable share in producing them. As a specimen of these confessions, we may mention that of Agnes Thompson, who was implicated in the supposed detected conspiracy of two hundred witches with Dr. Fian, "Register to the Devil," at their head, to bewitch and drown King James on his return from Denmark, in 1590. Agnes confessed that she and the other witches, her comrades, "went altogether by sea, each one in her riddle or sieve, with flagons of wine, making merry and drinking by the way, to the kirk of North Berwick, in Lothian, where, when they had landed, they took hands and danced, singing all with one voice—

"Commer goe ye before, Commer goe ye ;
Gif ye will not go before, Commer let me :"

and that Giles Duncane did go before them, playing said reel on a Jew's trump ; and that the devil had met them at the kirk." The silly monarch, who was present at their confession, expressed some doubts as to the last part of it ; but, taking Agnes aside, he affirmed that she "declared unto him the very words which had passed between him and his queen on the first night of their marriage, with their answers to each other ; whereat the king wondered greatly, and swore by the living God, that he believed all the devils in hell could not have discovered the same.*
—ED.

* *Newes from Scotland*, reprinted in the *Gent. Mag.*, vol. xlix., p. 449 and quoted in Drake's *Shakspeare*, vol. ii., p. 476.

importance to these foolish terrors, by bringing
the sacred character of the law to bear upon them,
they rendered this general apprehension incurable.
The multitude no longer doubted the guilt of men
who were so rigorously prosecuted ; enlightened
individuals swelled the ranks of the multitude,
either from the influence of the general panic, or
lest they should themselves become suspected of
the crimes whose existence they denied.   How
can we otherwise account for the lengthened and
deplorable annals of sorcery, whose daily records
tell of acts perfectly impossible, but which the accused confessed, the witnesses affirmed, the doctors
established, and the judges visited with punishment
and death ?   It was, for instance, supposed, that
the physical insensibility of the whole, or some
part of the body, was a sure sign of a compact with
the devil.   In France, in 1589, fourteen pretended
sorcerers, who were declared incapable of feeling,
were, for this cause, condemned to death, on the
testimony of the surgeons who formed part of the
legal commission.   On an appeal from these unfortunate beings, another examination was ordered
by the Parliament, at that time assembled at Tours.
The sentence was stayed by the sensible men who
conducted the second inquiry, and who reported
that the accused were imbecile or deranged (perhaps in consequence of the misery they had endured), but in other respects physically possessing
a keenly sensitive nature.*   For once, truth was
triumphant, and the lives of the poor wretches
were saved.   But this was a singular instance.

The course of the seventeenth century again saw
a great number of prosecutions for sorcery ; till at
length the progress of knowledge—the great benefit
of civilization—drew the film from the eyes of the

* *Chirurgie de Pigray*, lib. viii., chap. x., p. 445.

supreme authorities. The Act of the Parliament of France, of 1682, decrees that sorcerers shall be no longer prosecuted, except as deceivers, blasphemers, and poisoners—that is to say, for their real crimes; and from that time their number has diminished every day.*

This discussion may appear superfluous to those impatient spirits who believe it but loss of time to refute to-day the error of yesterday; forgetting that the development of the sources of error form an essential part of the history of the human mind. Beside, although the better instructed throughout Europe have ceased to believe in witchcraft, is this progress so very remote; has the light already shone on so vast a circle that this subject merits only to be consigned to oblivion? Scarcely a hundred years have elapsed since a book appeared in Paris, recommending the rigor of the laws, and the severity of the tribunals against sorcerers, and against those who were skeptical as to the existence of witchcraft and magic; yet this book has received the approbation of the judges of literature.†

. We have already related the punishment of a pretended witch, who was burned at Wurtzburg, in 1750. At the same period, in an enlightened country, the rage of popular credulity survived the rigor of the magistrates, who had ceased to prosecute for a chimerical crime. " Scarcely half-a-century has elapsed," writes a traveler, an enthusiastic admirer of the English, " since witches have been drowned in England. In the year 1751, two old women, suspected to be witches, were arrested, and, in

---

* Dulaure, *Histoire de Paris*, tome v., pp. 36, 37.

† *Traité sur la Magie*, par Daugis (in 12mo., Paris, 1732), extracted, with an eulogium on it, in the *Journal de Trévoux*, September, 1732, pp. 1534–1544.

the course of some experiments made on these
unfortunate creatures by the populace, they were
plunged three several times into a pond, and were
drowned; this occurred near Tring, a few miles
from London."* Notwithstanding the vicinity of
the metropolis, it does not appear that any steps
were taken to punish the actors in these two murderous assaults, to which the traveler gives the
gentle name of experiments.†

* *Voyage d'un Français en Angleterre* (2 vols. 8vo., Paris, 1816.
tome i., p. 400).

† It is curious to trace the influence of the belief of witchcraft
in England and Scotland, at different periods. It had attracted
the attention of government in the reign of Henry VIII., in the
thirty-third year of which a statute was enacted which adjudged
all witchcraft and sorcery to be punished as felony, without benefit of clergy. This statute did not regard these crimes as impos
tures, but as real, supernatural, demoniacal gifts, and consequently
punishable. In the subsequent reign, Elizabeth, the queen, suffered "under excessive anguish by pains in her teeth,"* which
deprived her of rest, a circumstance which was attributed to the
sorcery of a Mrs. Dyer, who was accused of conjuration and
witchcraft on that account; indeed, the belief had infatuated all
ranks, and extended even to the clergy. Bishop Jewel, in a ser-
mon preached before the queen, in 1558, made use of the following
expressions: "It may please your grace to understand that witches
and sorcerers, within these few last years, are marvelously increased within your grace's realm. Your grace's subjects pine
away, even unto the death; their color fadeth, their flesh rotteth,
their speech is benumbed, their senses are bereft: I pray God
they never practice further upon the subject."† Reginald Scott,
also, in his excellent work, entitled "The Discoveries of Witchcraft," says, "I have heard, to my greefe, some of the ministerie
affirme, that they have had in their parish, at one instant, xvii or
xviii witches; meaning such as could work miracles supernatur-
allie."‡ Were we not accurately informed of the deep root, and
consequently firm hold, which the idea of the existence of witchcraft had taken of the public mind at this period, the neglect of
Scott's work, and that of Johannis Wierius, *De Præstigiis Dæmo-
num*, would greatly astonish us. Both of these valuable productions were intended to free the world from the infatuation which
had seized upon it; to prove the falsehood of the accusations, and
even of the confessions; and to shield the poor, the ignorant, and
the friendless aged from falling victims to the arm of murder,

* Styrpe's *Annals*, vol. iv., p. 7.   † *Ibid.*, vol. i., p. 8
‡ *Discoverie of Witchcraft*, chap. i., p. 4.

After such an example, it may be understood how, in 1760, in one of the inland provinces of Sweden,* it required the authority and the courage of the wife of a great personage to save twelve families, under an accusation of witchcraft, from the fury of the populace.

In 1774, in Germany, where philosophy is so ardently cultivated, numerous disciples and followers of Gassner and Schrœpfer adopted their doctrines respecting miracles, exorcisms, magic, and

under the perverted name of justice, uplifted by terror and the darkest superstition. Scott informs us, that the whole parish of St. Osus, in Essex, consisting of "seventeene or eighteene, were condemned at once." On the accession of James to the English throne, the superstition of that weak and absurd monarch, which had been previously displayed in his "Demonologie," published at Edinburgh in 1597, brought forth a new statute against witches, which contains the following clause:—"Any that shall use, practice, or exercise any invocation or conjuration of an evill or wicked spirit, or consult, covenant with, entertain, or employ, feed or rewarde, any evill or wicked spirit, or to or for any intent or purpose; or take up any dead man, woman or child, out of his, her, or their grave, or any other place where the dead body resteth, or the skin, bone, or other part of any dead person, to be employed or used in any manner of witchcraft, sorcery, charme, or enchantment, whereby any person shall be killed, destroyed, wasted, consumed, pined, or bound in his or her body, or any part thereof: such offenders, duly and lawfully convicted and attainted, shall suffer death."* After such edicts as these, issuing from the highest authorities in the kingdom, can we wonder at the extension of the credulity of the people respecting supernatural agency; or at their faith in the power of those who professed to do "a deed without a name;" and who, as the silly monarch and royal author, to whom we have referred, sayeth, "gave their hand to the devil, and promised to observe and keepe all the devil's commandments."† The early Christians were not only dupes to these deceptions, but they preferred their assistance by means of prayers and benedictions to obviate the influence of the demon; and thus contributed to rivet the chains that already enslaved the human mind in the darkest superstitions.‡—Ed.

* En Dalécarlie.—Barbier, *Dictionnaire Historique*, p. 1195.

---

* This statute was not repealed till the 9th of George II., 1736.

† *Discoverie of Witchcraft*, book iii., chap. i., p. 40.

‡ The act of ducking supposed witches in England has been practiced more than once within the present century.

theurgy.*   In 1785, in the canton of Lucerne, J. Müller, the celebrated historian, and one of his friends, while peaceably seated under a tree and reading Tacitus aloud, were assailed by a troop of peasants, who had been persuaded by some monks that the strangers were sorcerers.   They narrowly escaped being massacred.† At the commencement of the century several sharpers were condemned, in France, for traversing the country and persuading the peasants that spells had been cast both on their cattle and on themselves; and, not satisfied with exacting payment for taking off the pretended spells, they raised violent enmities, and occasioned even murderous encounters, by pointing out the authors of these pretended spells.

It was still a matter of serious argument, in the schools of Rome, in the year 1810, as to whether sorcerers were mad or possessed.‡   They went further in Paris, for, in 1817, works§ were there published in which the existence of magic was formally maintained; and in which the zeal of the learned and virtuous, but mistaken men who formerly had caused sorcerers to be burned, was applauded.

Let the upholders of such doctrines applaud themselves; the doctrines are still dominant in those distant countries where colonization has oftener introduced the vices than the advanced knowl-

* Tiedmann, *Quæstione, &c.*, pp. 114, 115.
† C. V. de Bonstetten, *Pensées sur divers objets de bien public,* pp. 230–232.
‡ Guinan Laoureins, *Tableau de Rome vers la fin de* 1814, p. 228.
§ *Les Précurseurs de l'Anti-Christ.—Les Superstitions et Prestiges des Philosophes.*   See *Le Journal de Paris,* 28 Décembre, 1817. The maladies to which our author alludes are the consequence of malaria, arising from decomposing animal and vegetable matters.   If such accusations as he mentions occur in the French West-Indian Islands, they are happily unknown in the English.— ED.

edge of Europe. The elevated and arid soil of
the American islands, is, in summer, a prey to
maladies which attack the horses and flocks, and
do not even spare men. It can not be doubted
that they arise from the noxious properties of the
stagnant water, which they are obliged to make
use of; as a proof of which the habitations, near a
running stream, invariably escape the scourge.
Far from recognizing this fact, the planters persist
in ascribing their losses to sorcery, practiced by
their slaves; and, consequently, the unlucky individuals on whom chance fixes the suspicion are
condemned to perish by torture.*

But, to find examples of such horrible extravagance, it is unnecessary to cross the ocean. In the
year 1617, in a country village of East Flanders, a
father murdered his daughter, who was only ten
years old, "because," he asserted, "she was a sorceress." For a similar motive he intended the
same fate for his wife and sister.† It was pleaded
in excuse that he was insane. What awful insanity
was that which converted the husband and father
into an assassin! How fearful the credulity that
led to such a delirium! Can we qualify the cul-
pability of those who awaken, or who dare to encourage it!

In 1826, the town of Spire was much scandalized
by a circumstance that was more deplorable from
the character given to it by the position of those
with whom it originated, and from the moral consequences which might have ensued. The bishop
of that town died at the age of eighty-two years,
and had bequeathed twenty thousand florins to its
cathedral. He was not buried in a chapel of his
church, as his predecessors had been; nor would

* I got this fact from an eye-witness.
† *Le Journal de Paris, Jeudi*, 3 Avril, 1817. p. 3.

the clergy take part in his obsequies, because they accused the venerable prelate of sorcery.*

How can one, after this, be surprised at the ignorant credulity of the multitude, with such an example from their spiritual advisers?

In the peninsula of Hela, near Dantzic, a woman was accused by a charlatan of having cast a spell over a sick person. She was seized, and tortured several times in the course of two days; twice they tried to drown her; they ended by murdering her with a knife, because she refused to acknowledge herself to be a witch, and because she declared herself incapable of curing the sick person.†

In France, also, justly proud of its enlightenment, of its civilization, and the gentleness of its manners, this error has been fruitful. A country-woman of the neighborhood of Dax having fallen ill, the friends who were with her were persuaded by a quack that her illness was the result of a spell, thrown upon her by one of her neighbors. The peasants seized on the accused individual, and, after violently beating her, thrust her into the flames to compel her to dissolve the spell; there they held her in spite of her cries, her screams, and assertions of innocence, and at last drove her from the house only when she was on the point of expiring.‡

This crime, which was committed eleven years ago, has lately been repeated in a village in the department of Cher. The victim, who was accused of bewitching the cattle, will probably die, owing to the atrocious treatment she has met with.§ It is true that justice will pursue her murderers,

* *Le Constitutionnel du 15 Août*, 1826.
† *Le National du 29 Août*, 1836.
‡ *Le Constitutionnel du 26 Juillet*, 1826.
§ *Le National du 6 Novembre*, 1836.

and punish them; but of what use is the condemnation of a few grossly ignorant peasants, while the source of the evil remains unremoved? Has the time not yet passed for maintaining the opinion that it is well for the people to remain in ignorance, and to believe whatever is told them without examination? In the schools open to the lower classes, can no one venture to expostulate, or to forewarn and forearm them against the dangers of a blind credulity? Even in the vicinity of the capital, the country districts are infested with books on witchcraft. I speak of what I have myself witnessed. One, among others recently printed, particularly attracted my observation, from the typographical character, the whiteness of the paper, the state of preservation, and the general neatness of the volume, so uncommon in the rough hands of a herdsman. With various absurdities, and extracts from conjuring books, less innocent recipes were interspersed: for example, one for the composition of the waters of Death, a violent poison, described as being capable of transmuting all metals into gold; another for procuring early abortion; and a third for a more active medicine, should the mother have felt the infant move: so true it is, as we have already observed, that lessons of crime have been almost always mixed up with the absurd fancies of sorcery!

Is this error, then, to be left to root itself out? Is it not rather the duty of the higher classes to strive against the principles that lead to it, until the progress of knowledge shall afford a guard to men of simple and limited understanding? Should they not endeavor to save those who wildly believe themselves to be endowed with supernatural power from the consequences of this belief, and release the credulous who, through fear of this power, are

tormented by anxieties equally formidable in their
issue, and ridiculous in their origin? Or, is this a
mere speculative question of philosophy? The
age is not long past since peaceable individuals
were dragged to punishment by a multitude agitated by that excessive terror which is so much the
more difficult to cure because it has no real foundation; an age in which a single word, a vague
rumor, were sufficient to constitute the same person
at once an accuser, a judge, and an executioner.
Do not these superstitious terrors, which convert
man into a ferocious animal, place a powerful engine in the hands of those whose interest it is to
excite him, whose aim is the subversion of order
and of government? Should the opinions I have
proffered affix upon me the charge of profaneness
from some fanatical hypocrites, I can only answer,
I am obeying my conscience in endeavoring to expose the shameful absurdity of a belief as contrary
to the best interests of society, as to all which true
piety teaches of the power, the wisdom, and the
goodness of God.

CHAPTER III.

Influence of the Imagination, seconded by physical Accessories,
in producing an habitual Belief in marvelous Narrations, by
Music, by the Habit of exalting the Moral Faculties, by unfounded Terror, and by Presentiments.—Sympathetic Emotions
increase the Effects of the Imagination.—Cures produced by
the Imagination.—Flights of the Imagination effected by Diseases, Fastings, Watchings, and Mortifications.—Moral and
physical Remedies successfully opposed to these Flights of the
Imagination.

To the physical causes which involved pretended sorcerers in deplorable errors, was added an
auxiliary which alone is sufficient to produce the
evil—namely, Imagination.

Such is its power, that some men have ascribed to its wanderings the origin of all magical illusions; but this is going too far. Imagination combines the impressions it has received; it does not create.* In the phantoms of sleep or the reveries of waking hours, it presents nothing which has not either been seen, or felt, or heard. Terror, melancholy, uneasiness, or preoccupation of mind, easily produces that intermediate state between waking and sleeping, in which dreams become actual visions. Thus, proscribed by the triumvirs, Cassius Parmensis fell asleep, a prey to cares too well justified by his position. A man of an alarming form appeared to him, and told him he was his evil genius. Accustomed to believe in the existence of supernatural beings, Cassius had no doubt of the reality of the apparition; and by superstitious minds such

* This definition of our author, although critically correct, yet does not embody the idea generally entertained of imagination, which may be truly said to create, inasmuch as it selects qualities and circumstances from a great variety of different objects, and, by recombining and disposing them differently, forms a new creation peculiarly its own. It is true that its influence is chiefly confined to objects of sight; and we must admit that "we can not, indeed," as Addison remarks, "have a single image in the fancy that did not make its first entrance through the sight." Were we, therefore, capable of analyzing every illusion, we should most probably be able to trace, at least, many of its components, although perhaps not the whole, to objects which had previously made a lively impression upon our sight. It admits of intellectual combinations and the association of abstract ideas, without which none of those conversations and reasonings that are carried on in dreams would occur. This view of imagination, however, does not weaken the position of our author; and there can be no doubt that, in a mind not under the control which education bestows, dreams and the most extravagant illusions acquire a powerful influence in regulating its affections and exciting its passions. Much depends on the physical condition and health of the individual at the time; and to the state of the nervous system may be ascribed the pleasurable or distressing nature of illusions, whether the effect of simple revery or of dreaming: the influence which they exert on our conduct, or apparently on our destiny, depends much on the degree of superstitious credulity which governs the individual.—Ed.

a vision is regarded as the certain warning of that violent death which an outlaw can scarcely escape.

The same explanation may be applied to the vision which appeared to Brutus, without intimidating him, on the eve of the battle of Philippi; and still more forcibly to the dream of the Emperor Julian.*

The night preceding his death, a genius seemed to retire from him with an air of consternation. He recognized in the specter the genius of the empire, whose image might be seen in every thing around him : reproduced upon the coin; reverenced by the soldiers upon the center of his standards; and doubtless also placed in his tent.   Uneasy at the famine which afflicted his troops; certain that, even in the bosom of his army, a religion opposed to his own faith raised up numerous enemies, and perhaps assassins; on the eve of a decisive battle; is it surprising that the enthusiastic disciple of the theurgian philosophy, whose doctrine assigned so important an office to the genii, should have seen such a vision in a perplexing dream ?   Julian believed that he actually saw the genius of the empire sad, and ready to abandon him.

Let us take another example.   An aged woman was mourning for a brother whom she had just lost: suddenly she thought she heard his voice, which, by a blamable deception, was counterfeited near her.   Seized with fear, she declared that the spirit of her brother had appeared to her radiant with light.   She would not have seen such a vision if her memory had not, from her childhood, been filled with stories of ghosts and apparitions.

These stories may be traced to the most ancient times, and then they were not counterfeited.   Let

* Ammian. Marcell., lib. xxv.

us remember that in the sanctuaries, in the time of Orpheus, they invoked the dead.   Even in ancient Judea these phantasmagorical apparitions abounded, the first accounts of which were then neither founded on dreams, nor upon the wandering of the imagination, nor upon the desire of deceiving; the individuals did actually see what they asserted they had seen, and which, as they were constantly stimulated by such narrations, or the recollection of them, and overcome by sorrow yet full of curiosity, they both feared and desired to behold.

In the mountains of Scotland, and in some countries of Germany, the people still believe in the reality of apparitions, which are said to be warnings of an approaching death.*   One sees, distinct from

* *Phantasmagoria, or Collection of Stories, &c.*, translated from the German (2 vols. 12mo., Paris, 1812), vol. ii., pp. 126–142. These apparitions are denominated "Wraiths," or "Taisch," which means simply visions; and the persons beholding them are called seers.   They are generally prophetic of evil, but not always; as births, marriages, and many other events, are said to be foretold by these beholders of the shadows "of coming events." In the Highlands of Scotland, at one period, they were generally and firmly believed.   Although many seers might be in the same place or apartment, yet all of them did not see the same vision, unless they touched each other, when it became common.   The gift was also inherent: it could not be taught; but Mr. Aubrey says it was taught in the isle of Skye.

Every Highlander believes that he has an attendant genius or spirit, which is always present with him from the cradle to the grave.   This spirit is a counterpart of himself, in form, in dress, and in every other respect; but, although thus peculiarly his attendant, yet the spirit may be separated from him for a time, and may perform acts, when distant from him, which his principal shall execute at some future time.   Thus, if the person is likely to die, or to perform some act that may endanger life, his wraith may appear to his distant friends, and thus communicate the sad news, or anticipate the event.   In a few words, the Highland wraith is the *simulacrum* or *imago* of the ancient Romans.   The visions may be of the specter alone, who may be seen either by the individual himself, or by his friends, or by strangers; but, when the attendant genius appears to his principal, his back only is seen: on other occasions the vision may consist of a number of persons or things; for example, the whole ceremony of a funeral or a marriage may be displayed.

II   E

one's self, as it were, another self, a figure in every respect resembling one's own in form, features, gesticulations, and attire.   To produce a similar

The inhabitants of the Western Islands and of St. Kilda were especially liable to be affected by these impressions. The apparitions were generally exact resemblances of the individuals, in person, in features, and in clothing. They attacked the individuals some months before they sickened of the disease of which they died. A man on a sick bed was visited by a lady, the wife of the clergyman of St. Kilda, and was asked by her if at any time he had seen any resemblance of himself; he replied in the affirmative, and told her that, to make further trial, as he was going out of his house of a morning, he put on straw-rope garters, instead of those he formerly used; and having gone to the fields, his other self appeared in straw garters. The conclusion of the story is, that the sick man died of that ailment; and the lady no longer questioned the truth of such presages.— (Sir W. Scott, *A Legend of Montrose*, chap. xvii., note *Wraiths.*)

In such cases, it is evident that the illusion was truly the result of imagination, operating under the influence of derangement of the nerves, the body being already in a state of incipient disease. The uneasy sensations of approaching disease would naturally awaken in a mind educated in the belief of such apparitions, the idea of some impending evil, and imagination would readily operate in completing the illusion.

It is also probable that, as the wraiths or apparitions of themselves, which are seen by these islanders, always appear in the early morning, and in mountainous districts subject to fogs, they may be the result of an optical deception, such as occurs at the Brocken, one of the Hertz or Harz Mountains, and occasionally in Cumberland. St. Kilda is the most northern of the Hebrides, and consists of an unequal mountainous ridge, the highest point of which, Benochan, rises thirteen hundred and eighty feet above the level of the sea; and, as in the Harz, the southwest wind, which prevails, brings with it fogs. As many of our readers may not be aware of the nature of the Specter.of the Brocken, we shall abridge the lucid account of it, from Gmelin,* given by Sir David Brewster.—(*Letters on Natural Magic.*) We may remark that this specter seems to have been observed at a very early period, as the blocks of granite on the summit of the Brocken are called the sorcerer's chair and altar; a spring of pure water, the magic fountain; and the anemone, on its margin, the sorcerer's flower—names which are presumed to have originated in the rites of the great Saxon idol, Vortho, who was secretly worshiped in the Brocken. This mountain was visited by Mr. Hane, on the 23d of May, 1797. "The sun rose at four o'clock, a.m., through a serene atmosphere, which afterward became clouded with vapors brought by a west wind. A quarter past four, Mr.

* *Göttingen, Journal der Wissenschaften,* 1798, vol. i., part iii.

miracle is not beyond the resources of art. It will be necessary, in the first place, to place a concave mirror, or segment of a large-sized sphere, at the back of a deep closet; and to dispose a lamp at the top of the cabinet, in such a manner that its light may not pass straight through, but, on the contrary, fall with all its brilliancy upon the spot where it will be necessary to place yourself, in order to obtain the best possible effect from the mirror. To this spot conduct, without his knowledge, an uneducated man, one given to revery and the terrors of mysticism; contrive that the folding-doors of the closet shall suddenly open, and pre-

Hane, looking toward the southwest, observed at a great distance a human figure of monstrous size. His hat having been nearly carried away by a gust of wind, he suddenly raised his hand to his head; the colossal figure did the same. He next bent his body; the spectral figure repeated the action, and then vanished. It soon, however, returned in another spot, and mimicked all his gestures as before. He then called the landlord of the inn, when, after a short time, two colossal figures appeared over the spot where the single figure had previously appeared. Retaining their position, these two spectral figures were joined by a third; and all three mimicked the movements of the two spectators. These specters appeared standing in the air." Similar aerial figures have been several times observed, among the hills surrounding the lakes in Cumberland.

These spectral illusions, so admirably calculated to impress the credulous with their supernatural origin, "are merely shadows of the observer, projected on dense vapor or thin, fleecy clouds, which have the power of reflecting much light." They are most frequently seen at sunrise, when the sun throws its rays horizontally, when the shadow of the observer is thrown neither upward nor downward. Sometimes, "owing to the light reflected from the vapors or clouds becoming fainter farther from the shadow, the head of the observer appears surrounded with a halo;[*] which affords another reason for strengthening the belief in the reality of the specter. The St. Kilda specter, with its straw garters, is thus easily explained." We refer our readers to Brewster's little volume, to which we are indebted for the above explanation of the specter of the Brocken.

Time and superior education, however, will gradually expel such superstitions: they have ceased to prevail even at St. Kilda.—ED.

---

[*] Brewster l. c., pp. 153, 154.

sent to him the deceptive glass. He will see his
own image come forth from the depth of the darkness, and advance toward him radiant with light ;*
and in such a shape that he will think it possible
to take hold of it, but in advancing for that purpose
it will disappear. He can not explain this vision
naturally ; he does not attempt it ; he has seen it,
actually seen it ; he can not forget it. The recollection of it pursues him, besets him, and soon,
perhaps, his imagination becomes so excited that
the phenomenon is spontaneously reproduced without the aid of the exterior cause.† The disorder
of the mind is communicated to the nerves. The
credulous man languishes, wastes away, and at
last dies. The records of his unhappy end survive him. Invalids, or people with a tendency to
disease, hearing the legend repeated, meditate upon
it ; their reveries are impregnated by it ; and they
end, at last, by seeing the vision which they have
heard related from their youth ; and being persuaded that it is the forerunner of death, they die
of their own conviction.‡

* "I approached the closet; the two doors opened without
the least noise ; the light which I held in my hand was suddenly
extinguished ; and, as if before a mirror, I saw my own image
advance from the closet ; the light which it spread illuminating a
large portion of the apartment."—*Fantasmagoriana*, tome ii., pp.
137, 138.

† This explanation is perfectly correct in reference to spectral
illusions within a house or a temple ; but those of the second
sight seen in the morning, and in the open air, can only be explained as in the foregoing note.—ED.

‡ No better explanation can be given of the fulfillment of the
prediction of these seers : death, when predicted, and the prediction when believed will take place. Such creeds assimilate every
event to themselves ; even the seer himself is the dupe of his
credulity, a circumstance less wonderful than the confessions
of witchcraft, or of the insane German *werewolf*, Peter Stump,
who murdered sixteen persons, from an idea that he was one
of the sorcerers termed *werewolves*, who, by means of an ointment
and girdle, were believed to become real wolves ; tearing to

If such is still human credulity, can we suppose that, in less enlightened times, the Thaumaturgists, endowed with so many means of acting upon the imagination, would have allowed so powerful an instrument for extending the empire of the mar-velous to have remained idle ?* Supported by some real, but extraordinary facts, the recital of prodigies and apparent miracles everywhere governed credulity; or rather it formed, as in the present day, almost all the instruction allotted to the vulgar, and prepared their eyes beforehand for seeing every thing, their ears for hearing every thing, and their minds for believing every thing.

Thus prepared, thus excited by some powerful cause, where will the influence of imagination stop ? By turns it is terrible and seducing, but always ready to confound us with unforeseen phenomena, and intoxicate us by fantastic marvels; to suspend or excite the action of our senses to the highest possible degree; to withdraw the play of our organs from the empire of our will, and the regular course of nature; to impress upon them emotions and an unknown strength, or to render them rigid and immovable; to excite the mind to folly, or even to frenzy; at one time creating objects far above the tameness of humanity, and at another raising terrors more dangerous than the perils which they represent: such are the flights, such the freaks of the imagination; and ruled, in its turn, by the disorder fallen upon our physical functions, it originates fresh errors, new fears, more powerful deliriums and torments, until remedies purely material, by curing the body, restore to the

pieces and devouring men, women, and children. This wretched maniac was inhumanly tortured with red-hot pincers, and broken on the wheel.—ED.

* See vol. i., chap. xiii., upon the subject of the optical illu-sions produced by the ancient Thaumaturgists.

mind that calm which the diseased condition of the nervous system had taken from it.

What pretended miracles would not a skillful Thaumaturgist work with a power susceptible of such various application, and endowed with so irresistible an influence ? ˙ Let us not speak of contracted minds only, or of men as ignorant and weak as the unfortunate beings whose miseries we have just retraced; let the strongest-minded man suppose himself, unconsciously, exposed to every cause which can . act upon his imagination : will he, we may inquire, dare to affirm that these influences will not operate upon him; that his moral strength will triumph, and that there shall be no perturbation in his heart, no confusion in his thoughts ?

The ancients were not ignorant of the advantages which, under various relations, could be taken of the influence of the imagination.   This fascinating and powerful agent explains an immense number of the wonders described in their histories. Our path, however, is traced out, namely, to render these marvels credible, by opposing to them analogous facts observed in modern times, facts in which imposture has not been more suspected than the intervention of a supernatural power.

No less calm than persevering in her mystic reveries, the celebrated Madame de Guyon declared to Bossuet, her accuser and judge, and also related in her life,* that she had received from God such an abundance of grace that her body could not bear it; and that it was necessary that she should be unlaced and placed upon her bed, in order that some other person should receive from her the superabundance of the grace which

* *Vie de Mme. de Guyon, écrite par elle-même*, tome ii., chap. xiii.–xxii. ; tome iii., chap. i.

filled her. This communication, she asserted, was effected in silence, and often upon the absent; and could alone relieve her feeling of excess. The Duke de Chevreuse, a man of serious and austere manners, also affirmed to Bossuet that he had felt this communication of grace when seated near Madame de Guyon; and he ingenuously asked the prelate if he did not experience a similar sensation.[*] Entitled at once to ridicule, and equally to compassion, these two persons were not very unlike the prophets and·pythonesses, who are described to us as being so subjugated by the god whose presence filled their whole being, as to be forced to utter the oracles, which he himself placed in their mouths, to be announced to the world.

Let the excitement increase, and man will fall into a state of slavery capable of making him not only believe in assumed miracles, but in his power of working them, because it withdraws him as much from the empire of reason as from that of physical impressions. This ecstasy has attracted the attention of physiologists, and provoked some learned researches, the results of which will probably be confirmed by ulterior observations.

To examine it in this light would carry us too far from our subject; we must, therefore, limit ourselves to those facts immediately connected with it. We are assured that the Hindoos can fall at pleasure into ecstasy, a state to which the Kamschatdales, the Jakoutes, and natives of North and South America are very prone. It has been observed, that since the persecutions exercised by Europeans in the formerly happy countries of Tahiti and the Sandwich Islands, the imagination of the followers of the ancient religion has been

* Burigny, *Vie de Bossuet* (12mo., Paris, 1761), pp. 274, 275 280.

much excited.* This ecstasy, or trance, is in some
degree a benefit to an ignorant and superstitious
people; it gives them instantaneously the power
of forgetting their miseries, beneath the weight of
which they drag on a languishing existence. We
may, in this point of view, compare it to intoxication, to the heavy torpor produced by stupefying
drugs, which have been sometimes used by unhappy beings to enable them to bear the agonies
of torture.† Volney attributed the extraordinary
courage exhibited in the midst of most frightful
torments by the natives of Northern America, to
the effects of a state bordering on ecstasy.‡

Ecstasy has, above all, the advantage of supplying to the believer, all that the coldness of the testimony has left defective in the descriptions of celestial happiness. Man being, by reason of his
weak nature, susceptible of prolonged pain and
short enjoyments, can much more easily imagine
the torments of the infernal regions than the joys
of heaven. This ecstasy does not describe these
pleasures, nor prove their future existence; it
causes them to be actually tasted. That the an-

* Ferdinand Denis, *Tableau des Sciences Occultes*, pp. 201–205.
† See chap. i., vol. ii.
‡ *Œuvres complètes de Volney*, tome vii., pp. 443–450. The
Editor is of opinion, that this degree of insensibility to corporeal
suffering depends on directing the mind powerfully to some
object, or train of recollection, capable of abstracting it wholly
from the sensations produced upon the nervous system by extra-
neous impressions. It is well known that directing the mind to
the seat of disease will augment both the diseased action going
on in the part, and also increase to a degree of acute suffering
any pain previously felt in the part. Thus, independent of the
counter-irritation produced by a blister, much of its beneficial
influence arises from the attention being directed to a new seat
of pain. On this principle, Protestant martyrs, by concentrating
their thoughts on the eternal triumphs they are about to enjoy
for their constancy in their faith, have felt little or nothing under
the tortures of the Inquisition, or the consuming flames of the
stake.—ED.

cients should have studied the cause and known
the power of this ecstatic fervor is hardly to be
doubted;* and if it was necessary to lead some ardent imaginations by secondary agents, the Thaumaturgists had at their control the pomp of ceremonies, the splendor of illusions, the charm of pa-
geants, and the seductions of melody. Music alone
was sufficient to plunge many young and tender
souls into the most delicious illusions. It was
from that source that Chabanon† twice in his youth
experienced feelings similar to the descriptions of
the ecstasies of the saints. " Twice," said he,
" when listening to the notes of the organ or to
sacred music, have I thought myself transported
into heaven; and this vision had something so real
in it, and I was so carried out of myself while it
lasted, that the actual presence of the objects could
not have had upon me a stronger effect." Had
this young man, in less enlightened times, been
placed under the discipline of Thaumaturgists,
who were desirous of cultivating this inclination to
revery, the momentary ecstasy would have become an actual durable vision, which he would no
more have doubted than his own existence, and
the truth of which he would have attested with all
the obstinacy of a convinced man, and all the enthusiasm of a martyr.

We have already spoken of the magical influence
of harmonious sounds.‡ We can also recall to remembrance how Alexander and Erick le Bon§ were

* Tertullian, *De Ecstasi.*
† Chabanon, *Tableau de quelques Circonstances de ma Vie, &c.—*
Œuvres posthumes, pp. 10, 11. ‡ Refer to chap. vii., vol. i.
§ Saxo-Grammat., *Hist. Dan.*, lib. xii., pp. 204, 205. Erick le
Bon, or St. Erick, was a Swedish nobleman of the name of Ind-
wardun, connected by alliance with the royal families of Sweden
and Denmark. He was elected to the throne of Denmark in
1155. He marched against Finland, which he subdued, solely to
convert the inhabitants to the Christian faith; and left the Bishop

excited to a deadly anger by warlike songs. The feeling experienced by these two heroes is still produced upon soldiers when marching to battle to the sound of warlike instruments.

Alone, without exterior aid, without physical impressions, the imagination can warm itself to a degree of fury, to the pitch of delirium.

To be convinced of this fact, it will be sufficient to attempt upon ourselves a similar experiment; and in disposing ourselves either for or against any object occupying our thoughts, we shall be surprised at the degree of anger or tender feeling to which this voluntary illusion would soon lead us. Let us ask ourselves whether it is not necessary for the dramatic author to identify himself with the impassioned character he personifies, in order to portray the real expression of his feelings. Where such is not the case, eloquence and poetry offer him but insufficient resources; we perceive, at once, that it is he, and not his hero, that speaks. The actor, in his turn, can not succeed if he does not actually become the character he represents, as far at least as the theatrical regulations permit him. The costume, the attendance, the presence, and language of the personages whom he is to struggle against or defend, second him in his illusion; he is moved, before he dreams of having excited our emotions; his cries come from his heart; his tears are often not feigned. What then would be the effect, if a personal interest, actually deep and present, were to be attached to the passions and sentiments he expressed? He would then actually be what he assumes, and with more truth,

of Upsal in the country to found churches, while he himself framed a code of laws for them. He was killed by a party of Danes, who had unexpectedly landed on the coast, under Prince Magnus, in 1161. The fact mentioned in the text merely demonstrates the highly excitable condition of his nervous system.—Ed.

perhaps, or at least more energy, than the personage whose transports he reanimates. Let us go
further, and freeing the impassioned being from the
restraint imposed by public observation, place him
in the situation in which I have several times observed a young woman placed, who was endowed
with a powerful organization and a very excitable
and lively imagination. It would have been more
than imprudent to have confided to her the character of a heroine, chanting the song of war, and
precipitating herself armed upon the enemies of
her country. This single thought, a weapon of
which she might possess herself, some words, some
verses that she might recite, would suddenly intoxicate her with fury strangely contrasting with her
gentle and amiable disposition. The most loved
being would not long have been safe from her
blows. This sudden and formidable excitement
inspires the belief that what has been related of the
Scandinavian heroes is perfectly credible. " They
were seized, from time to time, with a fit of frenzy.
They foamed with rage, made no distinction of
persons, but struck at random, with their swords,
friends, enemies, trees, stones, animate and inanimate objects ; they swallowed burning coals, and
threw themselves into the fire. When the fit was
at an end, they suffered long from extreme exhaus
tion."* If, as the author I have just quoted seems
to think, this was the effect of an intoxicating beverage, the Sagas, which contain so many examples
of the fact, would sometimes have alluded to the
causes of it. I have no doubt that these furious
movements proceeded from the habitual state of
the imagination rendering it liable at times to an
excessive excitement. The peculiar sentiments of

* Depping, *History of the Expeditions of the Normans, and their
Settlement in France in the tenth century*, vol. i., p. 46.

these warriors, who knew no happiness but that of
seeing the blood of their enemies or their own
blood flow, and whose paradise was open only to
heroes dying in battle, were quite sufficient to ex
cite this transient frenzy: we are nearly as much
astonished that they were not continually a prey
to it.*

Will not an excess of terror sometimes produce
the same delirium as an excess of courage? Why
not, if reason is equally disordered by both? The
Samoyedes, says a traveler, are exceedingly susceptible of fear.† If they are unexpectedly touched, or if their minds are struck by some unforeseen
terrifying object, they lose the use of their reason,
and are seized with a maniacal fury. They arm
themselves with a knife, a stone, a club, or some
other weapon, and throw themselves upon the
person who has occasioned their surprise or fright;
and, if unable to satisfy their rage, they howl, and
roll upon the ground like an enraged animal. We
must here observe, that the original cause of these
peculiarities is the fear the Samoyedes entertain
of sorcerers; and the unhappy beings, tormented
by the delirium which is the result of it, are consequently looked upon as sorcerers. What a fer-
tile mine for the exploits of a worker in miracles!

More generally fear places the weak man completely in the power of him who inspires him with
the passion. If, as many observers have thought,
fear is the real operating principle in all that has
been related of serpents and other animals charming the feeble bird they intend to make their prey,

---

* The same degree of wild enthusiastic fervor was lately witnessed by a British officer, who was traveling in Algeria, at the
festival of a sect termed Arouates. The ceremonies consisted in
the most frantic exhibition of actions almost preternatural, but
evidently the result of a highly excited imagination.—ED.

† Wagner, *Memoirs of Russia*, &c., p. 207.

the look of a strong, threatening man ought to exercise a similar influence over weak minds; nor can they, in fact, withstand it. Their enchained faculties leave them powerless, senseless, under the influence of the charm. In the legends of every country there is nothing more common than the inevitable power which the fascinating glance of a magician has exercised. This power is not entirely chimerical; although mean or common in its origin, yet it has an unbounded ascendency over the timid imagination.

And does not, we may inquire, man himself conspire to aid such an ascendency, when, at the very moment that he is attempting to fortify himself by plausible reasonings, he spontaneously gives himself up to deadly terror? Without any exterior circumstance to cause his folly, a weak mind (often so on this point only) is filled with one fixed idea; for example, that such or such an age will inevitably lead to the end of life! Such a disease must terminate fatally! How many of these vain presentiments have rendered inevitable the event which seemed to justify them. They operate continually and destructively upon the weakened nerves, which would have recovered their natural vigor if they had not been influenced by these mournful apprehensions.

If fear, instead of spontaneously rising in a soul where reason can still struggle against it, should be the result of a formidable power, the limits of which we dare not assign, its effects will be no less sure and terrible than those of steel and poison. To prove this assertion, a recent example can be joined to the testimony of all the facts offered to us in ancient history. There exists in the Sandwich Isles a religious community pretending to a power, obtained from heaven by the prayers addressed to it, of destroying every enemy they wish to overcome. If any one incurs its hatred, they announce to him that imprecations against him will be commenced; and not unfrequently this declaration is sufficient to cause the unfortunate individual exposed to their anathema to die of fright, or to commit suicide.*

The influence that sympathy and a propensity to imitation† exercise upon the organs, is also felt

* Lisianski, *Voyage round the World in* 1803–1806.—*Bibliothèque Universelle, année* 1816.—*Littérature*, tome iii., pp. 162, 163.

† A thousand instances might be brought forward to demonstrate the influence of imitation. One of the most remarkable was the dancing mania which prevailed all over Europe in the fourteenth century, and which actually grew into a real epidemic. It is only requisite to relate two or three instances of more recent date in this kingdom. At a cotton manufactory, at Holden Bridge, in Lancashire, a girl, on the 15th of February, 1787, put a mouse into the bosom of another girl, who was thereby thrown into convulsions, which lasted for twenty-four hours. On the following day, six girls, who had witnessed these convulsions, were affected in a similar manner, and on the 17th, six more. The alarm became so great, that the whole work was stopped, under the idea that some particular disease had been introduced in a bag of cotton opened in the house. On the 18th three more, and on the 19th eleven more girls were seized. Three of the whole number, namely, twenty-four, lived two miles from the factory, and three were at another factory at Clitheroe, about five miles off, but who were strongly impressed with the idea of the plague, as the convulsions were termed, being caught from the cotton. Dr. Sinclair relieved all the cases by electrifying the affected girls. The convulsions were so strong as to require four or five persons to hold the patients, and to prevent them from tearing their hair and dashing their heads on the floor or on the walls.*

Upward of a century ago, a woman in Shetland, laboring under epilepsy, was attacked with paroxysms of the disease in the church; the result was, that many adult females and some children became affected in a similar manner; and the disease has continued to occur very frequently, ever since, during divine service. When Dr. Hibbert visited the island of Unst, and was attending the kirk of Baliasta, a female shriek was heard; but the person was carried out by the desire of the clergyman, who also requested any woman who felt that she might be similarly affected to leave the church. Dr. Hibbert says, "On leaving the kirk,

* *Gentleman's Mag.*, 1786, p. 268, quoted in Hecker's *Epidemics*, trans. by D. Babbington, p. 141.

upon the imagination like the contagious effects of
laughter, yawning, tears, depression, and enthusiasm. A widow who was affected with an hysteri-
cal melancholy, committed actions so strange that
she was supposed to be possessed with a demon.
It was not long before some young girls about her
were similarly attacked. They were cured as
soon as they were taken from her; and the widow
herself, under the treatment of an able physician,
recovered her reason with her health.* How many
stories of demons could be reduced to as few words.
We should be wrong if we supposed there was
nothing but deception in the history of the convulsions of St. Medard,† and those of other people
who fell at once under the influence of the evil
spirit. The greatest number of these men were,
on the contrary, honest in intention, but necessi-
tated to this imitation from their excitable organization, weak minds, and heated imaginations.
The poets have probably not exaggerated in their
descriptions of the fury with which the Bacchants
were seized when celebrating their orgies. The
greater part of these Bacchants were more morally
than physically intoxicated. They only imitated
involuntarily the transports of some priestesses;
but whether the latter kept within the bounds of
and played an arranged part, or whether, placed
under the influence of the imagination, excited by
spirituous liquors, songs, instruments of music, and
the cries, and the mystic disorders that surrounded

I saw several females writhing and tossing about their arms, on
the green grass."*—ED.

   * Fromann, *De Fascinationæ, &c.,* p. 55.

   † St. Medard was a native of Salency, in Picardy. He was
descended of a noble family, and flourished in the fifth and sixth
centuries. He was inaugurated Bishop of Noyon in 530, and died
in 561, not at a very advanced age.—ED.

    * *Description of the Shetland Islands,* 4to., p. 461.

them, they were themselves the first to feel that all which their example inspired in others may be questioned.

The imagination is not always hurtful, for how many unhoped-for, sudden, and prodigious cures have been effected by it. Our medical books are filled with facts of this nature, which among an unenlightened people would easily pass for miracles. It requires also some effort of reason to see nothing but what is natural in these sudden effects of the influence of imagination. Man is so accustomed to look for the marvelous wherever the cause does not strike upon him as forcibly and closely as the effect.*

* In the fourteenth century a disease appeared in Europe which induced those afflicted with it to leap and dance. It was called St. Vitus's dance, from a firm-rooted belief that the shrine of St. Vitus possessed the power of curing it; and, solely from the influence of this belief on the mind, many were cured. The legend whence this belief arose, taught that St. Vitus, before he bent his neck to the sword, at his martyrdom, prayed that the Deity would protect from the dancing mania all who should solemnize the day of his commemoration, and fast on its eve; whereupon a voice from heaven was heard saying, " Vitus, thy prayer is accepted."

The cures effected by the royal touch, and the money (716, see *Excerpta Historica*, p. 87, &c.) given to each person touched, were due solely to the influence of confidence operating as a powerful tonic on the animal system, laboring under the relaxation on which scrofula chiefly depends ; the anticipation also of benefit caused an increase of nervous energy equivalent to that effected by physical excitants. The celebrated Flamstead, the astronomer, when a lad of nineteen, went into Ireland to be *touched* by a celebrated empiric, named Greatracks, who cured his patients, without medicines, " by the stroke of his hand." Flamstead says, " he was eye-witness of several cures," although he himself was not benefited. (Bailey's *Life and Observations of Flamstead*.) He awaited, but did not anticipate the result.

A more impudent quack than Greatracks has seldom appeared ; he flourished in the seventeenth century. The belief in his power general, from the most highly born and educated, to the most abject and illiterate mendicant, all sacrificed at the altar of Credulity, and relied on the healing touch of Greatracks. In a letter to Lord Conway, who sent for him from Ireland on account of the health of Lady Conway, this prince of impostors thus expresses

Animal magnetism, in which all the real phenomena are produced by an excited imagination,
was first cried up by charlatans as a physical agent;

himself:—" The virtuosi have been daily with me since I writ to
your honor last, and have given me large and full testimonials,
and God has been pleased to do wonderful things in their sight,
so that they are my hearty and good friends, and have stopped
the mouth of the court, where the sober party are now most of
them believers, and my champions. The king's doctors, this day
(for the confirmation of their majesty's belief), sent three out of
the hospital to me, who came on crutches; but, blessed be God!
they all went home well, to the admiration of all people, as well
as the doctors. Sir Heneage Finch says that I have made the
greatest faction and distraction between clergy and laymen that
any one has these thousand years." Such was his boast; there
is retribution in this world as well as in the next; the reputation of Greatracks soon afterward declined as suddenly as it had
risen.

But we need not go to the seventeenth century for examples of
the power of imagination as a curative agent. In the early part
of the present century, a Miss Fancourt was cured of a spine complaint, in answer to the prayers of a Mr. Greaves. She had been
ill eight years, and during the last two years had been confined to
her sofa. She was apparently cured; she again walked; and the
only question was, how was the cure effected? Dr. Jervis, a very
sensible physician, remarks, " that her disease had probably been
some time previously subdued, and only wanted an extraordinary
stimulus to enable her to make use of her legs. Both my friends,
Mr. Travers and the late Mr. Parkinson, concurred in thinking
that there had been nothing in the illness or the recovery but what
might be accounted for by natural causes." Mr. Travers, in a
letter on the subject, says—" Credulity, the foible of a weakened,
though vivacious intellect, is the pioneer of an unqualified and
overweening confidence; and thus prepared, the patient is in the
most hopeful state for the credit, as well as the craft, of the pretender." On the same principle are to be explained the cures
performed by the metallic tractors, mustard-seed, brandy and salt,
the prayers of Prince Hohenlohe, the embrocations of St. John
Long, the miracle performed by mesmerism on my talented friend
Miss Martineau, and a thousand cases in which hysteria played
a notable part, and which only required full confidence in the pre-
scriber to effect a complete cure.

The means employed as the remedial agents in these cases are
very varied; but they were all fully confided in by the patients;
and in that confidence lies the secret of their success. Music, as
in the dancing mania, has often performed wonders. Democritus
affirms that diseases are capable of being cured by the sound of a
flute, when properly played. Asclepiades employed the trumpet
to cure sciatica; its continued sound, he affirmed, makes the

II.   F

and has become in the hands of fanatics and impostors one branch of modern theurgy.*

When the imagination of an invalid has been much struck by details of the efficacy of some remedy which is naturally inefficacious, it may in such a case become truly salutary. Thus, " an invalid may be relieved by magical ceremonies, if he be convinced beforehand that they will effect his cure."† Have not these words of an ancient physician been verified in the happy applications of animal magnetism, Perkinism, the sympathetic powder, and jugglings of the same kind, that both in ancient and modern times have been seen by turns to triumph or fall into contempt ?‡

fibers of the nerves to palpitate, and the pain vanishes. Even the great Bacon believed in the power of charming away warts. —ED.

* The magnetic sleep, and the miraculous effects it produces, were predicted by the enthusiast Swedenborg, in the year 1763, when he said, " Man may be raised to the celestial light even in this world, if the bodily senses could be entombed in a lethargic slumber," &c. (*Of Angelic Wisdom*, p. 357.)   This conclusion belongs to the partisans of Swedenborg ; but they hastened to add, that we must not implicitly believe all that the *somniloquists* or *somnambulists* have stated, that all is not good that is revealed : they depend upon that verse of St. John's 1st Epistle, chap. iv., v. 1, " Believe not every spirit, but try the spirits, whether they are of God."   They recommend, above all, no dependence upon those somnambulists who would *dispute* with Swedenborg his office of messenger of God, or who would speak against his doctrine.   (Daillant Latouche, *Abrégé des Ouvrages de Swedenborg*, pp. 55, 58.

† *De Incantatione libellus* (inter libros Galeno ascriptos), " *Quando mens humana rem amat aliquam*," &c.

‡ It would be well if they always fell into contempt ; but wherever ignorance and superstition enslave the mind, there credulity erects her temple.   At so late a period as 1837, the Honorable Robert Curzon, jun., traveling in the East, arrived at Nagadi, and had a conference with the bishop.   In the midst of it, a tall figure, with a heavy chain tied to his legs, entered the apartment, waving a brazen censer in his hand, with which he made an attack upon the party, and was with some difficulty secured and carried off.   " He was the son of the bishop, and, being a maniac, had been *chained down before the altar of St. George—a sovereign remedy* in these cases ; only he pulled up the staples of his

The imagination, although having so powerful an effect upon our bodily organs, is in its turn subjected to their deranging influence when disease has disturbed the harmony of their functions.

Four hundred years before the Christian era, Carthage was a prey to one of those endemics which the ancients denominated *plagues:* agitated by a frantic transport, the effect of the disease, the greater part of the inhabitants flew to arms to repulse an imaginary enemy, who they believed had penetrated into the city.*

The shipwrecked mariners of the Medusa, when exhausted by fatigue, hunger, and affliction upon the raft to which they had been so cruelly abandoned, experienced ecstatic illusions, the charm of which contrasted frightfully with their desperate situation.† In these two instances, the moral disorder may have been augmented by sympathy and the propensity to imitation. But more recent and individual instances are not wanting. The mother of the regent, the Duke of Orleans, relates, in her correspondence, an anecdote of a lady of her acquaintance, which seems the height of absurdity, yet has nothing improbable in it if we look upon it as a vision produced, during the lying-in of a wom-

chain, and came away with the censer, before his cure was completed."* Is it wonderful, indeed, that the deceptions of the Asclepiades should have succeeded, when we observe charlatanism flourishing and patronized by the aristocracy, and even by the educated and learned, in our own times? In the temples, during the influence of the Asclepiades in Greece, the patients slept on goat-skins; and when they were supposed to be asleep, but known to be kept awake by the novelty of their situation, a priest, dressed as Æsculapius, accompanied by young girls, trained to represent the daughters of the god, entered and delivered a solemn medical opinion, which the result confirmed in proportion to the credulity and intellectual imbecility of the hearers.—ED.

* Diodod. Sic., lib. xv., cap. ix.
† *Relation du naufrage de la Méduse,* 1st edit., pp. 72, 73.

an, by the delirium accompanying the milk-fever.[*]
A young man, victim to bad habits, had fallen into a
marasmus;[†] he was tormented with phantoms, and
complained that he heard the sentence of his eternal condemnation perpetually sounding in his ears.
General Thiebault, a man equally distinguished by
his mind and military talents, during the weakened
state which followed an inflammatory disease, was
attacked by visions, the more strange from the fact
of his enjoying undiminished reason, and that none
of his senses were altered.   The fantastic objects,
nevertheless,which annoyed him, and which he knew
did not exist, struck so forcibly upon his sight, that it
was as easy for him to enumerate and describe them
as the real objects by which he was surrounded.[‡]

We shall be little astonished to see how the
Thaumaturgists, in every country, debilitated the
corporeal organs in order to rule the imagination
more surely.   Mortifications and fasts were an
essential part of the ancient initiation, to which it
was absolutely necessary to submit before receiving
the answer of several oracles, and above all, of
those which were revealed only in dreams.[§]

[*] *Mémoires sur la Cour de Louis XIV.*, &c., edit. 1823, pp. 74, 75.
[†] The patient was under the care of Dr. Marc in 1843.
[‡] M. le Lieutenant-General Thiebault has permitted me to relate his case.   Let us observe that similar hallucinations have
been experienced by very important persons.   The learned Glé-
ditsch, three hours after noon, clearly saw in a corner of the
Academy-hall, at Berlin, Maupertuis, who had died at Basle some
time before.   He attributed this vision to a momentary derangement of his organs ; but in speaking of it, he affirmed that the
vision was as perfect as if Maupertuis had been placed living before him.—(D. Thiebault, *Recollections of a Residence at Berlin,*
vol. v., p. 21, 5th ed.)   "The maternal grandfather of Bonnet,
when in perfect health, independent of all exterior impressions,
saw the figures of men, birds, and boats produced, moving, growing, decreasing, and disappearing.   His reason could not have
been affected, as he was quite aware it was an illusion."—(La-
place, *Essai Philosophique sur les Probabilités*, pp. 224–226.)

[§] Before consulting the oracle of Amphiaraus, at Oropas, in

We can not be ignorant how the disposition for, and liability to see, phantoms, is increased by an irritation of the visual organs, caused by long vigils or by a steady contemplation of any luminous body, particularly when the mind is disordered or the body weakened. The principal trial to which the Sannyasi (meditative Hindoos) are subjected, is that of looking fixedly at the sun. It is not long before they have visions, see sparks of fire, flaming globes, meteors; the end of which is, not unfrequently, that they lose their sight, and even their reason.*

To these powerful auxiliaries, the strength of which is increased by solitude and darkness, is added an intoxication produced by the sacred food and drinks; and thus, already a prey to beliefs, to fears, and to superstitious hopes, and given up to so many causes of excitement, how would it be possible for any man, even the greatest master of his reason, to defend his imagination from the power of such superstitions? And without the

Bœotia, the votaries fasted a whole day, and received the answer in a dream.—Philostrat., *Vit. Apollon.*, lib. ii., cap. iv.

* Dubois, *Mœurs et Institutions des Peuples de l'Inde*, tome ii., pp. 271-274. The Sannyasi are Bramins of a very strict order, who have renounced the society of wives and children, altogether forsaken the world, and adopted the vow of mendicity, to subsist solely upon alms. The duty of a member of this sect is to seek solitude; to subdue every passion; to shun the slightest approach to pleasure, or any earthly enjoyments; and to concentrate his whole mind in meditation upon holy things, and, among others, the constant perusal of the Veda. The penances to which he is to subject himself are numerous, and truly ridiculous. Thus—he is to slide backward and forward on the ground; to stand a whole day on tiptoe; to continue a whole day in motion, rising and sitting alternately; to expose himself to hot fires in the warmest weather; to look fixedly for hours upon the sun; and to feed entirely on roots and fruits. Such are the rules imposed on a Sannyasi; and such the idea of human perfection, which Superstition has impressed on the minds of her Hindoo votaries. Under such discipline, in addition to that mentioned in the text, it is not surprising that visions should be seen and believed.—ED.

assistance of other artifices, would not the union
of these means be sufficient to make a superstitious
man, shut up in a cavern without an opening, such
as has received the name of the *Purgatory of St.
Patrick*, believe that he was in an immense place,
surrounded by all those apparitions which the
monks of Ireland had beforehand promised to his
terrified imagination ?*

Instructed by observation of the intimate connection between every part of our being, the ancients well knew that the imagination could produce diseases apparently supernatural, which often
defied the *art*, and always the precautions of the
physician ; and that also, on the contrary, it could
effectually struggle against a really diseased state
of the organs, with a success equal to that effected
by physical remedies. They armed the imagination against physical evils, and forced it to be productive of as much benefit as it sometimes was of
evil.

During the dog-days in Egypt, an epidemic disease, which is attributed to the influence of the
atmosphere, prevails. As a remedy for it, the
priests were accustomed, after solemn ceremonies
and sacrifices, to light numerous wood-piles with
fire taken from an altar dedicated to an ancient
deified sage.† This proceeding was no doubt useful, as it increased the circulation of the air, and
tended to purify it ; but fire taken from the domestic hearth would have been as efficacious. In
this instance, therefore, they addressed themselves
also to the imagination. These religious mum-
meries, and the sacred fire, tended to increase the

---

* Gerard Boate, *Natural History of Ireland*, pp. 137–141, of the
French translation.—Twiss, *Travels in Ireland*, pp. 128, 129.
† Ælian, *Var. Hist.* (quoted by Suidas), verb: ἐναύειν—'Ἰαχεν
'Ιερογραμματεῖς. ·

persuasion among the people, that a protecting god would come to their relief. The Roman people were cut off in numbers by a pestilential disease, which would not yield to any known remedy: the pontiffs, therefore, ordered, in the name of Heaven, a celebration of the public games and festivals.* This remedy, which appears so strange to us, was, nevertheless, found so efficacious, that it was resorted to more than once. Let us suppose that the endemic disease† was of the nature of those pestiferous fevers, which often resulted in Italy, from the crowding together of a numerous population in confined dwellings; or from privations and fatigue; and also from variations of the temperature, to which the citizens were exposed during their military expeditions. Under such circumstances, a general terror would be spread; it would freeze every soul, and thereby add doubly to the deadly power of the scourge. Were not the games which kept the population in the open air, and agreeably occupied the mind; the festivals, or numerous sacrifices of animals, presenting means of substituting a more substantial and wholesome food, to that provided by habitual parsimony; and the ceremonies which reassured the imagination, and promised that the gods would throw a compassionate glance on their obedient worshipers, sufficient to combat the progress, and accelerate the disappearance, of the malignant contagion? To prostrate the people before the altar, believing that they owed to the gods their miraculous deliverance, was a course frequently resorted to; and when cures were effected, it was indeed a miracle

---

* Valer. Maxim., lib. ii., cap. ii., § iv., A.U.C. 389.

† Endemic diseases are those that originate in some circumstance connected with the locality in which they appear: they are not contagious.—ED.

in the sense of the ancients; an immediate, but assuredly not a supernatural benefit from the gods.

We could recall to remembrance, without trouble, innumerable examples of physical remedies employed to cure supernatural diseases, as far, at least, as we should continue to translate into modern meaning the ancient expressions. As every benefit was ascribed to the benevolence of the gods, so were all evils supposed to emanate from their vengeance, or from the malevolence of evil genii. What ought we to recognize in the evils attributed to this latter cause? Nervous infirmities, epilepsy, hysteria, the symptoms of which were developed, or at least increased, if not originated, by a disordered imagination. Hellebore cured the daughters of Proteus of a madness with which the anger of the gods had afflicted them. When the Samoyedes are by terror thrown into a paroxysm of frenzy which they regard as the effect of enchantment, and as the characteristic sign of sorcery, they are cured by having the hair of the reindeer burned under their nostrils.* The Hebrew exorcists ejected demons from the human body by the smell of the smoke of the burning baaras-plant. Ælian described this plant under the name *cynopastes;* and Josephus attributed to it the power of expelling demons and of curing epilepsy.† The mode of treating these maladies did not differ greatly from that now employed. Like the Hebrews, the Thaumaturgists of antiquity, the Samoyedes, and those Magi who, two centuries ago, dared to oppose medical art by their pretended magical

* Wagner, *Recollections of Russia*, p. 207.
† Ælian, *De Nat. Animal.*, lib. xiv., cap. xxvii. One of the sea algæ, which the same author compares to the cynospastos (*ibid.*, cap. xxiv.), contained a very strong poison. It was perhaps this last quality which induced the Thaumaturgists to reserve to themselves the exclusive possession of it.

*fascinations,** we also use fumigations and ammo-niacal odors when fighting against diseases of the nature of epilepsy, hysterics, hypochondriacism, and those mournful results of a disordered imagination under which reason is prostrated. The apparent miracle would disappear, if we were to recall to mind that it was the custom of the ancients to personify the principles of good and evil.

CHAPTER IV.

Medicine formed a Part of the Occult Science : it was not long exercised by the Priests ; Diseases were supposed to be sent by Malevolent Genii, or the irritated Gods ; the Cures were considered Miracles, or Works of Magic.—Credulity and the Spirit of Mystery attributed marvelous Properties to Inanimate Substances ; and Charlatanism assisted this Species of Deception.—Counterfeit Cures.—Extraordinary Abstinences.—Nutritious Substances taken in an almost imperceptible Form.—Apparent Resurrections.

CARRIED away by our subject, we have already entered the province of science in which promises will always have the greatest power over the imagination, namely, the science of the physician.

Medical science is, although it may be thwarted by unforeseen anomalies, founded upon much positive knowledge. It has not, however, been able to overcome the diseases of the intellect in a manner equal to its influence over those of the body ; neither has it placed us upon our guard against those numerous secrets used by the Thaumaturgist to disarrange the play of our organs, to deceive our senses, and to terrify our imaginations.

Although originating in the temples, and revealed as an emanation from the Divine Intelligence,

* See the indication of this medicine in Fromann, *De Fascinatione*, pp. 955–958.

yet medicine did not infringe upon the province
of other sacred sciences. In treating of it, we
need not diverge from the empire of the wonder-
workers; for, everywhere, cures were long esteemed miracles, and physicians were regarded as
priests or as magicians.*

Physicians, under some circumstances, were even
looked upon as gods. In Armenia,† under the
name of Thicks or Haralez, the gods were said to
revive those heroes who died in battle, by sucking
their wounds. Angitia,‡ the sister of Circe, established herself in Italy only in order that she might
merit altars there, by applying her salutary science
to the diseases that desolated that country. Formerly in Greece, and even after the siege of Troy,
the sons of the gods and the heroes alone understood the secrets of medicine and surgery;§ and
even to a late period Æsculapius, the son of Apollo,
was there worshiped as a deity.‖

* In the earliest periods of society the character of priest and
physician is always combined in the same person. The Payes of
Brazil are priests, exorcists, and physicians; they cure diseases
by sucking the affected part, and spitting into a pit, to return to
the earth the evil principle, which, they assert, is the cause of
disease. The Hebrew priests, according to the Mosaical account
of the Jews, were also physicians; the Asclepiades, the priests of
Æsculapius, were the first physicians of the Greeks; and the
Druids those of the northern nations.

† Cirbied, *Mémoires sur l'Arménie.—Mémoires de la Société des
Antiquaires de France*, tome ii., p. 304.

‡ Solin., cap. viii.

§ Ælian, *De Nat. Animal.*, lib. ii., cap. xviii.

‖ The original seat of the worship of Æsculapius was at Epidaurus, where he had a splendid temple, adorned with a gold and
ivory statue of the god, who was represented sitting, one hand
holding a staff, the other resting on the head of a serpent, the
emblem of sagacity and longevity; and a dog crouched at his feet.
This temple was frequented by harmless serpents, in the form of
which the god was supposed to manifest himself. He had, also,
temples at Rhodes, Cindos, Cos, and one on the banks of the
Tiber. According to Homer, his sons, Machaon and Podalirius,
treated wounds and external diseases only; and it is probable
that their father practiced in the same manner, as he is said to

In Egypt theurgy divided among thirty-six genii, inhabitants of the air, the care of the different parts of the human body; and the priests practiced a separate invocation for each genius, which they used in order to obtain from them the cure of the particular member confided to their care.* It was from Egypt also that the formularies which taught the use of herbs in medicine originally came; and these formularies were magical.† The magicians of the islands of Sena cured invalids by others deemed incurable.‡ The Scandinavian virgins were instructed, at the same time, in magic, medicine, and the treatment of wounds.§ Diodorus, who has often attempted to extricate history from its medley of fables, looks upon the science of Medea and Circe as natural, as a profound study of all remedies and poisons; and he relates that the former cured the son of Alcemenes of a furious madness.‖

For a long time after the age of Hercules and the heroic times, invalids in Greece sought relief from their sufferings from the descendants of Æsculapius in the temples of that god, which an enlightened policy had raised on elevated spots and salubrious vicinities.¶ Those men who pretended in

have invented the probe, and the bandaging of wounds. His priests, the Asclepiades, practiced, however, incantations; and cured diseases by leading their patients to believe that the god himself delivered his prescriptions in dreams and visions; for which impostures they were roughly satirized by Aristophanes in his play of *Plutus.* It is probable that the preparations, consisting of abstinence, tranquillity, and bathing, requisite for obtaining this divine intercourse, and, above all, the confidence reposed in the Asclepiades, were often productive of benefit.—ED.

* Origen, *Contr. Cels.*, lib. viii.
† Galen, *De Simpl. Médicam. Facult.*, lib. vi., proem.
‡ Pomponius Mela, lib. iii., cap. vi.
§ C. V. de Bonstetten, *La Scandinavie et les Alpes*, p. 32.
‖ Diod. Sic., lib. iv., cap. ii. et xvi.
¶ Plutarch, *Quæst. Roman.*, § cliv.

right of their birth to hold the gift of curing, finally learned the art of it, by preserving in the temples the history of those diseases, the cure of which had been sought from them.* They then added to their number disciples, whose discretion was secured by the trial of a severe initiation. By degrees, the progress of philosophy raised the mysterious veil behind which they would have still concealed the science. Hippocrates at last placed medicine on a real foundation, and taught its precepts in his immortal works. Its doctrines, till then imprisoned in the archives of the Asclepiades, were given entire to swell the patrimony of perfectible civilization. From this moment the priests ought to have renounced their pretensions to the healing art;† but they were careful to prevent the science from being entirely divested of its heavenly

* The temple of Cos was rich in votive offerings, which generally represented the parts of the body healed, and an account of the method of cure adopted. From these singular clinical records, Hippocrates is reported to have constructed his treatise on Dietetics. It is a curious fact, that many similar votive offerings of legs, arms, noses, &c., are hung up in the cathedral of Aix-la-Chapelle, and some other continental churches, as records of cures performed by the holy relics in those sacred edifices. The crutches of the Countess Droste Vischering, also, are hung up in the cathedral of Treves, in memory of the sudden and miraculous cure of a contraction of the knee-joint, which had long withstood all medical skill, by the mere sight of the seamless coat of our Savior, before which she prostrated herself, and was instantaneously cured. But although the crutches attest the cure, and the countess walked from the church to her carriage, merely leaning on the arm of her grandmother, yet, like most other miraculous cures, it was only a temporary alleviation; and her walking was an effort of sudden excitement, the result of muscular energy, produced by the confidence of obtaining relief from the miraculous power of the holy coat. She became once more a cripple. These facts display the melancholy truth, that many pagan customs were engrafted on Christianity, and are still employed by the Church of Rome to delude the ignorant and superstitious, in order to support her powers.—ED.

† Coray, *Prolegomènes* of the French translation of Hippocrates treatise on air, water, and places

•

and magical origin. The greater number of the thermal waters, more frequently used then than in the present day, remained consecrated to the gods, to Apollo, to Æsculapius, and, above all, to Hercules, who was surnamed *Iatricos*, or the able physician.*

Those philosophers who never left the temples incurred accusations of dealing in magic, when by natural means they cured their fellow-beings of the evils which desolated their abodes : this hap-

* The sacred character of healing springs is a relic of classical and Druidical superstition that still remains. In Fosbrooke's *British Monarchism* (477) we learn that, "on a spot, called Nell's Point, is a fine well, to which great numbers of women resort on Holy Thursday, and, having washed their eyes in the spring, they drop a pin into it. Once a-year, at St. Mardrin's well, also, lame persons went, on *Corpus Christi* evening, to lay some small offering on the altar, there to lie on the ground all night, drink of the water there, and on the next morning to take a good draught more of it, and carry away some of the water each in a bottle at their departure.* At Muswell Hill was formerly a chapel, called our Lady of Muswell, from a well there, near which was her image ; this well was continually resorted to by way of pilgrimage.† At Walsingham a fine green road was made for the pilgrims, and there was a holy well and cross adjacent, at which pilgrims used to kneel while drinking the water.‡ It is remarkable that the Anglo-Saxon laws had proscribed this as idolatrous.§ Such springs were consecrated upon the discovery of the cures effected by them.‖ In fact," Fosbrooke properly adds, "these consecrated wells merely imply a knowledge of the properties of mineral waters, but, through ignorance, a religious appropriation of these properties to supernatural causes."

I may add to this record, that Holywell, in the county of Flint, derives its name from the Holy Well of St. Winifred, over which a chapel was erected by the Stanley family, in the reign of Henry VII. The well was formerly in high repute as a medicinal spring. Pennant says that, in his time, Lancashire pilgrims were to be seen in deep devotion, standing in the water up to the chin for hours, sending up prayers, and making a prescribed number of turnings ; and this excess of piety was carried so far, as in several instances to cost the devotees their lives.—ED.

* *Antiq. Repertory*, vol. ii., p. 79.
† Simpson, *Agreeable Historians*, vol. ii., p. 622.
‡ *Beauties of England* (old edit.), vol. ii., p. 118.
§ Brompton and Script, 123.
‖ Decem., *Scriptures*, 2417.

pened to Empedocles. An endemic disease raged
in Selinuntia; Empedocles saw that it arose from
the hurtful vapors exhaled from the stagnant waters of a sluggish river; and to remedy the evil
he changed the course of two brooks, and by conducting them into the bed of the river, he increased
the current of the waters; after which, as the river
ceased to be stagnant, it ceased to exhale the pestilential miasma; and, consequently, the plague
disappeared.*

If, in the second century of our era, the Emperor Adrian succeeded in relieving himself for a
time from an aqueous congestion which swelled
his body,† it was said to have been effected by
some magic art. Tatian, a sincere defender of
Christianity, who lived about the same time, does
not deny the wonderful cures effected by the
priests of the temples of the Polytheists; he only
attempts to explain them by supposing that the
pagan gods were actual demons, and that they introduced disease into the body of a healthy man,
announcing to him, in a dream, that he should be
cured if he implored their assistance; and then,
by terminating the evil which they themselves had
produced, they obtained the glory of having worked
a miracle.‡

These opinions were not peculiar to a civilized
people. Less enlightened nations have believed
that diseases were signs of the vengeance or the
malevolence of beings superior to humanity; consequently, priests and magicians were everywhere
selected as physicians. Among the Nadoessis and
Chippeways the three titles of priest, physician,
and sorcerer, were inseparable, and they are so

* Diogen. Laert. in *Empedocl.*
† Xiphilin in *Adrian.*
‡ Tatian, *Assyr. Orat. ad Græcos* p. 157.

still among the Osages.* The priest-magicians were the only physicians of Mexico.† In the heart of the Galibis nations, the Payes are priests, physicians, and magicians ; and they form a corporation, the admission into which can only be obtained by submitting to a very painful initiation.‡

Christianity could not, in Asia and Europe, entirely destroy the prejudices which had prevailed under the reign of Polytheism. They reappeared with renovated strength in the dark ages ; when, in spite of the antipathy which the Jews inspired in the Christians, the Israelites were almost the only surgeons to princes and kings : and the remarkable cures they effected seemed the results of some mysterious influence. This opinion was strengthened by the credulous concealment of their prescriptions, which were probably borrowed from the Arabians ; and they evidently were not unwilling that their Christian adversaries should deem them possessed of supernatural secrets. It was not long before some of the indiscreet supporters of Christianity brought forward miraculous cures to oppose to the influence of the Jews. Like the ancient temples, many of the Christian churches displayed within their walls holy springs, the waters of which were reputed to possess great healing virtues. The belief of the Christians in their healing powers partly originated from a sincere confidence in their adopted faith, and partly from failure of any other resource. It may, however, have been a legacy of Paganism, hastily accepted by men, who would rather sanctify an error than allow confidence to exist in a proscribed religion.

* Carver, *Travels in North America*, p. 290.
† Joseph Acosta, *Natural History of the Indies*, book v., chap. xxvi.
‡ Noël, *Dictionnaire de la Fable*, art. *Payes*.

Whatever might be the reason, when these healing
springs were resorted to, the sick could derive no
benefit from them unless they submitted to the
regulations of the priests.   The diseases sometimes yielded to the regimen, to time, and to the
calm that hope and a pious confidence, aided by
the imagination, produced; sometimes, however,
they resisted their influence, but the failures were
attributed to the sins and the want of faith in the
patient: hence the miraculous virtue which was
proved by cures in some cases was not, therefore,
nullified by the failures in others.

The institutions were conformable to the *opinion*
that all cures were effected by the direct interposi-
tion of the divinity; and they long survived it.
The Christian physicians who, in conjunction with
the Arabians and the Israelites began to spring up,
formed part of the clergy, long after the idea of
any thing supernatural in their art had exploded.
"The professors of medicine," says Et. Pasquier,
" were formerly all *clerks;* and it was not till the
year 1542 that the *legate* in France gave them
permission to marry."*   Toward the same time

* Et. Pasquier, *Recherches de la France*, liv. iii., chap. xxix.—
Until this period, the four instructing faculties of the university
were condemned to celibacy.   In 1552, the doctors in law obtained, like the physicians, the permission to marry.   But it was
long after the first dignities in this faculty were accorded to the
canons and priests.   In many of the Protestant cantons of
Switzerland, in the present day, it is necessary, before being
promoted to the chair of the public establishments, to give proof
of theological talent.   The pretext for this arrangement was,
that these establishments had been endowed at the expense
of the ancient religious foundations.   This motive would not,
however, have been decisive without the established prejudice
that the instructing body should belong to the church and the
sacerdotal corporation.*
Richard Fitz-Nigel, who died Bishop of London, A.D. 1198, had
been apothecary to Henry II.   The celebrated Roger Bacon,
who flourished in the thirteenth century, although a monk, yet

* Tiedmann, *De Quæstione, &c.*, p. 122.

Paracelsus, who, during his travels in Africa and the East had acquired secrets which secured him great superiority over his competitors, renewed the example which had been given by Raymond Lully and other adepts, and presented himself as instructed and inspired by a divinity.* Had his life been prolonged and his conduct less light, who would have dared to say that there might not have been found a public credulous enough to have recognized his assumptions?†

The habit of associating a supernatural power to the natural action of remedies, particularly those

practiced medicine. Nicolas de Farnham, a physician to Henry III., was created Bishop of Durham; and many other doctors of medicine were at various times elevated to ecclesiastical dignities.—ED.

* Tiedmann, *De Quæstione, &c.*, p. 113.

† The birth-place of Paracelsus is not accurately known, but it is supposed to have been Einsiedeln, in the canton of Schwyz. He was born in 1493. He was the son of a physician, who instructed him in alchemy and astrology, as well as medicine. He displayed early an ardent desire for knowledge; not such, however, as is derived from books, but such as he could pick up wherever it could be procured, without being very difficult of acquirement, or without much nicety being shown as to the source whence it came. For this purpose he traveled over the greater part of Europe, and also into Africa and Asia. He was chosen professor of medicine at Basil in 1526; and at his first lecture he publicly burned the works of Celsus and Avicenna, asserting that they were useless lumber. He was a man of the most irreligious character and immoral habits, a glutton and a drunkard; and in falsehood, vanity, and arrogance, unequaled. He pretended to possess the philosopher's stone, asserted that he imprisoned a demon in the pummel of his sword, and that he had discovered the elixir of life. His medical writings are specimens of credulity and imposture. He was a believer in magic, and boasted of having conversed with Avicenna, in the vestibule of the infernal regions. He had, however, the merit of introducing into medicine the use of mercurials, and several metallic remedies, and greatly improved pharmaceutical chemistry. He left Basil in less than a year after his appointment; and, after having undergone many hardships and vicissitudes, he died in great poverty at Salzburg, in the Tyrol, in 1541, in the forty-eighth year of his age, giving the lie to the impudent boast of his possessing the elixir of life and the philosopher's stone.—ED.

II   G

which were kept secret, has been preserved to the present day. The best physicians have proved that the only effectual remedy against the bite of a rabid animal is cauterization of the wound with a red-hot iron : and this remedy has been employed for many centuries in Tuscany, and also in some provinces of France. But in the former place, the iron which they heat is one of the nails of the true cross ;* and in the French provinces it is the key of St. Hubert,† which is, however, only useful in the hands of those persons who can trace the illustriousness of their genealogy to this noble saint. It is thus a kind of heir-loom or hereditary possession, similar to that assumed by the Psylli and the Marses, and the descendants of Æsculapius.

We must again repeat what we have so often before stated, that it was originally rather a feeling of pious gratitude than a spirit of deception, which united the idea of an inspiration and the gift of the divinity to the recipes and salutary operations of medical science. Upon the banks of the river Anigrus was a grotto dedicated to the nymphs. There resorted persons afflicted with herpes, who, after prayers and a previous friction, swam across the river, and by the favor of the nymphs were cured. Pausanias,‡ who relates this apparent miracle, adds that the waters of the Anigrus exhaled a fetid odor; that is to say, they were charged with sulphureted hydrogen gas, and were, there-

* Lullin-Châteauvieux, *Lettres écrites d'Italie*, tome i., p. 129.
† Particularly in the village of La Saussotte, near Villeneuve, department of the Aube. At the abbey of St. Hubert, in the diocese of Liège, the intercession of the saint is alone sufficient to effect the cure, provided it is seconded by some religious ceremonies, and a diet which will reassure the imagination.—*Voyage Littéraire de D. Martenne et de D. Durand*, part second, Paris, 1724, pp. 145–147.
‡ Pausanias, *Eliac.*, lib. i., cap. v.

fore, antiherpetic. Our physicians succeed in curing it by means of the same agent, without the
ceremonies, and without speaking of miracles.

But the ancient teachers and the rulers of the
people were often obliged to speak of and sanction
salutary precepts, through the illusion of the marvelous, whether necessary to overcome, as in Es-
thonia and Livonia, the apathy of men stupefied
by slavery and misery, by commanding them, in
the name of the gods, to combat the epizootics,
which in their ignorance they deemed the effect of
sorcery, by fumigating their stables with asafœt-
ida ;* or whether, in the midst of a society rich
and abandoned to pleasure, they attributed to a
particular stone the property of preserving the purity of the voice, provided the singer, who would
profit by its salutary virtue, lived in chastity.†

The pride and interest attached to exclusive possession involved the concealment of the secrets
which were valuable enough to be preserved under a supernatural veil.‡ Juno recovered her virginity every year by bathing in the fountain of
Canathos,§ and it is said that the women of the
Argolides bathed there with the same hope. It is
certain, however, that the Argians, in relating the
prodigy, mention that, in order to be relied upon,
some occult ceremonies practiced in the worship
of Juno|| were requisite. According to tradition,

---

* Debray, Sur les Préjugés et les Idées Superstitieuses des Livo-
niens, Lettoniens, et Esthoniens.—Nouvelles Annales des Voyages
tome xviii., p. 3.   † Solin., cap. xl.

‡ This is very natural, at a period when the whole of the art
of curing disease was supposed to depend on the possession of
such secrets. The sick, on this account, were carried on biers,
and exposed on the highways, for the inspection of the passers-
by, and to obtain from them prescriptions.—Ed.

§ A fountain of Nauplia.—Ed.

|| Pausanias, Corinthiac., cap. xxxviii.—Nöel, Dictionnaire de la
Fable, art. Canathos.

the goddess, immediately after her nuptials, bathed in an Assyrian fountain, the waters of which immediately contracted a very delightful odor.* Does not this last trait denote that both in Syria and Greece the property which had caused the myrtle to be dedicated to the goddess of love, and used by women to repair the exhaustion of child bearing, was known ?†

But we are informed, that the priest administered the beneficial effects with mysterious ceremonies only, offering them as a miracle resulting from these ceremonies.

The books of the ancients are inexhaustible on the healing and magical properties of plants. The greater number have, no doubt, originated in the love of the marvelous; and many have obtained reputation from no greater reason than an inaccurate translation of the name of the plant. We must nevertheless observe, that modern writers have not been more reasonable upon this subject than the ancients. The herb *scorzonera*, for instance, derived its name from the exterior color of its stalk, *scorzo nero*. It is quite evident that this name has been taken from *scurzo*, the Spanish for viper; and the *scorzonera*, from that circumstance, is regarded as a powerful antidote for the bite of the viper.‡

* Ælian, *De Nat. Animal.*, lib. xii., cap. xxx. The Greeks pretended to recognize Juno (Hera) in the goddess of Assyria, the celestial virgin spouse of the sun, who, at the period when Gemini make the equinox of the spring, was every year found a virgin by her husband, when the summer solstice led him again to her.

† Rabelais (livre i., chap. xliv.) puts for this reason abundance of myrtle-water in the baths of the ladies of the abbey of Thélème. For myrtle-water, in the first editions, published during the life of the author, the reimpressions have erroneously substituted water of myrrh.

‡ *Dictionnaire de Furetière*, art. *Scorsonère*. Plants were valuable as remedies only when collected under the influence of certain planets; they were also required to be collected on certain

Charlatanism, in short, in order to conceal from view the action of natural agents, in medicines as in other branches of the occult sciences, attributed a magical efficacy to points of an insignificant nature.   An adept, quoted by Fromann,* pointed out a remedy for consumption and the sweating sickness, which was in itself simple enough, but was not to be prepared with common fire.   A saw was to be manufactured from an apple-tree struck by lightning, and was to be used to saw the wood of the threshold of a door through which many people had passed, until the continued friction of the instrument upon the wood had produced a flame.†   The extravagance of the proceeding inspired a pious confidence in those who resorted to the remedy, and the difficulty of executing it well secured, beforehand, in case of failure, the infallibility of the medicine.   This instance is one of the strongest that can be cited, but it recalls millions of others.

To cure dislocations, and displacements of the thigh-bone, Cato‡ prescribes the application of splinters, so disposed as to replace and support the injured member in its natural position.   He then points out some words which are to be used during the operation.   These unintelligible words were possibly nothing more than the same direction expressed in another language : expressions upon which, though no longer understood, the magical efficacy of bandaging was supposed to depend.

The sacred words may, in a similar case, have been a prayer by which the use of any natural remedy was accompanied, and to which the suc-

days.   This superstition, indeed, was upheld until the seventeenth century ; and directions were given for collecting the plants, in the Herbals of Turner, Culpepper, and Lovel.—Ed.

* Fromann, *Tract. de Fascinatione*, pp. 953–964.

† *Ibid.*, pp. 363, 364.

‡ Cato, *De Re Rustica*, cap. clx.

cess was thought to be due. Men who pretended
to be endowed with secret powers taught that it
was possible to stop a hemorrhage from the nose
by repeating an *Ave* or a *Pater*, provided that, at
the same time, the nostrils were compressed with
the fingers,* and linen steeped in cold water applied to the head. More frequently the pretended
miracle originated in the care which the Thaumaturgists took to make an inert substance the mask
of an efficacious medicine.

The *Kicahans*, subjects of the Burmese, and who
appear to have been driven by them to the mountains of Assam, go out after every storm in search
of aerolites, and if they find any, transmit them to
their priest, who preserves them as remedies sent
by heaven for the cure of every disease.†

The miraculous powers of the bezoars,‡ experienced and celebrated in Asia, for some time found

* Fromann, *Tract. de Fascinatione* (4to., 1675), lib. i., cap. xxix.
† *Nouvelles Annales des Voyages*, 2d series, vol. iii., p. 229. The
Parthian Magi carefully seek a stone which is only to be found in
places struck by thunder. They doubtless attribute great virtues
to it.—Plin., *Hist. Nat.*, lib. xxxvii., cap. ix.
‡ The bezoar is a concretion found in the intestines of the stag,
and sometimes of the goat. It was formerly supposed to have
the power, not only of curing diseases, but also of driving out poisons, whence the name, from the Persian words *Pad-zahr*, "expelling poison;" *pad* meaning to remove or cure, and *zahr* poison.
The Hindoos and Persians have still great confidence in its curative powers, especially that one which is formed in the stomach
of the *caprea acyagros*, the wild goat of Persia, which is sold for
its weight in gold. The bezoar was, at one time, in as high estimation in Europe as in the East ; and its value as a remedy was
enhanced by the marvelous manner in which it was supposed to
be produced. "When the hart is sick," says Garner, "and hath
eaten many serpents for his recoverie, he is brought unto so great
a heate, that he hasteth to the water, and there covereth his body
unto the very ears and eyes, at which distilleth many teares from
which the stone (the bezoar) is gendered." Bezoars consist almost entirely of phosphate of lime ; and, as curative agents, afford
an addition to the many thousand proofs of the influence of mind
over the body, and how truly efficacious imagination may prove
in removing disease.—ED.

credence in Europe; yet these bezoars have no more effect than the aerolites upon the nervous system, and could only be used like the latter to disguise the use of more active substances.

A Greek inscription,* which we believe must have been anciently placed in the temple of Æsculapius at Rome, and which perpetuates four cures effected by that god, presents us with four examples of the different ways in which credulity lends itself to the marvelous.   There is nothing surprising in stopping a hæmoptyses, spitting of blood, by the use of sweet kernels and honey,† nor even in the oracle that ordered it.   But when the god, in order to cure a pain in the side, prescribed a topical application, the principal ingredient of which was to be the cinders collected from his altar, it is easy to conjecture that his priests mingled some drug with those cinders.   If a salve, in which the blood of a *white cock* was added to honey, produced beneficial results, we may be permitted to think that the color of the bird was only of use to veil in mystery the composition of the remedy.   A blind man, after some genuflections, placed the hand that had been extended upon the altar over his eyes, and suddenly recovered his sight.   He had never lost it; and he probably executed this juggling at some critical moment, when it was of importance to revive the declining reputation of Æsculapius and his temple.

We could compile whole volumes with similar impostures.   Worn by the sufferings of an incura-

---

* J. Gruter, *Corp. Inscript.*, folio, Amstelodami, 1707, p. 71, insc. 1.

† Under the term sweet kernels is meant the bitter almond, or the kernels of the peach, both of which, when they are moistened, evolve hydrocyanic acid, which, operating as a powerful sedative, would arrest the flow of blood.   The honey, which is an excitant, was a bad addition.—ED.

ble disease, Adrian invoked death, and it was feared he would have recourse to suicide: a.woman appeared, who declared that she had received in a dream an order to assure the emperor he should soon be cured. Not having obeyed this order at first, she lost her sight; but, being warned by a second dream, she fulfilled her mission, and her eyes immediately reopened to the light.* But although Adrian died some months afterward, the witnesses of this trick were not the less disposed to believe in every other assumed miracle set before them.

The greatest of all prodigies to reasonable minds is, in my opinion, the belief in assumed miracles by the very men who have unmasked and unveiled the falsehood of such miracles. And, by a remarkable singularity, the superstitious man and the philosopher may each, in his own way, profit by a prodigy often repeated. The one sees in it a proof of the truth of his assertions, and the effects of the gifts of heaven, which display themselves in overcoming human reason; the other, finding this contradiction everywhere, maintains that it proves nothing, since, if it was applied to one real belief, it would allow a hundred false ones to triumph : and that its only principle is, therefore, the facility with which the human race ever abandon themselves to those who attempt to deceive them.

Credulity is, in fact, the disease of every age and of every country. The haunts of those mendicants who deceive the public by obtaining their sympathy for the most deplorable deceptive infirmities, were formerly called in Paris *Cours des Miracles*, because, on entering those quarters of the city, these wretches deposited the costumes of the different parts they acted. At once the blind saw, and the

* Ælian, *Spartian. in Adrian.*

cripple recovered the use of his limbs. Nearly a dozen of these " courts" exist in the French capital; and it is lamentable to add, that their inhabitants are sometimes employed by the priests and monks to give an authority to their relics, by vouching for the miraculous cures which these pretended invalids receive from their touch.* The name *Cours des Miracles*† having become popular, proves that no one was ignorant of the impostures which were every day enacted there, and yet, daily, these sharpers find dupes; and with a perfect knowledge of this habitual deception, supernatural cures are still believed.

Obstinate and ingenious in deceiving herself, Credulity is found intrenched behind well attested wonders, that have not been denied by experience. This is very well! but let science take from these marvels what belongs to itself, it will quickly aid the honest man in detecting that which appertains to imposture.

It is not by opposing to the boasts of the charlatan an immense number of proofs of his errors, however credible, but it is by demonstrating that these marvels may have occurred in the order of nature, that we can cherish any hope of curing mankind of an infatuation which has already cost him very dear.

When we hear accounts of those miraculous fasts, which men of superior intellect have endured for days and for weeks, we are tempted to class them

* When Louis XI. was ill, he sent for the holy man of Calabria, and fell upon his knees before him, begging that his life might be prolonged. The holy vial was sent to· him. and St. Pete.·'s vest from Rome ; but, alas! both confidence and faith were of no avail in this case. "The monarch," says Comines, " could command the beggar's knee, but not the health of it."—ED.

† Sauval, *Antiquités de Paris*, tome i., pp. 510–515, quoted by Dulaure, *Physical, Civil, and Moral History of Paris*. (1821, vol. iv., pp. 589–596.)

with the Oriental tales,* in which similar inconceiv-
able abstinences figure.   But as these narrations
are so numerous, can we attribute them wholly to
a desire to deceive, and affirm that they are altogether without foundation ?

Let us first of all remark that certain substances
possess, or have attributed to them, the property
of suspending the sensations of hunger and of
thirst.   Such, for instance, as the leaves of the
tobacco plant, and the leaves of the *cocoa* (a Peruvian plant).   People have gone so far as to say
that, if either of these plants be held in the mouth
by a man who has worked all day without eating,
they will prevent him from suffering from hunger.†

Matthiolus‡ attributes to the Scythians the use
of an herb agreeable to the taste, and so efficacious in supplying the place of nourishment, that its
effects had sometimes prolonged life for twelve
whole days.   Another herb sustained in a similar
manner the strength of those indefatigable cava-
liers' horses.   This apparent miracle may have
been the result of a desire to deceive, and may
have been effected by reducing substances eminently nutritious to a very small bulk.§   To the
use of such an art we may explain what was said

---

* *Les Mille et un Nuits*, nuits 137 et 139.

† J. Acosta, *Natural History of the Indies, &c.*, book iv., chap.
xxii. Opium has the same power of allaying the sensation of
hunger. The Turkish courier, who performs long and fatiguing
journeys without rest, on horseback, provides himself with a small
bag of opium lozenges, *Mash-Allah;* and, when greatly fatigued,
he alights, opens his bag, takes a lozenge himself, and having also
given two to his horse, remounts, and proceeds with as much
alacrity as when he set out; both horse and man are refreshed,
and the sensation of hunger is subdued.—ED.

‡ Matthiolus, *Commentar. in Dioscorid.—Epistol. Nuncupator*.

§ This opinion of our author is not very tenable; and, although
the period is much exaggerated, yet, it is not inconsistent with
experience, that the sensation of hunger may be destroyed, and
life sustained, by some description of herbs.—ED.

of Abaris, that he had never been seen to eat or to drink;* an art also which was successfully practiced by Epimenides, the cotemporary of Solon,† is well known in the present day, and has very recently been brought to perfection by a learned man.‡ It is nearly fifty years since the plan of giving nourishment of this kind to mariners was attempted in France : its small bulk would have enabled a much greater quantity than of any other provision to have been embarked at a time; it was, however, abandoned; for although the men thus fed did not suffer from hunger, yet they were found less capable of sustaining fatigue.

This would not be any inconvenience to the

* Iamblich., *Vit. Pythag.*, § 27. Abaris was a Scythian, the son of Seuthes ; he flourished during the Trojan war, and is supposed to have written some treatises in Greek. Many absurd fables are related concerning him : among others, that he received a flying arrow from Apollo, which gave oracles, and transported him through the air wherever he pleased ; that he returned to the hyperborean countries from Athens without eating, and that he made the Trojan Palladium with the bones of Pelops.—ED.

† Plutarch, *Sympos.*

‡ M Gimbernat. *Revue Encyclopédique*, tome xxxv., p. 235. More absurd stories are related of Epimenides than of Abaris. He was said to have entered into a cave, where he fell asleep, and slept for fifty-seven years ; so that, when he awoke, he found every thing altered ; and he scarcely knew where he was : a degree of ignorance which is surprising, as he is also reported to have been able to dismiss his soul from his body, and recall it at pleasure. During its absence, he affirmed that it had familiar intercourse with the gods, and obtained the gift of prophecy. In plain language, he was a man of genius, a poet, and a learned man, capable of great abstraction ; and, for the sake of justifying his pretensions of intercourse with the gods, he lived in great retirement, and chiefly upon herbs. So high was his reputation for sanctity, that, during a plague in Attica, 596 B.C., the Athenians sent for him to perform a lustration, by which the gods were appeased, and the plague ceased. He was a native of Crete ; and the Cretans paid him divine honors after his death. Notwithstanding his celebrity, however, he can only be regarded in the light of an impostor, living in an age of almost incredible credulity ; therefore every thing related of him must be received with doubt.—ED.

Thaumaturgists. A holy man, who lives without any, or very little excitement, commonly remains motionless in his cell, receiving the respect and adoration of those who seek him there ; and if, after a long period of trial, he should be found sinking from weakness, this circumstance would only increase the faith in the reality of his miraculous abstinence.

This difficulty, beside, could not have existed in earlier times. According to Edrisi,* the Berber tribes of the neighborhood of Roun prepared, with honey, and roasted and bruised corn, so nourishing a paste, that a handful eaten in the morning enabled them to march until evening without experiencing hunger. The Caledonians and the Meates,† who formed the greatest part of the population of Great Britain, understood, says Xiphilin, a method of preparing their food in a way so capable of sustaining their strength, that having taken a quantity equal to the size of a bean, they felt neither hunger nor thirst. The Scythians, doubtless, possessed the art of a process similar to this, and even extended it to the food of their horses ; but the miraculous herbs mentioned by Matthiolus were merely intended to delude others as to the secret of their real nature. But this secret could not have been unknown, at least to the learned portion, among people much more civilized than the Caledonians and Scythians ; its existence, therefore, renders such narrations credible, and divests them of their miraculous covering.

Far above the miracle of making man indepen-

* _Géographie d'Edrisi_, translated by M. Am. Jaubert, vol. i, p. 205.
† Xiphilin in _Sever._, Anno 209. In a story which appears to be of Oriental origin, the secret of composing pills, or an opiate endued with the same virtue, is attributed to Avicenna and another learned man. (_The Thousand and One Nights._)

dent of the most pressing wants of nature, is that
of restoring to him the life that he has lost.

It is agreed that there is nothing so difficult to
determine as the certain and irrefragable signs of
death ; and the special study of these signs, and a
complete experience of what is doubtful and positive in them, alone furnish the means of distinguishing between a real and an apparent death. To
restore to life a being who is threatened to be deprived of it by a too hasty burial would, in the
present day, be a benefit; formerly it was a miracle.

The laws and customs of an enlightened people
will always prescribe laws for ascertaining that
life is actually extinct. From time immemorial
the Hindoos have employed fire, the most certain,
perhaps, of all proofs, for, even if it does not rouse
the sensibility, there is a visible difference in the
action of burning when exercised on an inanimate
body, and that on one in which life still exists.*
It is not until after a portion of cow-dung has been
burned in the hollow over the stomach of the
corpse, that the funereal pile, which is to consume
it, is lighted. According to appearances, a similar custom formerly existed in Italy and Greece.
Tertullian† ridicules those spectacles in which
Mercury is represented as examining corpses, and
convincing himself by a red-hot iron that the exterior marks of death were not deceptive. This
custom must then have been at one time in full
force, but had fallen into disuse, and existed only

* Fodéré, *Dictionnaire des Sciences Médicales*, art. *Signes de la Mort.*

† Tertullian, *Apologetic.*, cap. xv. Cœlius Rhodiginus (*Lect. Antiq.*, lib. iv., cap. xxxi.) reads, as we do, *cauterio* in the text of Tertullian, and not *cantherio*. This last version, adopted by some modern writers, does not seem to me to offer any reason-able sense.

in mythological remembrances.   Democritus had, at an early period, asserted that there did not exist any certain signs of real death.*   Pliny† maintained the same opinion, and even remarked that women were more exposed than men to the dangers of an apparent death.   He cited numerous instances of apparent deaths, and among others, one mentioned by Heraclides, of a woman who revived after having passed for dead during seven days.‡   Neither did he forget the sagacity of Asclepiades, who, seeing a funeral procession pass by, exclaimed that the man who was being carried to the pile was not dead.§   To conclude, might not humanity have adopted this means of safety, to

---

* A. Cornel., *Cels.*, lib. ii., cap. vi.
† Plin., *Hist. Nat.*, lib. vii., cap. lii.   ‡ *Ibid.*
§ A. Cornel., *Cels.*, loc. cit.   Heraclides wrote a treatise entitled, *The Disease in which the Respiration is suspended.*   Asclepiades was a learned physician, and was the founder of a sect in medicine.   There can be no difference of opinion with respect to the correctness of the observations of these distinguished men. Numerous cases of apparent deaths have been recorded as having occurred in modern times.   The mention of a few will suffice to demonstrate the difficulty of determining the fact that death has actually triumphed over mortality ; unless the signs be of that unequivocal nature that they can not be mistaken—namely, the extinction of animal heat, that rigidity of the body in which the direction of the limb, when changed, remains, and commencing decomposition.   Francis Civile, a Norman gentleman, who lived in the time of Charles IX., twice apparently died, and was twice in the act of being buried, when he spontaneously revived at the moment in which the coffin was deposited in the grave.   In the seventeenth century, a Lady Russell apparently died, and was about to be buried ; but, as the bell was tolling for her funeral, she sat up in the coffin, and exclaimed, " It is time to go to church !"   Diemerbroesk (*Treatise on the Plague*, book iv.) mentions the case of a peasant, who displayed no signs of life for three days ; but, on being carried to the grave, revived, and lived many years afterward.   So recently as the year 1836, a respectable citizen of Brussels fell into a profound lethargy on a Sunday morning.   His friends, conceiving that he was dead, determined to bury him ; and on Monday he was placed on a bier, with all the usual accompaniments of the dead, previous to interment, in Catholic countries.   His body was placed in the coffin ; and, when the undertaker's men were about to screw down the lid,

which the instinct of tyranny instigated Nicoc-
rafes* to make use of, in order to prevent the inhabitants of Cyrene from feigning death, and by
thus leaving the town, to withdraw from his cruelty ?

Would it be absurd to suppose that the Thaumaturgists were so well acquainted with the distinction between apparent and real death as to take
advantage of it, and to boast the power of so brilliant a miracle as a resurrection : and consequently
they exerted themselves to lead to the disuse of the
salutary practice attributed by tradition to the god
Mercury.

It is at least certain that many Theurgists boasted of being endowed with the power of recalling
the dead to life.   Diogenes Laertius relates that
Empedocles resuscitated a woman,† that is to say,
"that he dissipated the lethargy of a woman attacked by uterine suffocation."‡

The biographer of Apollonius of Tyana more
cautiously expresses himself, relatively to a young
girl who owed her life to the care of this philosopher.   He says, that she had seemed to die ; while
ne confesses that the rain which fell upon her,

the supposed corpse sat up, rubbed his eyes, and called for his
coffee and a newspaper.*   From these, and many instances of a
similar description, it is evident that a temporary quiescent condition of the vital principle must not be confounded with real
death.   The immobility of the body, even its cadaverous aspect,
the coldness of the surface, the absence of respiration and pulsa-
tion, and the somewhat sunken state of the eye, are not unequivocal evidences that life is wholly extinct.   The only unequivocal signs are those mentioned above ; and, happily, in this
country, interment does not take place until some evidence of
putrefaction display themselves.—ED.

 * Plutarch, *Mulier, Fort. Fact.*, § x.
 † Diogen. Laert., lib. viii., cap. lvii. et lxix.
 ‡ Diderot, *Opinions des Anciens Philosophes*, art. *Pythagore-
Pythagoriciens.*

when she was in the act of being carried with her face exposed to the pile, might have commenced exciting her senses.   Apollonius had at least, like Asclepiades, the merit of distinguishing at a glance between real and apparent death.*

An observer of the seventeenth century† relates that a servant, finding, on returning from a voyage, his master dead, tenderly and frequently embraced the inanimate body.   Thinking that he discovered some signs of life in it, he breathed his breath into it with so much perseverance as restored respiration, and reanimated the apparently dead man. This was not regarded as a miracle ;‡ and, happily

* Philostrat., *Vit. Apollon. Tyan.*, lib. iv., cap. xvi. Apollonius began by asking the name of the young girl, doubtless in order to address her. He knew that of all articulated sounds which strike upon our ear, our own name is that which we most easily recognize, and which most quickly excites our attention.

† Petr. Borellus, *Hist. et Observ. Medic. Centur.*, iii., observ. lviii., quoted by Fromann, *Tractat. de Fascinatione*, pp. 483, 484.

‡ This mode of restoring the respiratory function in suspended animation is often successfully resorted to in the present day ; and as a medical man has often to determine the question of real or apparent death, it is consolatory to know, that he possesses the means of deciding with sufficient accuracy to authorize the adoption of the measures which experience has proved to be the most likely to restore animation when it is merely suspended. When death has actually taken place, it is surely unnecessary to say, that any human attempt to restore life would not only display the most outrageous arrogance, but prove indubitably ineffective. We believe most sincerely in the real miracle of raising Lazarus from the grave by our Savior, as firmly, indeed, as in the resurrection of our Savior himself; and, although we are ready to admit that the Almighty, for some special purpose, as in the case of the Apostles and the early promulgators of Christianity, might even now endow a mortal with such a supernatural gift, yet, all experience is against such an event. Many impostors, however, have presumptuously asserted their possession of this power ; and, even at so recent a period as that of the French prophets, it was assumed by these insane enthusiasts, who, not contented with the reputation of many cures performed upon nervous and imaginative individuals, by means of prayer, destroyed their reputation by indiscreetly staking it on the resurrection of Dr. Eames : a striking proof how readily the intellect may become the slave of fanaticism.—ED.

for the faithful servant, it was no longer the custom to attribute such an occurrence to magic.*

CHAPTER V.

Poisonous Substances.—Poisons, the Effect of which can be graduated.—Miraculous Deaths.—Poisons employed in Ordeals. —Diseases asserted to be caused by Divine Vengeance.—Diseases foretold.

FEAR is more permanent, as well as more exacting, than gratitude. It was easy for Thaumaturgists to inspire the former, in employing the agency of poisonous substances on organized bodies. Nature has produced these substances principally in those parts of our globe which were first inhabited; and the art of increasing their number and their power is not less ancient than civilization. What could have appeared more magical, what more miraculous, we may inquire, in the eyes of ignorant men, at least in apparent connection with its cause, than poisoning by prussic acid, by morphia, or by certain preparations of arsenic, had they been known in ancient times? The author of the crime would have appeared in all eyes as a being endowed with supernatural power; even perhaps as a god, who could sport with the life of weak mortals, and who with a breath could cause them to vanish from the face of the earth.

The ancient use, however, of this formidable knowledge at one time proved a blessing. The

* The subject of the powerful influence of mind over the body is of so much importance, especially at the present time, when the public is so open to the promises held forth by every pretender to the healing art, who blazons forth, in advertisements, the marvelous cures effected by his nostrums, that the Editor has added an essay upon that subject to the Appendix. (See note C.)—ED.

II.　　　　　　H

territory of Sycion was desolated by the ravages of wolves. The oracle, which was consulted, pointed out to the inhabitants the trunk of a tree, the bark of which it enjoined them to mix with the morsels of flesh which they threw to the wolves. These animals were destroyed by the poison. But the inhabitants could not recognize the tree, of which they had only seen the trunk. The priests reserved this part of the secret to themselves.

If in Greece, more than two thousand years ago, a man had fallen a victim to the influence of poison, or from an excess of intemperance, the incident in itself would not be interesting. But, when the short sojournment of that man on earth had cost more deaths and more evils to humanity than the greatest scourges of nature; and, nevertheless, when the illusion of conquests and the fallacy of vulgar opinions, had converted that monster polluted with innumerable crimes and vices into a model for heroes; when, in a word, that man was Alexander, the son of Philip, the problem becomes historical, and excites curiosity. Its solution interests us, from its connection with scientific ideas, the existence of which it enables us to reveal.

Ælian, Pompeus Trogas, and Quintus Curtius attribute the death of Alexander to poison.* The two latter add, that the poison was sent from Macedonia to Babylon, and was water from a spring at the foot of Mount Nonacris, in Arcadia. This water was so cold and so bitter that it occasioned death to both men and animals; it broke or corroded all vases, except those which were made from the hoof of an ass, or a mule, or a horse, or from the horn which the Scythian asses† have on

* Pausanias, *Corinthiac.*, cap. ix.
† We are told by Aristotle, that, in his time, there were no

, their forehead. One of these horns had been offered as a present to Alexander : he had dedicated it to Apollo, in the temple of Delphi, with an inscription, relating its wonderful property.* In this recital we may perceive some dubious or obscure expressions; and remark that substances are frequently qualified as being *hot* or *cold*, independent of their temperature. Instead of the horn of a fabulous animal, a vessel might have been substituted which, like many vessels that were used by the ancients, was in the shape of a horn, and perhaps, also, displayed the color of one, with its polish and its semi-transparency ; but which, being brought from Scythia, or Upper Asia,† might have been made of thick glass, or of porcelain sufficiently well baked, and calculated to resist the action of corrosive liquids. Without entering into such an inquiry, the narrators have detailed only the marvelous part of the recital, and have made of it a ridiculous story.

I suppose, without entering into any explanation, that the wonderful springs of which they boasted, and the water of which, we are told, corroded all metals with the exception of one alone, which they described simply by this property of inalterability, from the facility with which it was volatilized by heat, and a residue procured under the form of powder, perfectly white, and of extreme tenuity, was such as we need not refer to the land of fables. Such springs are at the doors of the French capital, at Enghien : and for distributing the water, pipes and taps of zinc are

asses in Scythia; some other animal, therefore, must have produced the horn sent to Alexander.—ED.

 * Ælian, *De Nat. Animal.*, lib. x., cap. xl.

 † The name of Scythia began to be applied to the northern parts of Asia, in the Macedonian period, and was employed at the time of the conquest of Asia by Alexander.—ED.

used,* because this metal appears to be the only one which does not decompose sulphureous waters.

Our incredulity would be redoubled, if an unaccredited author had made us acquainted, for the first time, with the *zagh;* that substance which is employed in the East for inlaying steel arms with apparent gold. It is drawn from a spring in the mountains of the Druses, and can only be preserved in vessels of lead, or of glass, or porcelain. *Zagh* is a mixture of the acidulated sulphate of alumina, and sulphate of iron,† the solution of which will corrode any other metal except lead.‡   This, and the preceding example, at once sets aside part of the improbability which pervades the recitals relative to the water of Nonacris.   Nothing precludes the *zagh* from being, as the Orientals assert, a production of nature.   In a work§ which does as much honor to his vast knowledge as to his philosophy, Seneca describes a spring near to Tempe in Thessaly, the waters of which are mortal to animals, and penetrate through iron and copper.‖   In Thrace, in the country of the Cyclops, also, there flowed a rivulet whose limpid water seemed to differ in

---

* *Revue Encyclopédique,* tome xxxv., p. 501.

† *Report of the Society for encouraging National Industry,* December, 1821, p. 362.

‡ Our author here labors under a mistake. Such a solution will not affect vessels of platinum, gold, or silver.—ED.

§ Senec., *Quæst. Nat.,* lib. iii., cap. xxv.

‖ It is probable that this spring contained either free sulphuric acid, or a highly acidulous salt of that acid. Modern chemistry has detected this acid in a free state, as well as hydrochloric acid, in the water of the Rio Vinagre, which descends from the volcano of Paraiè, in Colombia, South America. Sulphuric acid is also found in the waters of other volcanic regions. The sour springs of Byron, in the Genesse country, about sixty miles south of the Erie Canal, contain pure sulphuric acid. Such waters, therefore, would rapidly corrode both iron and copper, converting the former into green, the latter into blue vitriol—sulphates of both metals. —ED.

nothing from common water; yet every animal who drank of it instantly died.[*]

The water of Nonacris, which corroded iron, and cracked or dissolved vases of silver and of brass, and even those of baked clay,[†] could only have been a solution more charged with corrosive substances than the *zagh*, and the water of the stream of Tempe. I think, nevertheless, that it was a production of art. 1st. Because it was, according to Quintus Curtius, a production of Macedonia, and according to many other authors, of Arcadia also, which could not have been the case unless it was manufactured in both countries. 2d. Plutarch adds, that it was obtained under the form of a light dew,[‡] an expression which seems to characterize it as the production of distillation. 3d. At Nonacris, Herodotus says, they took an oath on the water of the Styx. Stobæus adds that, according to the general opinion, this water possessed the terrible property of punishing perjurers who had dared to swear by it.[§] If this fact is regarded as the employment of poison in ordeals, we may believe that the water of Nonacris and of the Styx was a production of occult science which rendered it, at will, either innocent or injurious. 4th. The water of Nonacris could not be detected by its taste, when mixed with wine, which was

[*] Arist., *De Mirab. Auscul.*

[†] Q. Curt., lib. x., cap. ultim.—Vitruv., *De Architect.*, lib. iii., cap. iii.—Justin, lib. xii., cap. xiv.—Pausanias, *Arcad.*, cap. xviii. —Plutarch in *Alexandr.*, cap. xcix.—Plin., *Hist. Nat.*, lib. xxx., cap. xvi.—Arrian, *De Exped. Alexand.*, lib. vii., cap. vii. Plutarch extends the dissolving virtue of the water of Nonacris to glass and to crystal. The ancients were anxious to exaggerate ; and the possessors of the secret probably seconded this disposition with all their power.

[‡] Plutarch in *Alexandr.*, cap. xlix.—Herodot., lib. vi., cap. lxxv.

[§] Herodot , lib. vi.—J. Stobæus, *Eclog. Physic. De Statu. animarum.*

not the case with the *zagh,* nor is it with the water
of Enghien, which can be detected, however small
the quantity, when mixed with wine or any other
liquid. It could not be suspected, says Seneca,*
either by its appearance or by its smell; similar
in this respect to the poisons composed by the
most celebrated poisoners, which could only be
discovered at the expense of life. In speaking
thus, does not Seneca describe a composition analogous to the *aqua Toffana* of the Italians;† especially when he adds, that its deleterious action is
exerted particularly on the entrails, which it con-
tracts and binds, and thus occasions death.

Setting aside historical discussion, it is sufficient
for us to draw the attention of our readers to the
extent of the apparent magical power which such
a secret had put into the hands of the Thaumaturgists. What could they not accomplish, if, joined
to the power of graduating the effect of poison,
they could determine the exact day when the vic-

---

* Senec., loc. cit.
† The *Aqua della Toffana,* or *Aquetta di Napoli,* was the invention of a woman of the name of Toffana, a celebrated secret poi-
soner, who resided at Naples in the end of the seventeenth and
the commencement of the eighteenth centuries. This water was
so powerful, that from four to six drops were sufficient to destroy
a man. It was sold in small vials, inscribed " Manna of St. Nicholas of Bari," and ornamented with the image of the saint. By
thus concealing her drops under the name of a miraculous oil for
curing diseases, then in high repute in Naples, Toffana long carried on her abominable trade of assisting heirs to their estates,
and wives to new husbands. This violation of a sacred name,
however, having raised a loud outcry against her among the clergy, the wretched woman was arrested, put to the rack, and afterward strangled. These drops were stated by Garelli,* physician
to the Emperor Charles VII., to be a strong solution of arsenious
acid in an infusion of the ivy-leaved toadflax, Linaria *cymbalaria,*
which was an unnecessary addition, as the arsenious acid is perfectly tasteless.—Ed.

---

* Hoffman quotes Garelli's letter to him, in his *Medicina Rationalis
Symptomata,* tome ii., p. 2; cap. ii., § 19, p. 185.

tim should fall? This art has existed at all times
in India, where the possession of it is not concealed.* "There are," says a personage in the Eastern Tales,† "all kinds of poisons. There are some
which take away life a month after they have been
taken; there are others which destroy it at the end
of two months; and there are others, the effect of
which is still more gradual." When a Hindoo
widow, in 1822, burned herself upon the funereal
pile of her husband, the Bramins said frankly to
the English observer whom we have quoted,‡ that,
had she been prevented or dissuaded from accom-
plishing the sacrifice, she would not have survived
the violation of her vow more than three hours,
as they had graduated, for that time, the strength
of the poison which they had administered to
her.

Ælian,§ who mentions the art of the inhabitants
of India in manufacturing poisons, the effect of
which is slow and graduated at will, ascribes to
them also the possession of a substance, a very
small dose of which will occasion almost sudden
death without pain. It was sent to the King of
Persia, who promised his mother that she alone
should share with him the possession of this valuable poison. In fact, it served as well for murderous political unions, as for the sacred vengeance
of the Thaumaturgists.

When the Church, scarcely delivered from the
persecutions of the Polytheists, was torn by disputes
on transubstantiation, which, to use the expression
of a great poet, caused Christians to perish martyrs

---

* The Hindoo poison is named *poest*, and is a preparation of
the poppy.—ED.
† *Arabian Nights' Entertainments*, 14th night. Story of the
Forty Thieves.
‡ See ch. i., vol. ii—*Asiatic Jour.*, vol. xv. (1823), pp. 292, 293.
§ Ælian. *De Nat. Animal.*, lib. iv., cap. xxx. et xli.

of a diphthong,* St. Athanasius† and his partisans had the imprudence to celebrate the *miracle* which

---

* Lorsque attaquant le verbe et sa divinité,
  D'une syllabe impie un saint mot augmenté,
  Faisait, dans une guerre et si vive et si longue,
  Périr tant de Chrétiens, martyrs d'une dipthongue.
  Boileau, *Satire* xii., vers. 199–202.

Omousios, unsubstantiate or of *equal essence*; *Omoiousios*, or of *similar essence*. The dipthong *oi*, which distinguished these two words from one another, was adopted by the Arians, and rejected by their adversaries.

† St. Athanasius was born in Alexandria, A.D. 206, of Christian parents. He received the most liberal education, and profited by it to a degree that admirably fitted him for the station in the Church which he afterward filled. Arius, his opponent, was a native of Cyrenaica. He had been expelled the communion of the Church by St. Peter, who had ordained him a deacon, on account of having joined the Meletians; but, having repented, he was readmitted by Achillas, who had succeeded St. Peter as Patriarch of Alexandria, and was ordained a priest and pastor to one of the churches of Alexandria. The ambition of Arius was disappointed when his patron was succeeded by St. Alexander; and he soon afterward began to preach the heresy known by his name, respecting the divinity of our Savior, which caused his second expulsion from the communion of the Church. St. Athanasius was then merely a deacon; but, in the Council of Nice, he combated so successfully the doctrines broached by Arius, and supported by the followers of the heresiarch, that, on the death of Alexander, he was elected Patriarch of Alexandria, A.D. 326. Soon after this event, the Meletians and Arians having joined, and St. Athanasius having had a sentence of deposition pronounced against him, through the means of Eusebius, Arius made a kind of retraction of his former opinions to Constantine, and was readmitted to the Church generally, but, nevertheless, he was refused to be admitted by the church at Alexandria. It is unnecessary to enter into the history of Arianism, and the various controversies, feuds, and even appeals to arms, which this heresy occasioned. On the recantation of Arius to Constantine, in a third confession of his faith, and his profession on oath to submit to the Nicene Creed, the emperor, in 336, commanded that the patriarch should leave his see in case he persisted to refuse admitting Arius to communion, and resolved that he should be received in a solemn manner. St. James, who was then at Constantinople, exhorted the people to have recourse to God by fasting and prayer for seven days; and on the eighth day, the Sunday on which Arius was to have been admitted, that wretched man was found dead in a privy. Socrates relates that he was taken ill of a bowel complaint during the procession. Some writers ascribed his death to poison; but as the Arians ascribed his death to the magical practices of his enemies, the accusation of poisoning was not believed.—ED

had freed them from Arius. Let the names be
suppressed; let the details alone of this unexpect-
ed death be recalled—those which have been transmitted to us by three church historians :* there is
no man, however indifferently educated, who will
not there recognize symptoms produced by violent
poison No physician would have hesitated to
counsel a circumstantial examination, in order to
clear up·some very plausible suspicions, and no
magistrate would have declined to order it. And
if it is added, that a few hours before the death,
St. Alexander, the adversary of Arius, was heard
addressing fervent prayers to heaven, that rather
than the heretic should be permitted to enter in
triumph into the Church, and his heresy with him,
he might be struck dead,† it is not surprising that
the partisans of Arius did not think his death natural, although they had supposed it to be a miracle, and that their accusations were sufficiently
public to induce one of their adversaries to think
it necessary to pass them over in silence.‡

Such, in those days of discord, was the transport
of zeal! The Christians, in the excess of joy which
the death of the Emperor Julian occasioned them,
indiscreetly published that his tragical end had
been foretold by marvelous dreams, and that they
perceived in it a signal miracle of the divine

---

* Socrat., *Hist. Eccles.*, lib. i., cap. xxxviii.—Sozomen, *Hist.
Eccles.*, lib. ii., cap. xxix., xxx.—Theodoret, *Hist. Eccles.*, lib. i.,
cap. xiv.

† Theodoret, *Hist. Eccles.*, lib. i., cap. xiv.

‡ Sozomen, *Hist. Eccles.*, lib. ii., cap. xxix. From what has
been already stated, the Editor can not avoid blaming our author
for great partiality, in insinuating the charge of poisoning against
the opposers of Arius. Such feuds in the Christian Church were
undoubtedly most unhappy at the time for the progress of the
true faith, and led to much of the apostasy that followed; but
there are no grounds for the accusation of the poisoning of Arius
—Ed.

vengeance. The philosopher Libanius,* the friend of the monarch, after his death, and under successors who had very little respect for his memory, boldly declared that Julian had fallen beneath the blows of a Christian assassin. To this imputation an orthodox writer replies, " The fact might be true; and who will blame that man, who, for his God and his religion, would have committed so courageous an action?"† This shameful glorying in crime, so contrary to the precepts of the religion which the writer believed, may, however, be natural; for it is natural that, in proportion to the keenness of the interests by which they are affected, men become eager, reject reason, and precipitate themselves into delirium and fury.

It must be lamented, that in every nation, the ancient priests enjoyed an influence equally infalli ble and mysterious in submitting the judgment of crimes to ordeals, more especially to those of beverages prepared by their hands; and which were generally deadly or innocent beverages, according to their wish to save or to destroy the accused person.

The Hindoo law, the most ancient of all, is the only one which dares frankly to utter the name— poison. The accused who submits to this ordeal, in taking the poison which he is about to drink, believes that it will change, if he is innocent, into a delicious draught.‡ This is a remarkable formulary, which, conformable with what we have else-

---

* Libanius was a native of Antioch, in Syria. He became so celebrated a teacher of rhetoric, that, although a pagan, yet he numbered some Christians among his scholars, and was on intimate terms with St. Basil. He was the personal friend of Julian; and, being adverse to the Christians, his assertions respecting the death of the emperor can, therefore, be scarcely regarded as worthy of much credit.—Ed.

† Sozomen, *Hist. Eccles.*, lib. vi., cap. ii.

‡ *Asiatic Researches*, vol. i., pp. 473, 486.

where declared, addresses itself to the physical agent as if it were a being endowed with supernatural power and knowledge; as, for instance, a genius, or a god.

Sometimes the trial was confined to swallowing the water in which the priest had bathed the image of one of the divinities,* which, although less formidable in appearance, yet was, in fact, as decisive.†

In Japan, the accused is obliged to swallow, in a cup of water, a piece of paper, on which the priests have traced magical characters and pictures; and this beverage tortures him cruelly, until he has confessed his crime.‡

Guided, probably, by ancient tradition more than by any knowledge which belongs to them, the Arabs practice similar trials.

The negroes of Issyny dare not drink the water into which the *Fetiche* has been dipped, when they

---

* Refer to vol. i. chap. vi.

† *Asiatic Researches*, vol. i., pp. 474–486. Upon the different ordeals employed among the Hindoos, namely, those of fire, of a weight, of freezing water, of scalding oil, of the serpent, of poison, &c., see Dubois, *Mœurs et Coutumes des Peuples de l'Inde*, tome ii., pp. 546–554. There is not one of them, the success of which does not depend on the will of the priests.

The Hindoo code of laws is a pure theocracy, the lawgiver being supposed to promulgate nothing but what was revealed to him by the divinity; hence the unconditional and implicit obedience which the people yield to their priests, who must be necessarily the interpreters of revealed laws. Princes are even subject to them; and. so far does the assumption of power by the Bramins extend. that we find these words in the *Institutes of Menu* :— "What prince could gain wealth by oppressing those (Bramins) who, if angry, could frame other worlds; and could give being to other gods and to other mortals."* After such an assumption in the priesthood, the degree of superstition and mental degradation which has kept the condition of man servile and stationary in India, will no longer excite surprise ; for, what follows so closely in the steps of superstition as popular ignorance, mental despotism. and barbaric tyranny ?—Ed.

‡ Koempfer, *History of Japan*, book iii., chap. v., p. 51.

---

* *Institutes of Menu*, chap. ix., v. 315.

affirm what is not the truth.* Before consecrated
water could inspire so great a fear, must there not
have been several examples to prove its deadly
efficacy ?

The initiated of *Para-belli*, a very powerful religious society in the interior of Southern Africa,
prepare, among the Qojas negroes, a water of
trial, which is thrown over the legs, the arms, or
the hands of the accused. If the water burns him,
he is declared guilty ; if it does not burn him, he
is innocent.† Is not the mysterious composition
of the water, and the care that is taken to wash the
limbs before they are exposed to its action, sufficient to explain the assumed miracle ?

Among the Qojas, and among numbers of other
African tribes, a person suspected of poisoning is
made to drink a very acid liquid, prepared by
scraping the inside bark of the *quony-tree*, from
which the sap has been first pressed out into water.
The accused who survives the trial is declared innocent; he who dies is pronounced guilty.‡ It
may be believed that the care with which the bark
is pressed, decides the fate of the accused. In
other countries, the accused is obliged to drink a
liquid prepared by the hands of the priests : in
Monomotapa he is condemned if he vomits it ; and
in the kingdom of Loango, if the liquid has a diu-
retic effect upon him, he is also condemned.§

Nations more advanced in civilization have authorized those trials in which the divinity is called
upon to work a miracle to manifest the truth. At
Rome, in the time of Cicero and Horace, a master
who suspected that his slaves had robbed him conducted them before a priest. They were each

---

* Godefroy Loyer, *Voyage to the Kingdom of Issyny.*
† O. Dapper, *Description de l'Afrique*, pp. 269, 270.
‡ *Ibid.*, l. c., p. 263.   § *Ibid.*, pp. 325, 326, 392.

obliged to eat a cake over which the priest had pronounced some magical words (*carmine infectum*). This plan undoubtedly discovered the author of the theft.[*] Near Tyana, an inexhaustible spring of very cold, but always bubbling water (water strongly gaseous), served to test the truth of vows. The truthful man drank of it with impunity; the man guilty of a false vow, if he dared to taste it, saw his body covered with blisters and abscesses, and was so deprived of his strength that he could not quit the place until he had confessed his perjury.[†]

Christianity has not altogether rejected these kinds of ordeals. The fountain of *Wieres*[‡] is still celebrated in Picardy. The unfaithful wife of St. Genoulf dared to plunge her arm into it, vowing that her conduct was irreproachable; but her arm immediately became withered. The fountain, however, is now less malicious, and all women wash their hands in it with impunity. It may, therefore, be believed that this ordeal has not been always harmless; and that, more than once, the terror which it inspired had restrained many from attempting it. This has often occured with other ordeals. The collections of anecdotes are replete with stories of·the guilty, who, by the fear of a miracle, have been induced to confess their crimes. Here we repeat the reasonings that we have already offered, that fear would not have been occasioned, if preceding experiments had not proved that the ordeal was sometimes well founded. It was so managed that the promised miracle should not exceed the powers of the Thaumaturgist.

---

[*] Acron. in *Horat. Epist.*, lib. i., epist. x., v. 9.
[†] Philostrat., *Vita Apollon.*, lib. i., cap. iv.
[‡] A fountain which is situated near Samer, department of the Pas de Calais.—*Mémoires de l'Académie Celtique*, tome v., pp. 109, 110.

Death was not the only revenge which was foretold by the interpreters of an irritated god.
Turning against his enemies the secrets of the
sacred science with which he was armed, with more
address and less danger to himself, the priest often
reserved to himself the power of producing a second miracle in favor of repentance.

A very bright light, such, for example, as the
Bengal fire, can dazzle the eye so effectually, that
the power of seeing will remain suspended for
some time. At the taking of Milet by Alexander,
when the soldiers entered the temple of Milet to
despoil it, so strong a light shone forth from the
sanctuary, that the soldiers were struck with
temporary blindness.* But the effect produced by
such a method of revenge is of very short duration ;
and its success depends too much on the concurrence of favorable circumstances to permit it to be
often practiced.

Near the river Archeloüs grew the plant *myope :*†
it is impossible to rub the face with it, without
losing the sight. The leaves of the *stramonium*
possess a property differing very little from the
myope. A young man, having accidentally spurted
a drop of the sap into his eye, remained for several
hours deprived of the use of the organ.‡ We
know, in this day, that the extract of *belladonna*,
diluted with water, paralyzes for a time the organ
of sight. To seize the propitious moment for
causing the poisonous substance to act, and for
working the miracle, requires nothing more than
address. Thus, with the talents of the juggler

* Valer. Maxim., lib. i., cap. i.—Lactant., *Divin. Instit.*, lib. ii.,
cap. vii.
† Plutarch, *De Nomin. Fluv. et Mont.*, § xxii. M. Vallot, of the
academy of Dijon, is of opinion that this plant was a kind of
tithymale, most probably Euphorbia *officinarum*.
‡ *Bibliothèque Universelle des Sciences*, tome iv., p. 221.

aiding the science of the Thaumaturgist, the histories of men miraculously struck blind, and as miraculously recovered, present nothing improbable.

Endemic diseases, which ravage a country, an
army, a city, sometimes assume so malignant a
character that ignorance believes, and policy *feigns*
to believe them as contagious as the pestilence.

Formerly, before the oracles were abolished,
desolated populations had recourse to them ; and
it was the wish of the oracles that the people
should always recognize in these diseases the vengeance of gods, justly irritated against their wor
shipers. This belief being once established, the
priest menaced countries rebellious to his com
mands with the invasion of the plague : more than
once he has announced the appearance of it at a
certain time, and his prophecy has been fulfilled.
It was, in fact, easy for him to found his opinion
upon probabilities, equivalent to certainty : it is
only requisite to have observed beforehand the
return of circumstances capable of reproducing
these diseases. It was this science in ancient
Greece which procured for Abaris* the reputation
of being a prophet. The same observations will,
at the present time, serve for similar predictions,
although the honest man will confine himself to
indicating precautions for preventing the evil ; and
he is afflicted if, in neglecting them, a triumph is
provided him of passing for a true prophet.† But

* Iamblich. in *Vit. Pythag.*, lib. i., cap. xxviii.

† In 1820, the port of Roquemaure (an arrondissement of Uzes,
department of Gard) was discovered to be surrounded by stagnant waters in those places where the Rhone had been turned
from its course. M. Cadet, of Metz, predicted that, from the
month of March, the country would certainly be ravaged by an
endemic fever, if, before summer, the river was not restored to its
old bed. The works could only be completed in autumn, and the
summer saw Roquemaure depopulated by raging fevers. (*Letter
from M. Cadet, of Metz, to the Minister of the Interior*, March 23.
1820.)

instead of the philosophical observer, let us substitute a Thaumaturgist; would not the coincidence
of the prophecy and of the disaster strike many
minds, even at this day, with a deep and religious
terror ?

CHAPTER VI. ,

Sterility of the Soil.—The Belief in the Means which the Thaumaturgists were supposed to possess for causing Sterility arose
particularly from the Language of Emblems.—Sterility produced
naturally.—Cultures which injure one another.—Substances
which are prejudicial to Vegetation.—The Atmosphere rendered Pestilential.—Deleterious Powder and Nitrate of Arsenic
employed as offensive Weapons.—Earthquakes and Rumblings
of the Earth foreseen and predicted.

THE threats of celestial anger were not alone
pointed at isolated individuals; they were not alone
confined to the production of transitory diseases :
they raised alarms in a whole people that the earth
would deny them its fruits; that mortals would
only inhale death from the air; that under their
feet the trembling earth would sink and open in
abysses; or that rocks, shaken from their foundations, would roll upon them and crush them to
atoms.

The habit of observation, assisted by reflection
and enlightened by reasoning, imparts to mankind
some plausible idea of the results of the different
cultures to which he devotes himself. Thales, in
purchasing beforehand a crop of olives, the fecun-
dity of which he had prophesied,* proved to the
Milesians that the philosopher depended only upon
his scientific skill to obtain wealth. If the Thaumaturgist also could thus predict an abundant harvest, he might be able to predict others less abundant; being enabled also to foresee a true famine,

* Diogen. Laert. in *Thalet.*

he has the power of threatening the people with it. Should the event justify his prophecy, he would be regarded not merely as the *interpreter*, but as the *agent* of the gods, who had thus punished guilty mortals by the scourge of famine.

Nevertheless, how distant is this point still from that absolute sterility with which the imprecations of a sacred man, or the maledictions of a perfidious magician, were formerly believed to strike *plants*, *trees*, or even the *soil!* This remark will scarcely escape a judicious reader, when he reflects that, according to the principle upon which I have constantly reasoned, some positive facts have given birth to the opinion of the possibility of this terrible means of vengeance. In the eloquent menaces that Æschylus ascribes to Eumenides* I can only perceive the expressions of poetic enthusiasm and the hyperbole which belong to the Oriental style.

In vain I recall to remembrance the inclination which man always has had to ascribe to the wrath of the gods scourges, the cause and the remedy of which nature has hidden from him. The edifice which I have attempted to raise is shaken, if the belief in apparent miracles has no other origin than some transient predictions and the dreams of a terrified imagination.

Let us first retrace the influence of the language of emblems, and then observe how its power has been effectual in misleading writers of veracity, when they have related similar menaces, the accomplishment of which they have themselves witnessed in foreign countries.

For a long period of time, when a conquered city was condemned to eternal desolation, salt was sown among the ruins; and, in the face of experience to the contrary, the property of rendering the

* Æschyl. in *Eumen.*, vers. 783, 786, 803, 806, &c.

II. I

earth unfruitful was for a long time attributed to salt. Let us turn our eyes toward those climates where, in immense deserts, salt is seen everywhere effloresced on the surface of the ground. There one privileged spot may be seen productive. An enemy invades it, disperses its inhabitants, fills up its wells, turns the course of its rivers, destroys the trees, and burns up its vegetation; and this previously fruitful spot is confounded with the desert which surrounds it; and almost immediately, under a burning sky, the despoiled soil becomes covered with the saline efflorescence, the forerunner of future sterility. The emblem of salt strewed upon the earth was most expressive, therefore, in those countries where this phenomenon was known: better than an edict, better than the sound of trumpets and the voice of heralds, it proclaimed the will of the destroyer; it announced that the country should remain uninhabited, without cultivation, and devoted to eternal sterility. The menace was not vain, even where climate and the effects of time did not hasten the work of violence.

What a conqueror is to a weak people, so is the wicked man to a defenseless fellow-being. The Roman law punished as a capital offense that which may appear to us as a trivial delinquency, namely, the act of putting stones on the inheritance of another person. But in the country to which this law belonged, in Arabia, *Scopelism*,* such was the name of the crime, was tantamount to the threat that whoever should dare to cultivate an inheritance thus insulted would perish by a violent death. That this mute language was understood, and that the field remained from that time uncultivated and

---

* *Scopelismus, lapidum positio—lapides ponere indicio futuros quod si quis eum agrum coluisset malo letho periturus esset," &c.—Digest.,* lib. xlvii., tit. xi., § ix.

sterile, was a sufficient reason for the seriousness of the punishment carried out against this emblematical threat. Let us transfer, without any explanation, the indication of this fact into a different order of things; the emblem of *Scopelism*, like that of salt, would soon be regarded as a physical agent capable of destroying the earth by rendering it unalterably sterile.

Sterility is known to be the result of natural causes. Agriculturists know that every perennial plant with a tap-root, such as the luzerne,* sown at the foot of young and delicate trees, injures their growth, and frequently destroys them. The Thaumaturgists were able to collect several observations of this kind ; and they thus acquired the power of predicting the unfruitfulness of trees, and the barrenness of cornfields, when the imprudence of the cultivator placed such mischievous neighbors near useful vegetables ; and, as may be supposed, their predictions were frequently fulfilled. The parable of the Gospel, which describes tares being sown in the night among the wheat, by the enemy of the proprietor,† evidently alludes to a known and even a common delinquency. No police, and especially no rural police, existed among the ancient nations ; hence every one was the guardian of his own property. It was then much easier than it is at this day to injure a field already sown, by treacherously scattering other seed over it, whether it was expected that the person thus acting would profit by the antipathy existing between diverse plants, or that the result would be the choking of the good grain by the excess of a useless plant.

From the judicial avowals of several pretended

---

* Medicago *laciniata*, a native of Syria.—ED.
† *The Gospel of St. Matthew*, chap. xiii., vers. 24–29.

sorcerers, it appears that, among the inventions taught in the *Sabbat*, the composition of powders for injuring every kind of crops, for drying up plants, and blasting fruits,* was included. All that has been related by these wretched beings as to their occupations there, we have considered as dreams; but as dreams founded upon the recollection of ancient practices. To the tradition of the possibility of the assumed miracle was attached the idea that it could still be worked.

A Chinese book,† the antiquity of which is undoubted, notices the crime of destroying a tree by watering it secretly with poisoned water. According to ancient traditions, individuals, envious of the fertility of their neighbors' fields, threw upon them a Stygian water‡ to destroy their fertility. Theophrastus, quoted by ·St. Clement of Alexandria, affirms, that if the shells of beans are buried among the roots of a tree recently planted, the tree decays.§ To obtain a similar result, even to a great extent, Democritus has directed that the roots of trees should be watered with the juice of the hemlock (conium *maculatum*), in which the flowers of the lupine have been steeped.‖ I am ignorant whether experience has ever confirmed these assertions; but they indicate that some efficacious secret was concealed under a veil, more or less dense, and that the ancients were not ignorant of the existence of a process capable of destroying plants and trees. Recent experiments have proved that, to succeed in procuring such an event, it is

* Llorente, *Histoire de l'Inquisition*, tome iii., pp. 440–447.
† *Le Livre des Récompenses et des Peines*, translated by M. Stan islas Jullien, p. 346.
‡ See the Scholiaste of Stace. in *Thébaid.*, lib. ii., v. 274, verbo *Telchines*.
§ St. Clement, *Alexandr. Stromat.*, lib. iii.
‖ Plin., *Hist. Nat.*, lib. xviii., cap. vi.

only necessary to spread upon the soil a combination of sulphur and lime, in the proportion of fifteen parts of the former to one of the latter; a combination which is found to be formed in the residue of the lixivium, which is used in making curd soap, and in the residue of the artificial fabrication of soda. It is also proved, by daily observation, that the waters proceeding from coal-pits, and from the workings of metallic mines, first change, and finally destroy vegetation, upon every soil which is watered by them: and is it not natural to connect these waters with that *Stygian* water, of which the Telchines, a race celebrated in the art of excavating mines, and of working brass and iron, were accused of employing for so guilty a purpose? But it matters little, as we have thus observed more than once, whether these mischievous properties were formerly known or discovered by the founders of modern sorcery: the *possibility* of their being known is unquestionable; and the belief established among the ancients, and verified by the assertions of Theophrastus and Democritus, is unrefuted, that a natural process was sufficient to realize this possibility.

Let us apply the same reasoning to the terrible art of rendering the air pestilential. Natural phenomena were doubtless, at first, attributed to the vengeance of the gods. Under the government of Marcus Aurelius, a temple at Seleucia was delivered up to be plundered; the soldiers having discovered a narrow aperture, entered it, and broke open a door which had been carefully shut by the Chaldean priests. Suddenly there was exhaled a lethiferous vapor, the disastrous effects of which extended itself to some distance.[*] It was, I believe, a gas similar to that which sometimes escapes

* Amm. Marcell., lib. xxiii.—Jul. Capitol. in *Ælio-Vero*.

from mines, and from deep and deserted wells.*
From two gulfs, one near to the borders of the
Tigris, and another situated near Hierapolis of
Phrygia, there arises, in the same manner, a vapor
mortal to every animal that inhales it.†

According to a tendency which we have already
noticed, art has attempted to imitate the modes of
destruction which nature produces; and, at different periods, certain traces have been found of these
means having been employed as offensive weapons.
In 1804, the French government accused the English sailors of having attempted to poison the
atmosphere of the coasts of Bretagne and of Normandy, by leaving on shore horns containing burning nitrate of arsenic.   Several of these horns being
extinguished, they were collected, and their con-

* The deleterious gas mentioned in the text must have been
chiefly, if not wholly, carbonic acid gas, which frequently accu-
mulates in old cellars that have been long shut up, especially if
they have contained any fermentable vegetable matter.   It was
not the *fire-damp*, or gas exhaled in mines, which consists almost
solely of light carbureted hydrogen, and which issues from fis-
sures in the beds of coal, and, being light, collects in the upper
part of the mines, owing to deficient ventilation.   This gas is very
explosive when mingled with atmospheric air, and, prior to Sir
Humphry Davy's invention of the safety-lamp, frequently proved
dangerous to miners, when the atmosphere of it sank so low down
in the pit as to be fired by their candles; but it is not so poisonous when breathed as carbonic acid gas, *fixed air*, which destroys
life even when mixed with an equal portion of pure atmospheric
air.   Carbonic acid gas causes a sensation of giddiness, ringing
in the ears, dimness of sight, drowsiness, and hurried respiration;
and the debility which also attends it comes on so suddenly, that
the person is unable to make his escape, and falls down insensible: hence the dread and horror which it must have occasioned
in the Roman soldiers, when their comrades nearest the door
were immersed in the flood of this gas which rolled from the
apartment.   This gas is also considerably heavier than atmospheric air; and, therefore, when those who fell first were attempted to be raised by their companions, the necessity of stooping
would bring them also into the same atmosphere, and thus increase the number of victims.. Ignorance would be most likely
to deem their deaths a punishment for the sacrilege.—Ed.

† Amm. Marcell., lib. xxiii.   The modern bambuk-calasi.—Ed.

tents having been chemically examined, no doubt remained of the nature of the composition with which they were charged.* The enemies of France, in this instance, only renewed and perfected an invention which, in Europe, followed close upon the invention of cannon. At that time, bombs and grenades were filled with a powder prepared for the purpose; and these projectiles, in bursting, diffused, to a great distance, an odor so deleterious, that it proved mortal to all who had the misfortune to inhale it. Paw, who has discovered in an Italian pyrotechnic the composition of this offensive powder, recollects that a trial of it was made in London with a melancholy result.† A long time before, if we may believe Strabo,‡ the *Soanes*, not contented with wounding their enemies with poisoned weapons, endeavored to suffocate, with poisonous exhalations, those warriors whom they were unable to strike. It is evident that this poisonous odor developed itself only in the enemy's ranks; for, if such had not been the case, it would have first destroyed the men who carried the weapons which concealed it. It will be necessary to distinguish these weapons from poisoned arrows, and to suppose that they were filled with a composition similar to the exploding powder; a composition which acted either on the rupture of the vessel containing it, or by the contact of fire. As this secret was known by the barbarians of the Caucasus, it might have been also known among more enlightened nations. Its nature might have

* See the newspapers of 1804.
† Paw, *Traité des Flèches empoisonnées* (inserted in vol. xii., in 4to., of the translation of Pliny's *Natural History*), pp. 460–470. Paw calls in question the efficacy of this offensive powder. We think, with him, that it was trifling, since the use of it was so speedily abandoned.
‡ Strabo, lib. xi.

been understood also by the Thaumaturgists, and
have been made the origin of a belief in the apparent miracles which rendered the air pestilential.

If the iniquity of man can injure the fertility of
the soil and the salubrity of the air, it is not so
easy for him to shake the earth, and to cause
mountains to roll upon the people, whom his hatred has devoted to destruction.   But if signs which
escape the observation of the unobserving vulgar
warn him of the approach of some great convulsion
of nature, and if he dares to predict it, whether
with the intention of calling his fellow-creatures to
prevent the sad consequences of the event, or to
induce them to see in it the effects of the vengeance
of the gods, what glory and what power will be
his share, when the event shall have confirmed his
prediction !

Iamblichus* attributes the possession of this wonderful sagacity to Pythagoras, to Abaris, to Epimenides, and to Empedocles.   At a much later
period, in the thirteenth century of our era, a monk,
wishing to persuade the Emperor Andronicus to
recall the patriarch St. Athanasius, threatened him
with divers scourges, and, among others, with that
of an earthquake; and three days had scarcely
elapsed when many shocks, not indeed dangerous,
were felt in Constantinople.†

Is it necessary to reject this recital, and the
assertion of Iamblichus; and should we forget
that Pherecydes, the first master of Pythagoras, in
tasting, or only in looking at the water drawn from
a well, announced to the inhabitants of Samos an
approaching earthquake?‡ or ought we, with Ci-

* Iamblich., *Vit. Pythagor.*, lib. i., cap. xxviii.
† Pachymer., lib. x., cap. xxxiv.
‡ Diogen. Laert. in *Pherecyd.*—Plin., *Hist. Nat.*, lib. ii., cap.
lxxix.—Maxim. Tyr., *Dissertat.* iii., ◊. v.—Cicer., *De Divinat.*, lib.

cero, to reply, that the thing is impossible ? Thucydides was enabled to discover the connection that exists between volcanic fermentations and earthquakes ; and the appearance of water, generally pure and clear, becoming suddenly muddy and sulphurous, was sufficient to enable him to foresee the phenomenon which he predicted. In 1693, at Bologna, in Italy, the waters became muddy on the eve of an earthquake.* This observation is not singular : the water of several wells became equally muddy a few days before the earthquake which was felt in Sicily in the month of February, 1818.† The symptoms of the approaching disaster might even appear much sooner. There was an eruption of a volcano at the summit of Mount Galoungoun, in the island of Java, on the 8th of October, 1822. In the preceding month of July, the waters of the Tji-Kounir, a river which rises in the same mountain, were seen to become troubled; they had a bitter taste, and exhaled a sulphureous odor; and a whitish scum‡ settled upon the legs of travelers who forded the river at that time. The prophecy of Pherecydes, founded upon observations of a similar description, was that of a sage, and not of an impostor.

From the passage quoted from Iamblichus, it may be concluded, that the art of foreseeing earthquakes was common among the first masters of the Pythagorean school. It must have been a portion of the secret science among the ancients.

i., cap. l.—Iamblichus (*Vit. Pythag.*, lib. i, cap. xxviii.) attributes this prediction to Pythagoras.
* *Histoire de l'Académie des Sciences, année* 1696.—Buffon, *Hist. Nat.—Preuves de la Théorie de la Terre*, art. xi.
† Agathino Longo, *Mémoire Historique et Physique sur le Tremblement de Terre, &c.—Bibliotheca Italiana,* September, 1818.—*Bibliothèque Univ. Sciences,* tome ix., p. 263.
‡ *Bulletin de la Société de Géographie,* tome xii., p. 204.

Pausanias, who believed these phenomena to be the effect of the wrath of the gods, enumerated, however, the signs which preceded and announced them.* Pliny adds to the indication of these signs, the number of which he does not omit to reckon, the fetor and the change of color of the water of the neighboring wells. He also discusses the proper methods of preventing the return of the scourge, and advances the plausible opinion, that they may sometimes succeed, by digging very deep wells in those countries where it has been felt.†

Let us suppose, that, in the island of Hayti, a strange population were to establish itself. While living under the most beautiful sky, and in the midst of productions of a fruitful and rather prodigal soil, let us imagine that a subterraneous noise, a tremendous sound, should occur to alarm their minds, and that the chief who conducted the colony to this shore, assembles them together. Let us then suppose that he announces to them that the gods, irritated with their want of submission to his commands, are going to shake the earth from the depths of the valleys to the summits of the hills. They would, probably, laugh at a prediction that appeared to belie the universal tranquillity; and they would give themselves up to indifference, to pleasure, and to sleep. But suddenly the threat is accomplished in all its horror. The terrified population simultaneously prostrate themselves, and the chief is triumphant. How often will not this phenomenon be renewed before experience teaches what at this day is known by the most ignorant of the blacks, that the noise known by the name of Gouffre, is a presage, as natural as it is certain, of an approaching earthquake, and not the

* Pausanias, *Achaic.*, cap. xxiv.
† Plin., *Hist. Nat.*, lib. ii., cap. lxxxi., lxxxii.

voice of an angry god, nor the announcement of his inevitable revenge!

It was a subterraneous noise of a particular kind which announced to a Peruvian observer the earthquake which desolated Lima in 1828,* and led him to predict it four months before it occurred.

Nine lusters before the above period, a similar prediction had proved the perspicuity of a French scholar. In 1782, M. Cadet, of Metz, observed very thick sulphureous vapors over all the plain which serves as a basis to Calabria. He concluded, from this appearance, that the country was threatened with an earthquake, and publicly predicted the disaster, which took place at the commencement of 1785.†

About the same time, a subterraneous road was dug through the Alpine mountains, called Tenda, with the intention of opening a direct communication between Piedmont and the province of Nice: the nature of the mountain rendered the soil easily penetrable to the filtration of waters. The same scholar announced the fast approaching falling in of the subterraneous passage, and solicited the suspension of the works; but the engineers did not dream of profiting by his counsels until the event proved how well his fears had been founded.‡

* M. de Vidaurre. This scholar revived the opinion of Pliny regarding the possibility of preventing earthquakes by digging very deep wells. See the *Moniteur Universel*, No. for August 27, 1828.

† The notes in which he had consigned his prediction were added to the archives of an agricultural society, founded in Corsica by the intendant, M. de Boucheporn. The latter, writing in April 23, 1783, to M. Joli de Fleury, then minister, recalls the prediction of M. Cadet, with details much anterior to the event. M. Denon also recalls it in a letter addressed to M. Cadet, dated April 19, 1783.

‡ M. Cadet, of Metz, *Histoire Naturelle de la Corse*, note *aa*, pp. 138–147.

Anaximander[*] foretold to the Lacedæmonians a subterranean concussion, and the fall of the Peak of Taygetes; doubtless his foresight depended on the observation of analogous symptoms as to the nature of the soil, as well as of phenomena which were the precursors of an earthquake. Anaximander, Pherecydes, the Peruvian observer, and our own countryman, were only philosophers; but had any one of them been a soothsayer, the adoration for the Thaumaturgist would have succeeded to the esteem for the sage.

CHAPTER VII.

Meteorology.—The Art of foreseeing Rain, Storms, and the Direction of the Winds; this is converted, in the Minds of the Vulgar, into the Power of granting or refusing Rain and favorable Winds.—Magical Ceremonies for conjuring a Hail-storm.

DIFFICULT to be foreseen, and followed by results still more difficult to be repaired, are the crumbling of mountains, earthquakes, and all great convulsions of nature; but they are happily rare. Such is not the case, however, with many atmospheric phenomena, attendant upon the course of the seasons, the months, and the days; phenomena, the occurrence, the repetition, and the variation of which promise to mankind enjoyments or privations, and the laws regulating which, although formerly inscrutable, have yet been at length partially revealed to persevering and reflective observation. The knowledge which has been acquired on this subject constitutes meteorology; a branch of science destitute of fixed principles, and without par-

---

[*] Plin., *Hist. Nat.*, lib. ii., cap. lxxviii—Cicer., *De Divinat.* lib. i., cap. i. Anaximander was a Milesian, a disciple of Thales, and a consummate mathematician for the period in which he lived.—Ed.

ticular truths, but which has been, in all ages, most powerful in acting on the credulity of mankind.* It influences the fate of the labors of the year; of the subsistence of the morrow, or that of to-day; and, stimulated by present sufferings, or by anxiety for the future, the curiosity which awakens the desire to know what may be expected from atmospheric phenomena becomes excusable to man, when we consider his hopelessness, the intensity of his fears, and the excess of his gratitude under such circumstances. Every menace would be listened to with religious submission; and all prognostics that call for salutary precautions against great disasters, or, in pressing urgency, reanimate almost extinguished hope, would be hailed as celestial inspirations.†

* The limited extent of information in meteorology, and the laws which regulate aerial phenomena and perturbations, is mortifying to the pride of science. When atmospheric changes occur of a violent and desolating nature, man becomes conscious how little he is acquainted with their causes; and how inadequate his means are even to shield himself from the fury of elements which he can not control. He is forced to tremble upon his hearth, the slave to the apprehension of anticipated evil; and, powerless, to await the spontaneous lulling of the sweeping tempest and the driving hurricane. It is, however, gratifying to know that, of late years, some progress has been made in the philosophy of storms; and we must, therefore, hope that a more effectual investigation into the origin and laws of these overwhelming disturbers of atmospheric quiet, may lead to some practical means of evading their fury, and foretelling their approach. Some progress, indeed, has been made in the latter: for example, in the hurricane which desolated Barbadoes in 1831, Mr. Simons, of St. Vincent, before it reached that island in its passage from Barbadoes, observed a threatening cloud in the north, of an olive-green color, which indicated an approaching aerial conflict. He hastened home, and, by nailing up his doors and windows, saved his habitation from the general calamity. If the power of predicting atmospheric conflicts formerly existed, when ignorance contemplated every acquirement which was not universal as a direct gift from Heaven, we can scarcely wonder that those who possessed meteorological knowledge were regarded as little less than divinities.—ED.

† Many valuable observations on the statistics and philosophy

" The cape of Good Hope is famous for its tempests and for the singular cloud that precedes them; this cloud appears at first like a little round spot in the sky; and sailors call it the bull's-eye.   In the land of Natal, a little cloud also forms itself like the bull's-eye of the cape of Good Hope, and from this cloud there seems to issue a terrible wind that produces the same effects.   Near the coast of Guinea, storms are also announced like those of the cape of Good Hope, by a small, black cloud; while the rest of the heaven is usually very serene, and the sea calm."*   Is it requisite to direct the attention of the reader to the consideration of the marvelous predictions produced by the knowledge of these symptoms of approaching storms, and the astonishment thereby created among men who could have no cognizance of them; or ask him if he would be astonished at Anaxagoras and Democritus in Greece, and Hipparchus at Rome, all three accustomed, no doubt, by observation, to judge of the state of the atmosphere, having in fine weather predicted abundant rains, which of course, when they fell, justified the clear-sightedness of the three naturalists?†   When a drought had lasted a long time in Arcadia, the priest of Jupiter Lycæus addressed prayers and offered a sacrifice to

of storms are contained in the treatises of Lieutenant-Colonel Reid, of the Royal Engineers; and those of Mr. William C. Redfield, of New-York; and there is much reason for hoping that the foundation having been laid by these able observers, a superstructure may be raised, honorable to science and practically beneficial to the human race.—Ed.

* Buffon, *Hist. Nat. Preuves de la Théorie de la Terre*, art. xv.

† Plin., *Hist. Nat.*, lib. xviii., cap. xxviii.—Diogen. Laert. in *Thalet.*—Cicer., *De Divinat.*, lib. i., cap. iii.—Aristot., *Polit.*, lib. i., cap. ii.   Hipparchus was an astronomer, who flourished between the 154th and 163d Olympiads.   He predicted the times of eclipses, discovered a new star, and also the precession of the equinoxes, and the parallax of the planets.   After a life of labor in the cause of science, he died 123 b.c.—Ed.

the fountain *Hagno;* and then toucned the surface of the water with an oak branch. Suddenly there arose a vapor, a mist, and a cloud, which soon dissolved into abundant rain. The priest, no doubt, did not attempt to operate the assumed miracle until promising circumstances guarantied success. Thus, in modern Europe, the priests never carry the shrines or images of saints in procession, or order solemn prayers for the restoration of fair weather or for rain, until they are able to reckon on the near approach of the one or the other.

Many atmospheric phenomena exercise so great an influence on agricultural labors, that to the art of foreseeing the one is naturally joined the hope and the possibility of divining the success of the other.* There is nothing at all improbable in a fact related by Democritus and Thales, who, it is said, were able to foretell what would be the produce of the olive-trees. These philosophers only made use of their success to prove to the detractors of study how science might lead to wealth. If they had pretended, however, that heaven had revealed its secrets to them, they would have been listened to with greater admiration. Science, cultivated by the followers of learning, or by the disciples of the priesthood, has been able to extend its foresight still further; and, consequently, observations on the habitual course of the winds and tides of certain latitudes, would enable either an

---

* Simple observation alone is often sufficient to enable such predictions to be successfully advanced. Sir Isaac Newton, one fine morning, taking an accustomed ride, was accosted by a cowherd, and assured that he would soon be overtaken by a shower. As the sky was cloudless and the sun brilliant, Sir Isaac disregarded the remark and rode on; but, before he had proceeded far, a heavy shower fell. The philosopher immediately rode back to ascertain the foundation of the prediction. " Well, sir," replied the countryman, "all I know about it is this—my cow always twirls her tail in a particular way before a shower."—ED.

oracle or a philosopher to announce the success or unfortunate issue of a voyage. Thus, in the present day, such issues have been predicted many years previously, by anticipating what obstacle the movement, which carries the icebergs to the east or to the west would oppose to the attempts of navigators to reach the Arctic Pole; and that as long a time as they would take for sailing from the west to the east would be required also for the voyage. But to an ignorant people, only accustomed to regard the physical sciences environed by the marvelous, these circumspect announcements of learned foresight would not have sufficed; in order to satisfy impatient desire, it was, therefore, necessary to transform these prognostics into positive assurances. Thus the priests of Samothrace* promised to those who came to consult them favorable winds and a happy voyage. If the promise was not realized, it was easy to exculpate the divinity, by alledging (whatever might have been the faults of the candidate, or the harm done to his boat) that he was guilty of some crime, or, what was worse, some want of faith.

The Druidesses of the isle of Sena also pretended to the power of appeasing waves and winds;† and, doubtless, it was by the same artifice they preserved their title to infallibility.

Empedocles and Iamblichus only repeated the language of the temples, when the one, in his verses, boasted of being able to teach the art of enchaining or loosing the winds, exciting the tempest, and calming the heavens;‡ while the other

---

* Samothrace is situated on the Thracian coast, and peopled by Pelasgians. It was so celebrated for its mysteries, that it obtained the name of sacred; and its shrines were resorted to by pilgrims from every country.—ED.

† Pomponius Mela, lib. iii., cap. vi.

‡ Diogen. Laert., lib viii., cap. lix.—St. Clem., *Alex. Stromat.*, lib. v

ascribes to Abaris and Pythagoras a power no less extended.*

Such promises were too flattering to credulity not to be taken in the most literal sense. Contrary winds were, at Ulysses' return, shut up in a leather bottle by Æolus, and liberated by the imprudent companions of the hero. The Laplanders believe that their magicians possess the power attributed by Homer to the god of the winds. Do not let us mock their ignorance; at least, it does not render them unjust or cruel.

The belief that endowed the adepts of philosophy with the power of arresting and enchaining the winds, existed in the fourth century, even among men enlightened by Christian knowledge. Constantinople, incumbered with an immense population, suffered from famine. Vessels freighted with corn were stopped at the entrance of the straits; they could only pass them by a south wind, and they still awaited this propitious gale. Jealous of the favors which the philosopher Sopater† received from Constantine, the courtiers accused him of having enchained the winds, and caused the famine; and the weak emperor had him put to the torture, and murdered.‡ It mattered little whether the denouncers themselves believed in the truth of the accusation; it is clear that the prince and the people regarded the thing as possible, and as a fact of which many examples were already known.

We shall no longer doubt this, when we find that

---

* Iamblich., *Vit. Pythagor.*, lib. i., cap. xxviii.

† Sopater was a native of Apamea, and like his master, Iamblichus, pretended to possess supernatural powers; so that, in some degree, he may be considered as having brought his death upon himself.—ED.

‡ Suidas, verbo *Sopater.*—Photius, *Bibliothec.*, cod. cli.—Eunapius, in *Ædesio.*—Sozomen, *Hist. Eccles.*, lib. i., cap. v.

II.   K

in the eighth and ninth centuries, among the number
of magicians proscribed by Charlemagne, some
were designated by the name of *tempestarii*, or
those who regulated storms, tempests, and hail.*

Did this superstitious belief, and the agitation
excited by it everywhere, disappear before the
progress of civilization? We believe not. On
one occasion, when excessive rains were unpro-
pitious to the labors, and destroyed the hopes, of
the agriculturist, the long continuation of these
evils were attributed by the multitude to the sorceries of a woman who had arrived in the country
to exhibit the spectacle, a hundred times repeated,
of an aerostatic ascension. This persuasion spread
and acquired so much force that the aeronaut was
obliged to take precautions for her safety, or to
run the risk of being burned alive by men about
as enlightened as those who formerly applauded
the murder of Sopater. Who, we may inquire,
were these men? They were peasants in the environs of Brussels, and the inhabitants of the town
itself; and the date of the event was so recent as
1828.† The same case may again occur in another
century, or in three centuries hence, or as long as
those, who, pretending to the exclusive right of
instructing the people, make them believe in magic
and sorcery. Those who have accorded to the
wonder-worker the power of inflicting plagues,
attributed to them, with not more reason, that of
being able to cure those produced by nature. In
order to confirm an opinion so favorable to their
credit, it is only necessary to remark, that the possessors of sacred science have disguised more than

* *De Auguriis et aliis Maleficiis.*—Capitul., lib. i., cap. lxxxiii.
(12mo., Paris, 1588.) See also Ducange, *Glossar.*, verb. *Tempestarii—Tempestuarii.*
† *Le Moniteur Universel* of the 23d August, 1828.

once the most simple operations under a magical veil.

They ordered, for example, the husbandman who desired that in the season his fruit-trees should be laden with fruit, to cover them with a band of straw on the night celebrated by the Polytheists as the renewing of the invincible sun; and in the Christian Church, as the coming of our Savior,[*] the night when the sun, supposed to be enchained for ten days by the winter solstice, begins to arise again toward the equator, and on which we often find cold suddenly and intensely developed. Experience has proved that this precaution will effectually protect trees from the hurtful effects of frost.

In the present day, natural physics are consulted for preservatives against hail : magic formerly was consulted for that purpose. The inhabitants of Cleone in the Argolide, imagined they could distinguish, from the appearance of the sky, the approach of frost that would endanger their crops ; and immediately they endeavored, by offering sacrifices to the gods, to avert the evil :[†] other nations sang sacred hymns for this purpose.[‡] These were only acts of piety ; like the secret taught by some theologians to avert the hail supposed to be conjured by witchcraft, which consisted in making signs of the cross, and such long continued prayers, that, in the interval, the rain might have time to cease.[§]

But, in ancient Greece, men pretended to obtain by enchantments[||] what elsewhere was only asked through the mercy of Heaven.[¶] Pausanias even

* Fromann, *Tract. de Fascionatione*, pp. 341, 342.
† Senec., *Quæst. Nat.*, lib. iv., cap. vi.
‡ Carmina.—Plin., *Hist. Nat.*, lib. xxviii., cap. ii.
§ Wierius, *De Præstigiis Dæmon.*, lib. iv., cap. xxxii.
|| St. Justin, *Quæst. et Respons. ad Orthodox*, quæst. 31.
¶ The inhabitants of Methana, in Argolis, when a strong south

declares that he himself witnessed the successful
issue of their magical operations.*   Until positive
experience has proved the still doubtful efficacy of
the paragreles,† we shall think that if the men who
boasted of success of this kind have sometimes
appeared to obtain it, hail would not have fallen
whether they had recourse or not to magical ceremonies for conjuring it.   It is not undesignedly
that we place modern attempts and ancient opinions in juxtaposition.   In the eighth century, they
hoped to avert hail and storms by pointing long
poles toward the skies.   This measure reminds us
of what was recently proposed, and, fifty years
ago, was accredited by Berthollon, the naturalist.

east wind blew up the Saronic Gulf, defended themselves from
it by the following spell.   They took a white cock, and having
cut the bird in halves, two men seized each a part, and then,
standing back to back, started off in opposite directions, made the
tour of the vineyard, and returning whence they set out, buried
the remains in the earth.   After this the wind might blow as it
listed, since it possessed no power to injure any man's property
within the consecrated circle.—Pausan., ii., 34, 2, quoted in *St.
John's History of the Customs, &c., of Greece*, vol. ii., p. 339.

* Pausanias, *Corinthiac.*, cap. xxxiv.

† In a Report read to the Académie des Sciences, in 1826, their
efficacy is represented as somewhat doubtful.   These instruments, more properly called paragrandines, are intended to avert
hail-storms ; and, according to Seignior Antonio Perotti and Dr.
Astolfi, they have succeeded in averting hail as efficiently as conductors in obviating danger from lightning.   Seignior Perotti re-
ports that, having fixed up several of them on a piece of land
containing sixteen thousand perches, both his corn and his vines
were protected, although fourteen hail-storms had occurred in the
current year, which did great mischief in the neighboring fields ;
and in an official notice to the government of Milan, by the gon-
faloniere of St. Pietro, in Casale, a very favorable account, also,
is given of these protectors from hail.   They are formed of metallic points and straw ropes, bound together with hempen or flaxen
threads.   If we admit that the ancients were acquainted with the
use of lightning conductors, we may imagine that they were also
aware of the value of the paragrandines, and employed them.
The protection from the effects of hail of certain fields by their
means might have been readily passed off as the result of super
natural influence.—ED.

But, as at the end of the poles just mentioned, pieces of paper inscribed with magical characters were affixed, the custom seemed to be tainted with sorcery, and was consequently proscribed by Charlemagne.

Did the sorcerers of that age, then, we may inquire, only revive the belief, and, perhaps, the practice, adopted in preceding ages? We may certainly reply in the negative. But what appears decided to us is, that processes, tending to the same ends, were very anciently described, written in hieroglyphics; and what is still more remarkable, they gave rise to an error already exposed by us.* The ignorant man, deceived by these emblems, imagined that by imitating, well or ill, what they represented, he should obtain the effect procured by the · success of the prescription which they served to disguise. We may thus explain two very ridiculous examples of Tuscan ceremonies, that, according to Columella,† the husbandmen, instructed by experience, employed to appease violent winds, and calm the tempest. Gaffarel furnishes us with a third example, in a magical secret, supposed to be efficacious in averting hail.‡ It is the height of absurdity; yet, such is the point to which man's credulity will ever conduct him, that whenever the results of science only, without its principles, are presented to him, and displayed as

* See chap. viii., vol. i.

† Columella, lib. x., vers. 341–345. Further on the author mentions a plan, probably efficacious for preserving the seed in the ground from the approach of insects. It is the employment of a mixture of the juice of bitter plants with the grain, together with the lees of ashes. (Ibid., vers. 351—356.) But directly after this, he relates a ridiculous secret for destroying caterpillars—a secret which the same author (lib. xi., sub. finem) pretended was taught by Democritus, but which is probably only a hieroglyphic put into practice.

‡ Gaffarel. *Curiosites inouïes*, chap. vii., § i.

the effects of supernatural power, and not as the
ideas acquired by the union of reason and experience, he believes and confides in the apparent
miracle.

CHAPTER VIII.

The Art of drawing Lightning from the Clouds.—Medals and
Traditions that indicate the Existence of that Art in Antiquity.
—Disguised under the Name of the Worship of Jupiter Elicius
and of Zeus Cataibates, it was known to Numa and many
others among the Ancients.—The Imitators of Thunder made
Use of it.—It may be traced from Prometheus ; it explains the
Fable of Salmonious ; it was known to the Hebrews, and the
Construction of the Temple of Jerusalem is a Proof of this.—
Zoroaster made Use of it to light the Sacred Fire, and oper-
ate in the Initiation of his Followers : his Experiments and
Miracles.—If the Chaldeans possessed the Secret, it was after-
ward lost among them.—There existed some Traces of it in
India in Ctesias's time.—Wonders resembling those performed
through this Art, which, however, may be otherwise explained.

OF all scourges that alarm men for the preservation of their wealth and their lives, the most
fearful, although, perhaps, the least destructive, is
thunder. The fiery clouds—the roaring wind—
the shaking earth—the dazzling lightning—long
peals of rolling thunder—or, suddenly, a frightful
crash, presaging the fall of celestial fire, redoubled
in the distance by the mountain echoes—all are
so conducive in producing terror, that even the
frequent repetition of these phenomena does not
at all familiarize us with them, nor lessen the alarm
of the multitude. Realizing every thing that a
poetic imagination can picture, and the menaces
threatened by the priesthood, they are the most
imposing of all the signs of divine wrath, and
in addition, they always present to the ignorant
the direct feeling that heaven is warring against
earth.

Trembling man will supplicate the gods, and

appeal to those privileged mortals whom the gods have deigned to instruct, in order to avert from his head this instrument of terror. The miracle which he would demand has been performed by the genius of the eighteenth century ;* but, we may ask, was it known to the ancients ?

At first sight it seems absurd to admit such a supposition ; for we are aware how little the ancients were in general acquainted with electricity. The horse of Tiberius, at Rhodes, we are told, threw off sparks when strongly rubbed by the hand ; and another horse is mentioned as being endowed with the same faculty. The father of Theodoric, and many others, had observed it on their own bodies :† yet these simple facts were ranked among prodigies. We may also call to remembrance the superstitious terrors that were formerly awakened by the fire of St. Elmo shining on the masts of ships, and the place the apparitions of light evidently held among the histories of supernatural events ; to these proofs of ignorance, we may add the absurd belief in the pretended

* Admitting that the ancients were acquainted with the means of drawing lightning from the clouds, the merit of the invention of protecting our dwellings from its direful influence is not the less due to Dr. Franklin. That philosopher, having demonstrated the identity of lightning and electricity, and that metals are its best conductors, recommended that pointed metallic rods should be raised some feet above the highest point of any building, and continued down into the ground, as the best mode of securing the safety of the edifice during thunder-storms. The pointed rods attract the lightning, which then passes along their surfaces, and is thus carried into the earth, instead of being scattered upon the building on which they are erected.—ED.

† Damascius in *Isidor. Vit. apud Phot. Biblioth.*, cod. 242. "In winter, at Stockholm, the accumulation of animal electricity is quite perceptible ; a great quantity is visibly discharged when people undress in a warm apartment."—James's *Travels in Germany and Sweden.—Nouvelles Annales des Voyages*, tome xxxv., p. 13. I have often, adds our author, made the same observation at Geneva ; and the Editor has done so, in this country, on drawing off silk stockings in a dark room.

preservatives against lightning.   Tarchon, in order to guard against thunder-strokes, as he terms them, surrounded his dwelling with the white bryony.* Here, however, a legitimate suspicion is aroused. Tarchon, the disciple of the mysterious Tages— Tarchon, the founder of the Theurgism of the ancient Etruscans, might very probably have alledged the efficacy of these ridiculous means, in order to enable him more effectually to conceal the true secret that preserved his habitation and temple from lightning.   A similar stratagem has, perhaps, been the reason why the property of averting lightning was attributed to the laurels that surrounded the temple of Apollo—a virtue regarded as real, in spite of the evidence throughout all antiquity to the contrary, and which caused the laurel to be consecrated, until nearly our own time, in all poetical language.

The same may be alledged of the apparitions of light, of which ancient histories discourse.   All can not be false; all can not be accidental.   We can produce all these brilliant phenomena in the present day : is it wise, therefore, we may ask, to deny that other ages have possessed the power of producing them ?   To balance the reasons for doubting, we may oppose many other reasons in favor of the supposition.   We will not argue from the numerous traditions on the art of turning away thunder.   Neither will we scrutinize the origin of the religious precept that ordered the Esthonians

* Columella, lib. x., vers. 346, 347.   In Hindostan, the property of averting thunder is attributed to certain plants; and this is the reason these plants are seen on all the houses.   The white bryony, bryonia *alba*, is a common weed in the hedgerows and the woods in the south of Europe, as well as in Hindostan.   It is a climbing plant, with five-lobed, angular, cordate leaves, with callosities on both sides.   The flowers are unisexual on the same plant, and the fruit berries of a black color in clusters.   It possesses acrid and purgative properties.—ED.

to close their doors and windows whenever there
was a thunder-storm, " for fear of allowing the evil
spirit that God was then pursuing to enter."* This
precept reminds us of the belief, not unfounded,
that a current of air, especially humid air, will
attract and ʼconduct the thunder-explosion. But
what is the reason of another precept, which commanded this people to place two knives on the
window-ledge, in order to dispel lightning?†
Whence arose the immemorial habit in the district of Lesneven,‡ of placing a piece of iron,
during a thunder-storm, in the nests of hens that
are sitting? Practices of this nature, when observed in only one place, are of little importance;
but when they are found in places at considerable
distances from one another, and among nations who
have had no communication with each other, it is
almost sufficient to prove that the science that dictated them was anciently possessed by men who
carried instruction among these ʼdifferent nations.
"In the castle of Duino (says P. Imperati, a writer
of the seventeenth century) there was a very ancient custom of proving lightning. The sentinel
approached an iron pike, or a bar of iron, erected
upon the wall, and the moment he perceived a
spark, he rang the alarm-bell, to warn the shepherds to retire to their homes." In the fifteenth
century, St. Bernardin, of Sienna,§ reprobated,
as superstitious, the precaution used in all ages of
fixing a naked sword on the mast of a vessel to
avert the tempest.

* Debray, on the Prejudices and Superstitions of the Livo-
nians, Lethonians, and Esthonians.—*Nouvelles Annales des Voyages*, tome xviii., p. 123.   † *Ibid.*
‡ Department of Finistère.—Cambry, *Voyage dans le Départ-
ment du Finistère*, tome ii., pp. 16, 17.
§ St. Bernardin was born at Massa, in 1380, and died at the
same place, in 1444.—ED.

M. la Boëssiere, in a learned commentary, whence
I have taken these two last quotations, and in which
he discusses the knowledge of the ancients in the
art of conjuring and dispelling lightning,* speaks
of many medals that are apparently connected with
his subject. One of them, described by Duchoul,
represents the temple of Juno, the goddess of the
air : the roof that covers it is armed with pointed
blades of swords. The other, described and engraved by Pellerin, bears, as its legend, *Jupiter
Elicius*. The god appears with lightning in his
hand, while below is a man who is directing a flying stag. But we must remark, that the authenticity of this medal is suspicious. Other medals,
also, described by Duchoul in his work on the
religion of the Romans, bear the inscription *XV.
Viri Sacris faciundis*, and the figure of a fish, with
bristly spikes, lying on a globe or partera. M. la
Boëssiere thinks that a fish, thus armed with points,
on a globe, was the conductor employed by Numa
to attract the clouds of electric fire. And, putting
together the image of that globe, with that of a
head covered with bristly hairs, they afford an ingenious and plausible explanation of the singular
dialogue between Numa and Jupiter, related by
Valerius Antius, and ridiculed by Arnobe, without
probably either of them comprehending its meaning.† The history of the knowledge possessed by
Numa in natural physics merits more particular
examination.‡

* *Notice sur les Travaux de l'Académie du Gard*, from 1812 to
1821, Nismes, 1822, 1st part, pp. 304–313. The paper of M. la
Boëssiere, read in 1811, was only published in 1822.
† Arnob., lib. v.
‡ Numa was more of a philosopher than a king, and cultivated
science long after he was invested with the imperial purple. Although a pagan, yet he had the wisdom to dissuade the Romans
from worshiping the deity through images, on which account no
statues nor paintings of the gods appeared in the Roman temples

In an age when lightning made frequent devastation, Numa, instructed, we are told, by the nymph Egeria, attempted to propitiate it (*Fulmen piare*) ; that is to say, setting aside the figurative style, to put in practice the means of rendering it less mischievous. He succeeded in intoxicating Faunus and Picus, whose names probably are used to designate the priests of the Etruscan divinities, from whom he learned the secret of making Jupiter, the Thunderer, descend upon earth : and he immediately put it into execution. From this time Jupiter Elicius was worshiped in Rome.*

Here the veil of mystery is too transparent not to be seen through. To render lightning less hurtful, and to make it descend without danger from the bosom of the clouds, was, both in effect and in end, obtained by Franklin's beautiful discovery, as well as by the religious experiment repeated many times with success by Numa. Tullus Hostilius was less fortunate. "They relate," says Titus Livy,† "that this prince, when perusing the notes left by Numa, found among them some instructions on the secret sacrifices offered to Jupiter Elicius. He attempted to repeat them; but, in his preparations for or celebration of them, he deviated from the sacred rite; and being thus exposed to the anger of Jupiter, aroused by a defective ceremony (*sollicitati prâva religione*), he was struck by lightning, and consumed in his own palace."

An ancient annalist, quoted by Pliny, explains this event much more explicitly, and justifies the liberty I have taken in deviating from the sense

for upward of one hundred years. He nevertheless imposed upon their credulity, and flattered their superstitious prejudices in many respects.—ED.

* Ovid, *Fast.*, lib. iii., vers. 285–345.—Arnob., lib. v.

† Tit. Liv., lib. i., cap. xxxi.—Plin., *Hist. Nat.*, lib. ii., cap. flii.; lib. xxviii., cap. iv.

commonly given to the words of Livy by his translators. "Guided by Numa's books, Tullus undertook to invoke the aid of Jupiter by the same ceremonies employed by his predecessor. But having performed imperfectly the prescribed ceremony (*parum rite*), he perished, struck by thunder."[*] Instead of the term ceremony, if we substitute the word experiment, we shall perceive that the fate of Tullus was similar to that of Professor Reichman. In 1753 this learned man was killed by lightning while repeating, with too little caution, one of Franklin's experiments.[†]

Pliny, in the exposition of Numa's scientific secrets, makes use of expressions which seem to indicate two distinct processes : the one obtained thunder (*impetrare*), the other forced it to lightning (*cogere*) ; the one was, doubtless, gentle, noiseless, and exempt from any dangerous explosion; the other violent, burning, and in the form of an electric discharge. It explains the story of Porsenna destroying the terrible monster who deso lated the territory of Volsinium ;[‡] an explanation, however, which can scarcely be received : because, although it is not absolutely impossible, yet it is very difficult and dangerous to cause a strong electric detonation to take effect at a very distant point; and there still remains the difficulty of drawing to this exact point the being whom it was

[*] Lucius Piso.—Plin., *Hist. Nat.*, lib. xxviii., cap. ii.

[†] He had constructed an apparatus for observing atmospheric electricity, and while intent upon examining the electrometer, a large ball of electric fire glanced from the conducting-rod, which was insulated, to the head of the unfortunate experimentalist, and instantly deprived him of life. His companion, Sokolow, an engraver, who was present to delineate the appearances that might present themselves, was also struck down, and remained senseless for some time ; the door of the room was torn from its hinges, and the door-case split.—ED.

[‡] Plin., *Hist. Nat.*, lib. ii., cap. liii.

intended to overthrow by the magical commotion. We shall propose, elsewhere, another explanation of this Etruscan apparent miracle. But, in the coactive process mentioned by Pliny, and the well known and well attested possibility of obtaining, either from an isolated thunder rod or an immense electrical battery, a discharge of such power that the luminous flash, the noise, and the destructive influence of it completely resemble the effects of lightning, do we not perceive the secret of these imitators of thunder who so often themselves became the victims of their own success; and who, on that account, were said to have fallen under the vengeance of the god whose arms they dared to usurp?

Among these we may name Caligula, who, according to Dion Cassius and John of Antioch, opposed lightnings to lightnings, and to the voice of thunder one not less fearful; and shot a stone toward heaven at the moment the lightning fell. A machine, not very complicated, would suffice to produce those effects so well suited to the vanity of a tyrant, ever trembling before the gods whom he sought to equal.

It is not in times so modern that we are to look for a mysterious idea which had already extended into all the temples.

On the contrary, we must trace it into antiquity: and we may first remark, that Sylvius Alladas (or Remulus), eleventh King of Alba after Æneas, according to Eusebius,[*] imitated the noise of thunder, by making the soldiers strike their bucklers with their swords; a fable as ridiculous as that afterward related by Eusebius of machines which the King of Alba made use of to imitate thunder. "This prince," says Ovid, and Dionysius of Hali-

---

* Euseb., *Chronic. Canon.*, lib. i., cap. xlv. et xlvi.

carnassus, "despising the gods, had invented a method of imitating the effects of lightning and the noise of thunder, in order to pass as a divinity in the minds of those whom he inspired with terror; but

"In imitating thunder, the thunderer perished."*

the victim of his impiety, according to the priests of his time; according to our ideas, only of his own imprudence.

Here then we perceive that the secret of Numa and Tullus Hostilius was known a century before their time. We will not attempt to fix the epoch when it was first possessed by the divinities, or rather by the Etruscan priests, whose successors taught it to the King of Rome, and to those from whom the King of Alba must have received it; but the tradition relative to Tarchon being acquainted with a mode of preserving his dwelling from lightning, enables us to trace it to this Theurgist, who was much anterior to the siege of Troy.

It is from these historical ages that we trace the fable of Salmonius. Salmonius, said the priests, was an impious man, blasted with lightning by the gods for having attempted to imitate thunder. But how unlikely is their recital! What a miserable imitation of thunder would the vain noise of a chariot going over a bridge of brass appear; while torches, to imitate lightning, were thrown upon victims who had been condemned to death!† How was it likely that the bridge, which could only be of a moderate size, would, by the noise of a chariot passing over it, astonish the people of

---

* "Fulmineo perut imitator fulminis ictu."—Ovid, *Metamorphos.*, lib. xiv., vers. 617, 618.—*Fast.*, lib. iv., v. 60; Dionys., *Halic.*, lib. i., cap. xv.

† Hygin., lib. i., fab. lxi.—Servius in *Æneid*, lib. vi., v. 508.

Greece !* Eustathius† advances a more plausible
idea: he describes Salmonius as a learned man,
clever in imitating lightning and the noise of thunder; and who perished the victim of his dangerous
experiments. In this perfect imitation we discover
the coactive process of Pliny—the art of attracting
from the clouds, and condensing the electric fluid
when on the point of a fearful explosion.

What confirms our conjecture is, that in Elidia,
the scenes of Salmonius' success,‡ and the catastrophe that put an end to his life, there may be
seen, near the great altar of the temple of Olympus,
another altar§ surrounded by a balustrade, and
consecrated to Jupiter Cataibates (*the descending*).
" This surname was given to Jupiter to indicate
that he demonstrated his presence on earth by the
noise of thunder, by lightning, by meteors, or by
apparitions."‖ In fact, many medals of the town
of Cyrrhus in Syria represent Jupiter armed with
lightning, with the legend *Cataibates* below him.
It would be difficult to mark more strongly the
connection between this word and the descent of
lightning. In the temple of Olympus also they
worshiped the altar of Jupiter the Thunderer (Ke-
raunios), raised in memory of the lightning that
had destroyed the palace of Œnomaus.¶ This

---

* Virgil, *Æneid*, lib. vi., v. 585, et seq.
† Eustath. in *Odyss.*, lib. ii., v. 234.
‡ Salmonius was a King of Elis, whose ambition led him to
desire that he should be thought a god; for which purpose he is
said to have taken the means mentioned in the text. But the
whole story is too absurd to deserve any reference being made to
it.—Ed.
§ Pausanias, *Eliac.*, lib. i., cap. xiv.
‖ *Encyclop. Method. Antiquites*, tome i., art. *Cataibates*
¶ Pausanias, loc. cit. Œnomaus was King of Pisa, in Elis.
He was informed by an oracle that he should perish by the hands
of his son-in-law; to prevent which, being a skillful charioteer.
ne determined to give his daughter in marriage only to him who
could outmatch him in driving, on condition that all who entered

surname and that of Cataibates present, howeve ,
different ideas to piety. It becomes difficult to
avoid confusion between Jupiter Cataibates and
Jupiter Elicius—that is, between the thunder tha.
descends, and the thunder constrained to descend.
It must be seen that we are obliged to reason from
analogy, in defect of positive traditions ; but the
analogy receives great strength when we recollect
that Jupiter Cataibates was worshiped in the places
where Salmonius reigned, a prince whose history
closely resembles that of the two kings who, at
Alba and Rome, fell victims to the worship of
Jupiter Elicius.

It is true, that there remain no proofs of Greece
having possessed, in past ages, any idea of the
chemical experiment that proved fatal to Salmonius ; but the worship of Jupiter Elicius existed
at Rome when the mysterious process used by
Numa had long ceased to be employed, and had,
indeed, been completely forgotten. A similar for-
getfulness could not hinder the worship of Jupiter
Cataibates from being kept up in Elidia.

Whenever we look back into the past, we find
the most certain vestiges of the existence of the
knowledge of the sciences.

Servius carries us back to the infancy of the
human race. " The first inhabitants of the earth,"
said he, " never carried fire to their altars, but by
their prayers they brought down the heavenly
fire."*   He relates this tradition when he is commenting on a verse where Jupiter is described by

the lists should agree to lay down their lives if conquered.   Many
had suffered, when Pelops opposed him.   He bribed Myrtilus, the
chariot-keeper of Œnomaus, who gave his master an old chariot,
which broke down in the course, and killed Œnomaus.   Pelops
married Hippodamia, the daughter of Œnomaus, and became
King of Pisa.—ED.
    * Servius in Æneid, lib. xii., v. 200.

Virgil as ratifying the treaty between the nations by a peal of thunder.* It would, therefore, seem that the priests regarded this miracle as a solemn proof of the guaranty given by the gods to the covenant.† From whom, we may inquire, had they received the secret? "Prometheus," says Servius,‡ "discovered and revealed to man the art of bringing down lightning (*eliciendorum fulminum*); and, by the process which he taught to them, they brought down fire from the region above (*supernus ignis eliciebatur*)." Among the possessors of this secret, Servius reckoned Numa and Tullus Hostilius. The former only employed the celestial fire for sacred purposes; the latter was punished for having profaned it.

The legend of the Caucasus, upon the rocks of which an expiation for the partial divulgement of an art so precious had for many centuries been pending, leads us toward Asia, over which country this art must have been diffused before it penetrated into Europe. The legend of Jupiter Cataibates has been, as we before observed, discovered on the medals of the town of Cyrrhus. Now it is hardly probable that the Greeks would have carried this worship into a distant land, the foundation of which could not have been posterior to the time of Cyrus. It is, therefore, allowable to suppose that the legend quoted was only a Greek transla-

---

* Audiat hæc genitor qui fulmine fœdera sancit.

                             Virgil, *Æneid*, lib. xii., v. 200.

† This use of the coactive process may explain the apparent miracle, more than once repeated by the poets, of claps of thunder being heard in calm weather.

‡ Servius in *Virgil, Eclog.* vi., v. 42. This passage, which has been overlooked by so many modern writers, had, however, struck, more than three centuries ago, an author who is never read but for amusement, but who may be well read for instruction: "Qu'est devenu," said Rabelais, "l'art d'évoquer des cieux la foudre et le feu céleste, jadis inventé par le sage Prométhée?"—Rabelais, liv. v., chap. lxvii.

II.   L

tion of the name of the thundering god; and that
the secret to which it alluded was not anciently
unknown in Syria.

The Hebrews, however, appear to have been
acquainted with it. Ben-David has asserted that
Moses possessed some knowledge of the phenomena of electricity; and M. Hirt, a philosopher of
Berlin, has brought forward very plausible arguments in support of this opinion. Michaelis* has
even gone further. He remarks—1st. That there
is no indication that lightning ever struck the Temple of Jerusalem, during a thousand years. 2d.
That, according to Josephus,† a forest of points
either of gold or gilded, and very sharp, covered
the roof of the temple, in a manner similar to that
of the temple of Juno as figured on the Roman
medals. 3d. That this roof communicated with the
caverns in the hill upon which the temple was
situated, by means of pipes in connection with the
gilding which covered all the exterior of the building; in consequence of which the points would
act as conductors. Now we can hardly suppose
that they accidentally performed so important a
function, or that the advantage to be derived from
them had not been calculated upon. It can not
be supposed that so many points had been placed
upon the temple merely for the birds to perch on;
nevertheless, it is the only use assigned to them
by the historian Josephus. We may, however,
readily consider his ignorance as a proof of the
facility with which the knowledge of important
facts is forgotten.

This secret certainly does not appear to have
survived the destruction of the empire of Cyrus;
and yet there is much reason for thinking that so

* *Magasin Scient. de Göttingen*, 3ᵉ année, 5ᵉ cahier, 1783.
† Fl Josephus, *Bell. Jud. adv. Roman.*, lib. v., car. xiv.

powerful an instrument for displaying apparent miracles was not unknown to Zoroaster and his successors.

Khondemir[*] relates that the devil appeared to Zoroaster in the midst of fire, and that he imprinted a luminous mark on his body: and, according to Dion Chrysostom,[†] when the prophet quitted the mountain where he had so long dwelt in solitude, he appeared shining with an unextinguishable light, which he had brought down from heaven; a prodigy similar to the experiment of the electric beatification, and easy to be produced in the entrance of a dark cavern. The author of the *Recognitions* (attributed to St. Clement of Alexandria,[‡] and St. Gregory of Tours)[§] affirms that, under the name of Zoroaster, the Persians worshiped a son of Shem, who, by a magical delusion, brought down fire from heaven, or persuaded men that he possessed that miraculous power. May we not ask whether these facts do not indicate, in other terms, the experiments on atmospheric electricity of which a Thaumaturgist might so easily avail himself, as to appear sparkling with light in the eyes of a multitude struck with admiration ![‖]

We have, in another work,[¶] attempted to distinguish the founder of the religion of the Magi from the princes and priests who, to insure the respect of the people, had assumed, after him, the

---

* D'Herbelot, *Biblioth. Orientale*, art. *Zerdascht.*
† Dion. Chrysost., *Orat. Borysthen.*
‡ Recog., lib. iv.
§ Greg. Turon. *Hist. Franc.*, lib. i., cap. v.
‖ The Editor is of opinion that the arguments of the author, on this part of his subject, are far from convincing, as they are founded altogether upon an assumption for which there is no tenable foundation. It is more probable that the accounts are wholly fabulous, and, consequently, require no comment.—ED.
¶ Eusèbe Salverte, *Essai Historique et Philosophique sur les Noms d'Hommes, des Peuples, et des Lieux.* Additional Notes, B.

name of Zoroaster. We are reminded of this distinction in relating what has been recorded respecting Zoroaster, by authors who were ignorant of this fact: for these writers would not have attributed to that prophet what belonged to his disciples, the inheritors of his miraculous science. Zoroaster, say they, perished, being burned up by the demon whom he importuned too often to repeat his brilliant miracle. In other terms, they describe a natural philosopher who, in the frequent repetition of a dangerous experiment, ended by neglecting the necessary precautions, and fell a victim in a moment of carelessness. Suidas,[*] Cedrenus, and the chroniclers of Alexandria relate that Zoroaster, King of Bactria, being besieged in his capital by Ninus, prayed to the gods to be struck by lightning; and when he saw his wish about to be accomplished, desired his disciples to preserve his ashes, as an earnest for the preservation of their power. The ashes of Zoroaster, says the author of the *Recognitions*, were collected and carried to the Persians, to be preserved and worshiped as a fire divinely sent down from heaven. There is here an evident confusion of ideas: they apply to the ashes of the prophet the worship that was never rendered by his disciples to the sacred fire which they had received from him. Must not this confusion have arisen from the pretended origin of the sacred fire, kindled, it was said, by lightning? "The Magi," says Ammianus Marcellinus,[†] "preserved perpetually, in their furnaces, fire miracu-

---

[*] Suidas, verbo *Zoroastres.*—Glycas, *Annal.*, p. 129.

[†] Ammianus Marcellinus was a celebrated historian, who flourished in the reigns of Constantine, Julian, and Valens. He is supposed to be correct in his statements; and certainly he displays less of the acrimony against Christianity than is usually found in the writings of pagan historians, although he enjoyed the favor of Julian, and was a warm advocate of Paganism.—ED.

lously sent from heaven.''* The Greeks, who bestowed on the first Persian chief the name of his country, also relate that in the time when Perseus was instructing some Persians in the mysteries of the Gorgons,† a globe of fire fell from heaven. Perseus took from it the sacred fire, which he confided to the Magi; and from this event arose the name that he imposed upon his disciples.‡ Here we recollect what was said by Servius of the celestial fire which the ancient inhabitants of the earth brought down on their altars, and which they only employed for sacred purposes. The resemblance between the two traditions shows us the origin of this fire that fell from heaven at the voice of the institutor of magic; and was destined to burn forever on the Pyres, in honor of the god who had granted it to earth.

* Ammian. Marcell., lib. xxiii., cap. vi.
† Three fabulous sisters, Stheno, Euralye, and Medusa, the two first of whom were immortal. Their bodies were stated to be covered with impenetrable scales; their hands were of brass, their heads covered with snakes, their teeth like the tusks of the wild boar, and their eyes capable of turning to stone all on whom they were fixed. The absurd traditions respecting them are unworthy of being mentioned; but it may be necessary merely to remind the reader that Perseus, being provided with a mirror by Minerva, winged shoes by Mercury, and a helmet which rendered him invisible by Pluto, attacked these damsels—cut off the head of Medusa, the only mortal of the three, and presented it to Minerva, who wore it on her ægis. Perseus was still more favored; for, after this conquest, he took his flight through the air toward Ethiopia, but dropping some of the blood from Medusa's head on Libya, the drops changed into serpents, which accounts for those that infest the Libyan deserts. Diodorus explains this fable by supposing that the Gorgons were a tribe of Amazons, which Perseus conquered in war. The Abbé Bannier supposed that the three sisters were three ships, belonging to Phareys, their supposed father, who traded with Perseus; and that these ships were laden with elephants' teeth, horns of fishes, and the eyes of hyenas; a supposition as improbable, as far as concerns the cargo of these ships, as the original tradition.—ED.
‡ Suidas, verbo *Perseus.* In the *Chah-namah* of Ferdousi, Houcheng, father of Djah-Muras, as Perseus is of Merrhus, collects also in a miraculous manner the sacred fire.—*Annales des Voyages.*

Two of the magical oracles* which Plethon has preserved and commented on seem to bear some connection with this subject. These oracles were attributed to the first disciples of Zoroaster, or to Zoroaster himself, which is not at all improbable, since antiquity possessed two hundred verses, the authorship of which was attributed to this prophet.†
They contain the following lines:

"Oh, man! the production of Nature in her boldest mode,
If thou dost more than once invoke me, thou shalt behold alone
that which thou hast invoked:
For, neither the heaven, nor its arched concavity, shall be visible
to thee:
The stars shall not shine;—the light of the moon shall be veiled;
The earth shall tremble; and lightning alone shall be presented
to thy sight."   Vers. 39–43.

Plethon, after having observed that man is properly called the workmanship of an intrepid nature, because he undertakes the most daring deeds, adds, "The oracle speaks in the character of the god to the initiated. 'If more than once thou dost invoke me, thou wilt see everywhere *me* that thou hast invoked; for thou shalt see nothing but lightning, that is, fire falling throughout the universe.'"

The commentary, which informs us that the last oracle relates to the initiations, refers us, by one of its expressions, to the second oracle, whence it is borrowed.

"When thou seest the holy and sacred fire devoid of form,
Burning and flying about everywhere into the depths of the universe!
Listen to the voice of the Fire!"   Vers. 46–48.

"When thou shalt see," says Plethon, "the divine fire that can not be represented under any form" (it is well known that the laws of Zoroaster

* *Oracula Magica*, edente Joanne Opsopoeo, 1589.
† Plin. *Hist. Nat.*, lib. xxx., cap. i.

proscribed all images), " give thanks, and full of
joy listen to the voice of the fire, which will give
to thee a very true and certain *prenotion* (knowledge of the future).

Through the obscurity of the text and its explanation, we seize upon an important feature in
the Zoroastrian initiations. If the initiated is fearless, he will invoke the god he worships, and will
soon see the god alone. Every other object disappears; he is surrounded by meteors and lightnings, which neither can nor may be depicted by
any image; and from the midst of which a loud
voice is heard, that pronounces infallible oracles.
From the preceding, we may conclude, with some
probability, that Zoroaster had ideas upon electricity; and possessed the means of attracting lightning, which he made use of to operate the first apparent miracles destined to prove his prophetic
mission; and especially to light the sacred fire,
which he offered to the adoration of his disciples.
Such being the case, may we not inquire whether
we are correct in adding, that in his hands, and in
the hands of his disciples, the heavenly fire became
an instrument for proving the courage of the initiated, for confirming their faith, and for dazzling
their vision by its immense splendor, impossible to
be gazed upon by mortal eyes; which is at once
the attribute and the image of the divinity.

A tradition (most probably known to the reader)
seems to attribute the death of Zoroaster to that
want of precaution to which many other victims
had fallen a prey. Another story presents in a
more noble aspect the prophet, or King of Bactria,
who, in order not to fall into the hands of a conqueror, decided to die, and drew down lightning
upon himself; and by this last wonderful effort of
his art, he gave himself an extraordinary death,

worthy of the envoy of heaven, and the institutor
of the fire-worship.*

* Zoroaster admitted no visible object of adoration except fire,
which he considered the only proper emblem of the deity. It is
said, that it is difficult to ascertain who the great institutor of fire-
worship was; as there were several, at least six, lawgivers of the
name of Zoroaster; but this opinion has been satisfactorily re-
futed by Hyde* and by Pasteret ;† and there is sufficient reason
for believing that there was only one Zoroaster or Zerdusht, the
founder of the religion of the Parsees. He was the son of humble, but nobly descended parents. He was born at Urmia, a town
of Azerbijan, about the year 589 b.c., in the reign of Lehrasp,
the father of Darius Hystaspes, or Gushtasp. It is unnecessary
to mention the prodigies that announced and appeared at the birth
of this extraordinary man. His early years, nevertheless, were
productive of nothing remarkable; but, at the age of twenty, he
secluded himself from the society of mankind, and in his retirement conceived the idea of effecting a religious reformation, and
restoring the faith of his forefathers in greater purity, and more
adapted for the exigences of his country, than he found it. The
Parsee authors teach that, in this retirement, he was taken to
heaven, and there received the following instructions from Ormuzd (the Principle of Good):—"Teach the nations that my
light is hidden under all that shines. Whenever you turn your
face toward the light, and you follow my commands, Ahriman
(the Evil Principle) will be seen to fly." He then received from
Ormuzd the Zend-Avesta and the sacred fire.
Setting aside this fable, Zoroaster repaired, about the age of
thirty, to the court of Darius Hystaspes, who soon was converted
to his faith, and became a zealous and efficient propagator of it.
He introduced it into every part of his dominions; and had its
precepts written upon parchment, which were deposited in a vault,
hewn out of a rock in Persepolis, and placed under the guardian-
ship of holy men. He commanded that the profane should not
be permitted to approach the sacred volumes. Darius not only
aided Zoroaster in the propagation of his faith in Iran, but his attempt to promulgate it in neighboring states involved him in a
war with Arjasp, King of Tureen. Instead of being killed by
lightning, as the tradition states, the prophet is said to have been
murdered during the persecution of the fire-worshipers by Arjasp.
His death took place in his seventy-sixth year, 513 b.c.
Of all the pagan faiths, that of Zoroaster, which acknowledges
the Supreme Being, and a good and evil principle, is undoubtedly
the most rational; and, if emblems of the deity are admissible,
the sun, or fire, is the most sublime of all visible emblems.
The ancient religion of Iran, which was the same as that of
Zoroaster, was established by Djamschid; and was, in truth,

* *Veterum Persarum et Majorum Religionis Hist.*
† *Zoroastre, Confucius, et Mahomet comparés.*

Thus we trace this great secret from the earliest period of history; and it perhaps existed even before it.

The Chaldeans, who aided Ninus in the war against the Bactrians, with all the power of their magic arts, must have possessed the same knowledge relative to lightning as their rivals, although the fact is not established by any historical docu ments. It might not be impossible for these priests to have lost it, perhaps from want of the occasion of using it; while it was preserved in the mountainous countries of Asia and Etruriá, that were much more exposed than Babylon to the ravages of lightning. The *magical oracles* that are attributed by Plethon to Zoroaster, or his disciples, are commented on by Psellus, under the name of the

fire-worship, which renders the supposition of our author re specting the knowledge of electricity by Zoroaster at least prob lematical; for, unless the traditional fable of his obtaining fire from heaven be admitted, we have no data for the assumption that he drew lightning from the clouds. It is more probable that the original fire of the altars was lighted by reflected mirrors, or by burning-glasses, as is now done in the houses of the Parsees in India, when their fires are accidentally extinguished, or allowed to go out: in which case, it may be said to be bestowed by the sun.

It is remarkable, that although the Parsees (fire-worshipers) in India are an active, rich, and intelligent class, and follow their religious faith without hinderance, yet, in Persia, they are a degraded and oppressed race. They have no temples, and no priesthood; and, according to Sir Kerr Porter, their whole worship "has sunk into nothing more than a few hasty prayers, muttered to the sun, as supreme god: and what they call commemorative ceremonies are now only sad confused shadows of their former religious festivals."[*]

The Parsees of India, in the emigration from the isle of Ormuz, where they had fled from the Mohammedan persecutions, carried with them the antus-byrum, or sacred fire, which is still preserved at Oodwarra, near Nunsarree; and from it all the fires in their temples have been lighted. It is intended as a sacred and perpetual monitor to preserve their purity. The Parsees are a tall, comely, athletic, and well formed race; and much fairer than the Hindoos, and wear a peculiar cap, which distinguishes them from the Hindoos.—ED.

---

[*] Sir R. K. Porter's *Travels in Persia*, vol. ii., p. 40.

Chaldaic oracles,* regarding them as emanating
from the Chaldean priests; and the explanation he
gives respecting those we have quoted, is only as-
trological and allegorical. The sages of Babylon
and the prophet of Ariema had probably drawn
from the same source. It is possible that the secret
alluded to by the oracles having been preserved
for a long time by the successors of Zoroaster, traces might be found in the doctrine of the Magi,
from which Plethon borrowed the idea developed
in his Commentary. The Chaldeans, on the contrary, would have thrown themselves into allegory,
and drawn their followers with them, in desiring
to solve an enigma the secret of which was lost to
them, and which could alone furnish the solution.

If we turn toward Hindostan, the cradle of civilization, we find the substance, and some of the
most striking expressions, of the two oracles in this
stanza of the *Yadjour-Veda:* "There the sun shines
not, neither do the moon nor the stars; the meteors do not fly about" (that is, in this place):
"God overwhelms these brilliant substances with
light, and the universe is dazzled by its splendor."† Zoroaster, who borrowed much from an-

* The compilation of Psellus differs from that of Plethon in
the order in which the oracles are disposed. There are also various readings and considerable additions. Beside, the Greek
verses are much more correct, which seems to indicate a less
faithful translation, or one taken from an original not so ancient.
† *Recherches Asiatiques*, tome i., pp. 575, 576. The Vedas are
the scriptures, or revelations of the Hindoos; and, like the
sacred parchments of Zoroaster, they must not be read by the
multitude, nor approached by the profane. They are supposed
to have proceeded from the mouth of Brahma, and to be intended for the universal sacrifice. They are supposed, however,
to have been scattered; but again brought together and arranged
by a sage, named Deráparáyana, or arranger, who flourished
more than five thousand years ago, or in the second age of the
world. He was assisted in his labor, and divided the whole of
the recovered fragments of the Vedas into four parts.
I. The *Rigveda*, which contains invocations addressed to deities

cient India, doubtless, in this instance, might have
changed the sense of the words, and applied a metaphorical picture of the divine splendor to the magi-

of fire, of the sun, the moon, the firmament, the winds, and the
seasons, whose presence is invited to the sacrifices intended to
supplicate their aid. Some of the *manhras*, or hymns contained
in it, display specimens of the most exalted poetry. The sun,
savitri, is addressed as the light of the Divine Ruler; but in an
allegorical sense as the divine light which sheds its rays over all,
and emanates from the Supreme Being. One of the hymns,
translated by Mr. Colebroke, contains expressions closely resembling those in the Book of Genesis, which describe the period
prior to the creation of this world. " Then there was no entity
nor nonentity; no world, nor sky, nor aught above it; nothing,
anywhere, in the happiness of any one, involving or involved;
nor waters deep and dangerous. Death was not; nor then was
immortality; nor distinction of day or night."* In another portion of the Veda, called Aitareya Brahaman's, we find this sentence:—" Originally this was indeed *soul* only, nothing else
whatever existed, active or inactive." He thought, " I will
create worlds." These, and similar expressions, are supposed
to imply the Monotheism of the Ramadam Hindoo faith, according to which, the creation of man arose from the circumstance
that every element begged from the Creator a distinct form, and
the whole chose a distinct body.

II. The *Yajish*, or, *Yadjour-Veda*, which relates chiefly to ob-
lations and sacrifices, one of the most splendid of which is " to
light," and another " to fire;" which induces the Editor to
attribute the Hindoo faith to the same origin as that of Zoroaster. All the hymns in this Veda relate to sacrifices and ceremonies. It is scarcely necessary to say that many of these are
of a character inconsistent with the original faith, and seem to
belong to an after-period; especially the bloody sacrifices to
Kali; indeed, the following is one of the texts of the Veda:
" O ye gods, we slaughter no victim, we use no sacrificial stake,
we worship by the repetition of sacred verses."—*Sámaveda San-
hitá*, p. 32, v. 2.)

III. *The Sámaveda* concerns the names of ancestors, and relates chiefly to a sacrifice termed Soma-Yâga, or moon-plant
sacrifice; to which the three highest classes of Bramins only are
admitted. The plant (sarcostema *viminalis*) must be pulled up
by the roots in a moonlight night, from the top of a mountain;
and, at the same time, the arani wood (premna *spinosa*) must be
collected for kindling the sacred fire. From the juice of the
sarcostema an intoxicating liquor, called sama, is prepared for
the oblation, and also for the consumption of the officiating
Bramins, after the fastings, during the sacrifice, have been
finished. The fire with which the altar is lighted is produced

* Colebroke's *Essays*, vol. i., p. 43.,

cal ceremony of initiation.   But Sir W. Jones is inclined to think that this stanza is a modern paraphrase of some text of the ancient sacred books."*

This explains why these terms do not exactly correspond with those of the magic oracles; and may be applied in a less explicit manner to the secret of attracting lightning from the clouds.   The paragraph might have been written at a period when this process had been forgotten and lost sight of; and, consequently, the proper sense of the sacred text also forgotten.

Elsewhere the following passage of the *Oupnek'-hat*, "to know fire, the sun, the moon, and lightning, is three fourths of the science of God,"† proves that the sacred science did not neglect to study the nature of thunder ; and by the possession

by the friction of one piece of the arani wood upon another ; and may, consequently, be regarded as being procured from the air. The following verses from one of the hymns demonstrate that this sacrifice was originally a kind of purifying sacrament, although it is now degenerated into a festival disgraced by excesses of all kinds: " That saving moon-plant, by its stream of pressed sacrificial viands, makes us pure.   That saving moon-plant makes us pure."—(Stevenson's translation of the *Sámaveda*, part i. ; *Prapathaka*, vi. ; *Dasiata* ii., v. 4, p. 94.)

IV. The *Athar'vana* contains incantations for the destruction of enemies, and is not much reverenced by the Hindoos on that account.

The real age of the Vedas is supposed to be much less than that assigned by the Bramins; and it probably does not extend beyond the year 200 B.C. It is singular that throughout these scriptures there is a decided allusion to the fall of man, who, although emanating from, and a part of the deity, had lost his primeval purity, to recover which a great and universal sacrifice was required. It is impossible not to perceive in these, and in all the earliest traditions of all nations, that the primeval faith of man was the belief in one God ; and that Polytheism arose out of the vices and backslidings of the human race ; and it is satisfactory to trace in the Cosmogony of so ancient a faith, and in its account of the fall of man, and the consequent necessity of a propitiatory sacrifice, a confirmation, if any were required of the truths of our own sacred volume.—ED.

* *Recherches Asiatiques*, tome i., p. 375.
† *Oupnek'-hat. Brahmen* xi.

of this knowledge the priests might indicate the means of averting it. Finally, this opinion is also strengthened by an historical fact. In the time of Ctesias, India was acquainted with the use of conductors of lightning. According to this historian,[*] iron placed at the bottom of a fountain of liquid gold (that is to say, a *sheet of gold*), and made in the form of a sword, with the point upward, possessed, as soon as it was fixed in the ground, the property of averting storms, hail, and lightning. Ctesias, who had·seen the experiment tried twice, before the eyes of the King of Persia, attributed to the iron alone this quality which belonged to its form and position. Perhaps they used, in preference, iron naturally alloyed with a little gold, as being less susceptible of rusting, for the same motive that leads the moderns to gild the points of lightning conductors. Whatever might be the intention, the principal fact remains ; and it is not useless to remark that, from that time, the ancients began to perceive the intimate connection between the electric state of the atmosphere and the production not only of lightning, but also of hail and other meteors.

If the question so often resolved be renewed, namely, why no vestiges of a knowledge so ancient can be discovered since the time of Tullus Hostilius, more than four-and-twenty centuries ago? we reply, that it was so little diffused, that it was only by chance, and in an imperfect manner, that it was discovered even by Tullus Hostilius, when perusing the memoirs left by Numa. Would not the dangers attached to the least error in repeating the processes in these memoirs,—dangers so often proved by fatal experience,—have been sufficient to cause the worship of Jupiter Elicius, and

* Ctesias in *Indic.* ap. *Photium. Bibl.*, cod. lxxii.

Jupiter Cataibates, to fall into disuse through fear ?

The destruction of the Persian Empire by the Greeks, anterior to the nearly general massacre of the Magi, after the death of Smerdis, might cause this important gap in the occult sciences known to the disciples of Zoroaster. In India, which has been so often the prey of the conqueror, analogous causes might exercise an inflence as destructive. In all countries, indeed, over what subject more than this would the veil of religious mystery have been thrown, and greater obstacles placed in the way of ignorance, so as ultimately to plunge it into oblivion ?

Other questions arise, more important and more difficult. We may ask, whether electricity, whatever were the resources which it afforded, would be sufficient to explain the brilliant apparent miracle of the Zoroastrian initiation ? Does it sufficiently explain what Ovid describes so accurately in the worship of Jupiter Elicius by Numa, namely, the art of making the lightning, and the noise of the thunder, seen and heard in a clear sky ?* Does it explain the terrible power of hurling lightning upon an enemy, such as attributed to Porsenna,† and which two Etruscan magicians pretended to possess in the time of Attila ? Certainly not ;— at least it is not within the limits of our knowledge, a limit which has, probably, not been surpassed by the ancients. To supply any deficiency, may we

---

* Ovid, *Fast.*, lib. iii., vers. 367–370.

† Porsenna was a king of Etruria, in whose tent, when the Etrurian army lay before the gates of Rome, Mutius Scævola put his hand into the fire, and allowed it to be burned, without any expression of suffering, in order to convince Porsenna that it was in vain to make head against a people who could display such fortitude and daring. Porsenna was supposed to possess many magical secrets.—Ed.

not suppose that, by a happy chance, the Thaumaturgists, profiting by the explosion of a luminous meteor, attributed it to the influence of their art, and led enthusiasm to look upon it as a miracle, although it was only a natural effect? May we not, for example, recollect how, according to an historian, when a miraculous rain quenched the thirst of the soldiers of Marcus Aurelius, the emperor, at the same time, drew down, by the influence of his prayers, lightning on the warlike machines of his enemy.* We may also transport the apparent miracles of one country into another; and discover at the present day, in a place consecrated through all ages to religion, a secret equivalent to the miracle of Numa. Naphtha, when dissolved in atmospheric air, produces the same results as a mixture of oxygen and hydrogen. Near Bakhou†

---

* "Fulmen de cœlo, precibus suis, contra hostium machinamentum extorsit."—Julius Capitolinus in *Marc. Aurel.*

† The town of Bakhou is the capital of a territory of the same name, situated on the southern extremity of the peninsula of Abesheron, on the west side of the Caspian Sea. The soil of the whole territory is saturated with naphtha; and the peninsula contains many volcanoes. Not far from Bakhou, a spring of white oil gushes from the cleft of a rock at the base of a hill; it is pure naphtha, and readily burns in the surface of water. The inhabitants of these districts sink a hollow cane, or tube of paper, about two inches into the ground, and by blowing upon a burning coal, held near the orifice of the tube, the gas lights, but the flame does not consume the paper, nor the cane. There are many wells of the same substance; and these, as well as the burning places, or Atesch-gah, as they are called, were generally shrines of grace; and many thousands of pilgrims and fire-worshipers resorted there to purify themselves. Notwithstanding the degradation of the Parsees when the Mohammedan religion was established in Persia, a few, as stated in the text, still find their way to the *Atesch-gah of Bakhou*, and spend five, seven, or even ten years on the spot, worshiping the sacred fire, and performing prayer and penitential exercises. This sanctuary, which is surrounded by four low walls, is a space about twenty feet square, and contains twenty cells, in which the priests and Ghuebres reside; and from each corner of the quadrangle arises a chimney, about twenty feet high, out of which a bright flame, three or four feet in height, con

is a well, the water of which is saturated with naphtha; if a mantle be extended, and held above the water for some minutes, and then some lighted straw thrown into it, there is suddenly heard, says the traveler whose words I quote, " a thundering noise, like that of a line of artillery, accompanied by a brilliant flame."* Restore to the Atesch-gah its ancient majesty, and for its little number of penitents and pilgrims, who still awaken religious associations, substitute a college of priests, clever in turning to the glory of their divinity phenomena, the causes of which are carefully concealed from the eyes of the profane, and, under the clearest skies, at their command fire and peals of thunder would issue from the wells of Bakhou. Let us admit that substances which are abundant in certain countries might have been transported by the Thaumaturgists into those countries where the action of them, being quite unknown, would appear miraculous. The Tiber might have seen, in the age when Numa invoked Jupiter Elicius, the same wonder which at the present day is famous on the banks of the Caspian.† The ceremonies, indeed, of the same magic worship, might be enhanced by the effects of a composition of naphtha, and by those of the lightning-conductors and electricity elicited by the artifice of the Thaumaturgist, always care-

tinually issues. The penances to which these deluded creatures subject themselves are so severe, that scarcely one individual out of ten who visit the shrine ultimately survives them.—ED.

* *Journey of George Keppel from India to England by Bassora.— Nouvelles Annales des Voyages*, 2ᵉ séries, tome v., p. 349.

† Native naphtha is, in the present day, exported to almost every part of Europe, from the neighborhood of the Caspian. It is a limpid, nearly colorless, volatile liquid, with a strong, peculiar odor. It is much lighter than water, having a specific gravity of 0.753; consequently it swims on that fluid, for it does not mix with it. Naphtha is very inflammable, and burns with a white flame, which evolves much smoke. It is a compound of carbon and hydrogen.—ED.

ful to make the treasures of his science impenetrable, and thence more respected.

But, in spite of the principle we have hitherto followed, it is with regret we admit that it affords only a partial or local explanation, applicable to some isolated facts. We prefer general facts, such as were for so long a period concealed within the bosom of the temple. In recalling to remembrance the brilliant or destructive influence of the different inflammable compositions, the existence of which is indicated by these facts, we shall measure the extent of the resources in the power of the possessors of the sacred science, calculated to enable them to rival the fires of heaven by the apparent miracles of terrestrial fire.

CHAPTER IX.

Phosphorescent Substances.—Sudden Appearance of Flames.— Heat developed by the Slackening of Lime.—Substances which are kindled by Contact with Air and Water.—Pyrophorus, Phosphorus, Naphtha, and Alcoholic Liquids employed in different apparent Miracles.—The Blood of Nessus was a Phosphuret of Sulphur; and also the Poison that Medea employed against Creusa.—Greek Fire.—This Fire rediscovered after many Attempts.—In Persia and Hindostan an unextinguishable Fire was used.

NOTHING is more striking to the vulgar than the sudden production of light, heat, and flame without any apparent cause, or with a concurrence of causes seemingly opposed to such an effect.

Art teaches the preparation of substances which emit light, without allowing any sensible heat to escape. The phosphorus of Bologna,* and the

* The Bologna phosphorus is a natural gypseous spar, or selenite which has the property of emitting light, when it is calcined for that purpose. It is powdered after calcination, and then formed into small cakes by means of a solution of gum-tragacanth; these cakes are dried, brought to a state of ignition, and then suffered

II.   M

phosphorus of Baldwin,* are known to the learned, but they now only figure in books, among the amusements of physics. The ancients were acquainted with bodies endowed with a similar property. Isidore† mentions a brown stone, which became luminous when sprinkled with oil.

The Rabbins, given up to the study of the Cabbala,‡ speak of a light belonging to saints, to the elect, upon whose countenance it shines miraculously from their birth, or when they have merited this sign of glory.§ Arnobus,‖ on the authority of Hermippus, gives to the magician Zoroaster¶ a belt of fire ; a suitable ornament for the institutor of the worship of fire. A philosopher of the present age would be very little embarrassed how to produce these brilliant wonders, particularly if their duration was not required to be much prolonged.

to cool. If kept from air and moisture, they shine like a burning coal when carried into a dark place, after being exposed for a few minutes to the light. In 1602, Vincentius Casciorolus, a shoemaker of Bologna, who had discovered the properties of this spar, showed it to Scipio Bezatello, an alchemist, and several learned men, under the martial name of *lapis solaris*, and as the substance called the *sol* of the alchemist, or philosopher's stone, fitted for converting the ignoble metals into gold.*—ED.

* Baldwin's phosphorus is nitrate of lime, which, after the water of crystalization has been evaporated, and the salt has become dry, acquires the property of emitting light in the dark.—ED.

† *Savinius lapis, oleo addito, etiam lucere fertur*, Isid., *Hispal. Origin.*, lib. xvi., cap. iv.

‡ The Cabbala is the work which contains the esoteric philosophy of the Jewish doctors, and which derives its name from the Hebrew word *kibbel, to receive ;* as the laws it contains were received by Moses from above.—ED.

§ Gaulmin, *De vitâ et morte Mosis*, not. lib. ii., pp. 233–325.

‖ Arnobus lived in the reign of Diocletian, and was converted to Christianity. In proof of his sincerity, he wrote a treatise in which he exposed the absurdity of irreligion, and ridiculed the heathen gods.—ED.

¶ *Nunc veniat quis, super* igneam zonam, *magus interiore ab orbe Zoroaster.*—Arnob., lib. i. It is without any reason that some commentators wish to read it thus: *Quin Azonaces magus, &c.*

* Beckman's *Hist. of Inventions*, trans., vol. ix., p. 423.

The Druids extended the resources of science much farther. The renowned person, who, in the poem of Lucan, proclaims their magical power, boasts of possessing the secret of making a forest appear on fire, when it does not burn.* Ossian paints old men, mixed with the sons of Loda, and at night making conjurations round a *cromlech*, or circle of stones; and, at their command, burning meteors arose, which terrified the warriors of Fingal; and by the light of which Ossian distinguished the chief of the enemy's warriors.† An English translation of Ossian observes that every bright flame, sudden, and resembling lightning, is called in Gaelic *the Druid's flame*.‡ It is to this flame that Ossian compares the sword of his son Oscar.§ Connected with the recital of the bard, this expression indicates that the Druids possessed the art of causing flames to appear, for the purpose of dismaying their enemies.||

We may join to the traits of resemblance already observed between the Celts and the ancient inhabitants of Italy, the fable of Cæculus, the founder of the city of Preneste. Wishing to make himself known as the son of the god Vulcan, he implored the aid of his sire, when suddenly an assembled multitude, who had refused to acknowledge his brilliant origin, were enveloped in flames, and the alarm quickly subdued their incredulity.¶

We may remark, that Cæculus, most probably, had chosen the place of assembly, and that the

---

* " Et non ardentis fulgere incendia sylvæ."—Lucan, *Phars.*, lib. iii., v. 420.
† *Ossian's Poems, &c.*, published by John Smith, 1780.
‡ *Ibid.*   § G. Higgins, *The Celtic Druids*, p. 116.
|| From one strophe of the *Hervorar Saga*, it may be inferred that this art was not unknown to the Scandinavian magicians. (See *Magasin Encyclop.*, 1804, vol. iv., pp. 250–260.
¶ Servius in *Æneid*, lib. vii., vers. 678–681.

Druids only exercised their power in sacred in-closures, interdicted to the profane, as in certain optical illusions where fire has often played a part; for these apparent miracles required a theater suit-able to those who worked them; and, in other places, in spite of the urgency of necessity, they would have experienced great difficulty in any attempt to produce them.

The instantaneous development of latent heat is not less likely to excite astonishment, particularly if water kindles the flames. Substances suscepti-ble of evolving heat, or of taking fire, in absorbing or in decomposing water, are numerous, and they have very often occasioned fires; such as were attributed, formerly, to negligence or to malice. Stacks of damp hay, and slates of pyrites,* moist-ened by a warm shower, will produce this phe-nomenon.†

* Pyrites consists of a natural combination of iron and sulphur. It is frequently found in seams of coal; and when it is exposed to moisture, the sulphur and the iron aid one another in decomposing the water, and attracting its oxygen, which changes the sulphur into sulphuric acid, and the iron into an oxide; and thus forming, by the union of these two, the sulphate of iron. During these natural processes the degree of heat developed is often sufficient to inflame the hydrogen, the other constituent of the water, as it escapes into the air.—ED.

† In ricks of hay thus consumed, the combustion is the result of fermentation, a fact which was known to the ancients: for Ga-len informs us that the fermenting dung of pigeons is sufficient to set fire to a house, a phenomenon which he has witnessed: and it is recorded, on good authority, that the fire which consumed the great church of Pisa was occasioned by the fermentation of the dung of the pigeons that had for centuries built their nests under its roof. Many other substances, also, cause spontaneous com-bustion. When recent charcoal is reduced to an impalpable pow-der, by rollers, it gradually absorbs air, which is consolidated, and heat is developed during the process equal to 360° of Fahrenheit, which soon causes the combustion of the charcoal. The inflam-mation is more active in proportion to the shortness of the inter-val between the production of the charcoal and its reduction into powder: and the free admission of air is indispensable.*—ED.

* Brewster's *Natural Magic*, p. 215.

Were the Thaumaturgists acquainted with phenomena similar to the latter? I reply, without doubt, they were. The prodigious heat which is emitted by quicklime sprinkled with water could not have escaped their observation. Now, let us suppose that a sufficient quantity of quicklime is hidden at the bottom of a pit, or kiln, and that the pit is then filled with snow: the absorbed snow will disappear; and the interior temperature of the pit or kiln will be so much more raised, owing to its being thus closely shut, that less of the ex panded heat will be allowed to escape—and an apparent miracle will be proclaimed. Thus, a writer of legends has ornamented the history of St. Patrick, by relating that the apostle of Ireland lighted a kiln with snow.

Theophrastus* gives the name of *spinon* to a stone which is met with in certain mines; and which, if pounded, and then exposed to the sun, ignites of itself, particularly if care has been taken to wet it first. The *spinon*, there can be little doubt, is merely an efflorescing pyrites. The stone named *gagates*† (true pyritic jet) is black, porous, light, friable, and resembles burned wood. It exhales a disagreeable odor; and, when it is heated, it attracts other bodies in the same manner as amber. The smoke which it exhales in burning relieves women attacked with hysterics; and it is kindled by means of water, and extinguished when immersed in oil. This latter peculiarity was also the distinguishing feature of a stone which, according to Ælian and Dioscorides,‡ ignited in a like manner, when sprinkled with water, and, in burn-

---

* Theophrast., *De Lapidibus.*

† Plin., *Hist. Nat.*, lib. xxxvi., cap. xix.—Solin., cap. xxv.—isid., *Hispal. Origin.*, lib. xvi., cap. iv. So named from being ob tained near the river Gagas, in Lycia.—ED.

‡ Ælian, *De Nat. Animal.*, lib. ix., cap. xxviii.

ing, exhaled a strong bituminous smell; but, as it was extinguished by blowing above it, its combustion seems to have depended on the escape of a gaseous vapor.*

Those three substances, whether they were the productions of art or of nature, might have sufficed to work miraculous conflagrations. But Pliny and Isidore of Seville have described a fourth, still more powerful: a black stone that is found in Persia, and which, if broken between the fingers, burns them.† This is precisely the effect produced by a bit of pyrophorus, or phosphorus stone; and this wonderful stone was probably nothing else. It is known that phosphorus, melted by heat, may become black and solid;‡ and the word *stone* ought not to impose more upon us here than

* Many instances of spontaneous combustion can be traced to the escape of carbureted and sulphureted hydrogen gases through rents in the earth. Near the village of Bradley, in Staffordshire, an unextinguishable fire has burned for seventy years, arising from a burning stratum of coal, to which the air has free access from beneath it. At Bedley, also, near Glasgow, a constant stream of inflammable gas issues in the bed of a river, which is occasionally set on fire, and, in calm weather, continues burning at the surface of the water for weeks together. It consists of a mixture of two volumes of hydrogen gas and one volume of carbon, so that it is little more than half the weight of atmospheric air.* The light which has been termed the " Lantern of Maracaybo," in South America, and which is seen every night hovering over a mountainous, desert spot, on the banks of the river Catatumba,† near its junction with the Sulia, is another example of the escape of inflammable gas issuing from the ground, inflamed, most probably, at first by electricity. In some places these gases are applied to domestic use, as at the salt mine of Gottizabe, near Rheims, in Fecklensburg.—ED.

† " Pyrites ; nigra quidam, sed attrita digitos adruit."—Plin. *Hist. Nat.*, lib. xxxvii., cap. 11.—" Pyrites ; Persicus lapis . . . . tenentis manum, si vehementius prematur, adurit."—Isidor., *Hispal. Origin.*, lib. xvi., cap. iv.

‡ It is not probable that it was phosphorus; but it might have been a natural pyrophorus, which took fire on the exposure of a fresh surface to the air.—ED.

the words *lake* and *fountain* when a liquid is spoken of. Custom has consecrated in our own language the words *infernal stone (lapis infernalis)* and *cauterizing stone,* * for a pharmaceutical preparation.

But were the ancients acquainted with phosphorus and pyrophorus? I reply in the affirmative, since they relate wonders which could have been produced by no other means than the employment of these substances, or by reactives, endowed with analogous properties. We shall have occasion to mention an ancient description of the effects of a combination of phosphorus, a description as exact as if it had been made at the present time by a modern chemist. As to pyrophorus, science possesses so many substances which ignite after some minutes' exposure to the air, that it may, without improbability, be believed that many of them were known to the ancients. Without mentioning bitumens as being highly inflammable, or petroleum, or naphtha, which take fire at the approach of a lighted candle, how many of the residue of distillations kindle spontaneously in a damp atmosphere. This property, to which no attention is paid, except to explain it by a general principle, was certainly never neglected by the performers of apparent miracles, since the art of distillation formed an important part of the sacred sciences.

We will not then hesitate to believe, though it may well astonish us, what history relates of a vestal threatened with the punishment reserved for those who allowed the sacred fire to go out, that she had only to spread her veil over the altar in order that the flame should suddenly rekindle, and burn more vividly than before.† From beneath the friendly veil, we may imagine that we perceive a grain of

---

* It is a preparation of pure potassa.—ED.
† Valer. Maxim., lib. i., cap. iv., § 8.

phosphorus or of pyrophorus to fall on the hot cinders, and supply the place of the intervention of the divinity.

Nor need we longer share the incredulity of Horace, respecting the apparent miracle which was worked in the sanctuary of Gnatia,* where the. incense kindled of itself in honor of the gods.† We also may understand how Seleucus, sacrificing to Jupiter, saw the wood-pile upon the altar ignite spontaneously to offer a brilliant presage of his future greatness ;‡ neither can we deny that the Theurgist Maximus,§ offering incense to Hecate, might have been able to announce that the torches which the goddess held would light themselves spontaneously, and that his prediction had been accomplished.||

Notwithstanding the precautions which the love of mystery inspired, and which was seconded by the enthusiasm of admiration, the working of the science was sometimes openly shown in its assumed miracles. Pausanias relates what he saw in two cities of Lydia, the inhabitants of which, subjected to the yoke of the Persians, had embraced the religion of the Magi. " In a chapel," he says, " is an altar, upon which there are always *ashes, that in color do not resemble* any others. The Magi placed

---

* A town of Apulia, about eighty miles from Brundusium.—ED.
† Horat., *Serm.*, lib. i., sat. v., vers. 97–190 ; Plin., *Hist. Nat.*, lib. ii., cap. vii.
‡ Pausanias, *Attic.*, cap. xvi.
§ This Maximus was a cynic, and a magician of Ephesus. He instructed the Emperor Julian in magic ; but refused to reside in his court. He was appointed pontiff in the province of Lydia. When his patron Julian went into the East, Maximus promised him success, and that his conquests should be more numerous than those of Philip. After the death of Julian, he was almost sacrificed to the fury of the soldiers, but escaped to Constantinople, where he was, soon afterward, accused of magical practices before the Emperor Valens ; and being condemned, he was beheaded at Ephesus, A.D. 366. || Eunapius in *Maxim.*

some wood upon the altar, and invoked I know not what god, by orisons taken from a book written in a barbarous language unknown to the Greeks: the wood soon ignited of itself without fire, and the flame of it was very brilliant."*

The extraordinary color of the cinders, which were always kept upon the altar, doubtlessly concealed an inflammable composition; simply, perhaps, earth soaked in petroleum or naphtha—a species of fuel still employed in Persia, in every place where these bituminous substances are common. The Magi, in placing the wood, probably threw there, without its being perceived, a few grains of pyrophorus, or of that stone which was found in Persia, and which was kindled by a light pressure. While the orison lasted, the action of either substance had time to develop itself.

The vine-branches which a priest placed upon an altar, near Agrigentum, lighted spontaneously in the same manner. Solinus† adds, that the flame ascended from the altar toward the assistants without incommoding them. This circumstance announces that between the vine-branches a gas escaped, and was lighted from below the altar, in a manner similar to that at Mount Eryx, where a perpetual flame is preserved on the altar of Venus.‡ The fumes of a spirituous liquor would have produced the same phenomenon. By the inflammation of an ethereal fluid, also, may be explained the power that Fromann attributes to the Zingari§ of

* Pausanias, *Eliac.*, lib. i., cap. xxvii.
† Solin., cap. xi.
‡ Refer to chap. iv., vol. i.
§ Zingari is the Italian appellation of that extraordinary race of mankind known as wanderers in almost every part of the world, but whose original home, or aboriginal region, is still a problem. In every country, although the same people, yet they have a distinct name. In England we term them *Gipsys*, from their supposed Egyptian origin; in France they are called *Bohemians*; m

making fire appear upon a single bundle of straw placed among many others, and of extinguishing it at pleasure.* In this manner school-boys amuse themselves by making alcohol burn in their hands : a puff of breath disperses the flame at the moment when they begin to feel the heat of it.

"It has been observed," says Buffon,† "that some substances thrown up by Ætna, after having been cooled during several years and then moistened with rain, have rekindled, and thrown off flames, with an explosion violent enough to produce even a slight earthquake." The composition of these volcanic productions may have been imitated by art, or the Thaumaturgist may have carefully collected and preserved those which nature had formed. One of the four stones inflammable by water, of which we have spoken, shall be explained elsewhere.

In fact we may remark, with a man whom science and his country have equally regretted,‡ that quicklime mixed with sulphur, by the heat which

Holland, *Heydens ;* in Germany, *Zigeuners ;* in Spain, *Gitanos ;* in Russia, *Tzengani ;* and in Italy, *Zingari ;* while the Oriental nations call them *Tschingenes.* From the time they first appeared in Europe, they pretended to possess magical science, and to have the power of looking into the future. The art of chiromancy, or telling fortunes by the inspection of the hand, however, is not of their invention, lectures having been read in colleges upon that absurd art long before the Gipsys appeared in Europe. With respect to their origin, the most probable opinion brings them originally from Hindostan. Their language has a close resemblance to the Hindostanee ; and it is supposed that they migrated from India in the beginning of the fifteenth century, when Timur-Beg invaded that country, and endeavored to establish in it the Mohammedan faith. Whatever may have been their origin, they are now little better than lawless wanderers, thieves, impostors, and the only pretenders to sorcery in Europe at the present time.—ED.

* Fromann, *Tract. de Fascinatione,* pp. 263, 527, 528.
† *Théorie de la Terre, Preuves,* § xvi.
‡ Cadet-Gassicourt, *De l'Extinction de la Chaux, &c.* Thesis sanctioned before the *Faculté des Sciences,* August, 1812.

it emits when sprinkled with water, first fuses, and then causes the combustion of the sulphur; that this mixture rapidly sets on fire mixed with sulphur and chlorate of potassa, and as suddenly ignites gunpowder and phosphorus; and that, in the latter case, there exists a physical means of fixing the precise moment when the developed heat will cause the combustion.

Let us transport ourselves among a people whose first historical centuries, owing to the marvelous recitals with which they are filled, are thrown back into the indefinite ages of mythology.

The impartial reader will follow us in the march of these recitals. Let him weigh well all the expressions which Dejanira* employs for describing the first effects of the *Blood of Nessus,* a marvelous philter, with which she impregnated the precious tunic that was to bring back the heart of her inconstant husband.† "Nessus," says she, " advised me to keep this liquid in a dark place until the moment when I wished to make use of it. This is what I have done. To-day, *in the dark,* with a flock of wool dipped in the liquid, I have dyed the

* Dejanira was the daughter of Olmus, King of Ætolia. She was married to Hercules, and traveling with him, on one occasion, being stopped by the swollen waters of the Evenus, she was conveyed across the river by the centaur Nessus, who no sooner, however, landed her on the opposite shore, than he offered violence to her person in the sight of her husband. Hercules, to revenge the insult, killed the centaur with a poisoned arrow. Nessus, in dying, bequeathed his tunic, stained with his poisoned blood, to Dejanira, observing that it had the power of reclaiming husbands from infidelity. The lady gladly accepted and preserved the tunic; and when Hercules proved faithless to her bed, she sent it to him; and he, having put it on, was burned to death. The romance of the legend is scarcely destroyed by the explanation given by our author.—Ed.

† Sophocl., *Trachin.*, act iv., sc. 1. To be more concise, I have blended together two passages very much like each other. Seneca (*Hercules Œtacus*, act iii., sc. 1) describes the same details, and particularly the efflorescence produced whenever the philter touched the earth.

188 COMBUSTIBLES INFLAMED

tunic which I have sent, after having shut it in a
box, without *its having been exposed to the light.*
The flock of wool, exposed to the sun upon a
stone, was spontaneously consumed, without having been touched by any one. It was reduced to
ashes, into powder resembling that which the saw
causes to fall from wood. I have observed that
above the stone on which I had placed it froth
bubbles appeared, like those which, in autumn, are
produced from wine poured from a height."

Let a chemist read these details, stripped of all
mythological recollections; what will he recognize
in this pretended philter, given by the hand of
vengeance, and which, from its consistence, color,
or some other property, received the appellation
of blood? I reply, a liquid preparation of phosphorus,* which, owing to the proportions of its
elements, inflamed spontaneously when it was exposed to the light and heat of the sun. The phos-
phoric acid produced from its combustion would
produce upon the stone the effervescence which
struck the eyes of Dejanira, and also the ashes
of the wool reduced to a dry and insoluble phosphate.

Hercules clothed himself with the fatal tunic;
then he sacrificed twelve bulls; but scarcely had
he taken the fire to the wood-pile on which the
victims were deposited, than he felt the effects of
the philter.† The vicinity of the flame, the chemist will say, and the humid heat of the skin of a
man who works with strength and activity before
a kindled pile will infallibly determine, though

* A portion of phosphorus, combined with one portion of sulphur, composes a phosphoret which remains liquid at the temperature of 10°, and is ignited at that of 25° of the centigrade
thermometer, 50° and 77° of Fahrenheit.
† Sophocl., *Trachin.*, act iv., sc. 2.

without visible inflammation, the decomposition of the phosphoret spread upon the garment. The compound being dried up, and therefore much more caustic, would act upon all parts of the body, disorganize the skin and the flesh, and, by inexpressible pains, cause the death of its unfortunate victim. Even at this day, when its nature is not unknown, it would be difficult to arrest the action once begun of these consuming substances: formerly it would have been impossible.

In discovering so perfect a uniformity between the picture painted by Sophocles and the illustrations of science, can it fairly be supposed that by chance alone the dreams or the imaginings of a poet should coincide exactly with the operations of nature? It is more reasonable to admit that the details of these marvelous facts were preserved in the memory of men, than that the poet would digress from the received tradition, of which he knew not the origin. There can be little doubt that this origin belonged to occult science, to magic studied in Thessaly, in the country of Nessus, from the time of the siege of Troy.*

Convinced that the Greek tragedian has described the effects of a secret preparation which, perhaps, in his time still existed in the temples, I have given to the blood of Nessus the property of inflaming spontaneously in the light, although this may not have been an essential condition of the phenomenon that it produced. Every potential cautery, spread in sufficient quantity upon the surface of the body, will exercise the same power; will cause the same pains, and soon occasion the same impossibility of taking off the garment which is daubed with it, without tearing the skin and the flesh, and without redoubling instead of diminish-

* Plin., *Hist. Nat.*, lib. xxx., cap. i.

ing the sufferings of the victim irrevocably doomed to death.*

The poison poured by Medea upon the robe which she sent to her rival, resembles, by its effects, that which Dejanira, without knowing its malignity, employed. But this myth presents, further, an impossible circumstance. From the fillet of gold offered with the dress to the unhappy Creusa, there shot unextinguishable flames.† As it can not be supposed that here there was an elevation of temperature, or the power of a burning sun, the spontaneous inflammation discloses the employment of naphtha, which takes fire at the approach alone of a lighted body. Many authors relate that Medea really rubbed the robe and the crown destined for Creusa with naphtha.‡ Procopius strengthens this tradition by twice observing that the liquor called naphtha by the Medes, received from the Greeks the name of the *oil of Medea*.§ Pliny, in fact, says that Medea having rubbed the crown of her rival, whom she wished to destroy, with naphtha, it caught fire at the instant when the unfortunate individual approached the altar to offer a sacrifice.||

In the tragedy of Seneca, Medea, after having announced that the " golden frontlet sent to Creusa inclosed a hidden fire, the composition of which

---

* Toward the end of the last century, a pharcomopolist of Paris, M. Steinacher, was called into a house under the pretext of giving relief to a sick person. Some people who pretended to condole with him, made a barbarous game of covering him with blisters, and holding him in this state during several hours. When he recovered his liberty, the most active and best directed means to relieve him were useless ; he languished for some time, and died in the most horrible torments; the authors of this crime remained unknown and unpunished.

† Euripid., *Medea*, act vi., sc. i.
‡ Plutarch, *Vit. Alexandr.*
§ Procop., *Histoire mêlée*, chap. xi.
|| Plin., *Hist. Nat.*, lib. ii., cap. 105.

she had learned from Prometheus, adds that Vulcan had also given her fire, concealed under the form of a light sulphur, and that she borrowed from Phaeton the flashes of an unextinguishable flame."[*] In withdrawing the veil from these figurative expressions, it is difficult not to perceive there a genuine Greek fire, which a grain of pyrophorus, or a little naphtha would kindle, when the fatal mixture was dispersed through the air, or by the vicinity of flame, such as that burned upon the altar which the wife of Jason approached.

We do not inadvertently add the Greek fire to the number of the weapons of Medea. According to every probability, we may ask, what was the foundation of the Greek fire? I answer, naphtha —the *oil of Medea;* and those *bulls* which vomited flame in order to defend the golden fleece that Medea's lover had delivered up to Jason—those bulls, the feet and the mouth of which were of brass, and which Vulcan had fabricated[†]—were they not machines adapted for throwing out the Greek fire?

Faithful to the method which we have followed, we shall endeavor to trace the history of this weapon, formerly so dreaded, from the earliest times when it was employed, till the latest records of it; when nothing announced that the discovery of it was still recent.

Two troubadours, one of whom flourished in the first years of the thirteenth century, mention the Greek fire. One of them says that it was extin-

---

[*] "Ignis fulvo . . clausus in auro . . latet obscurus . . quel mihi cœli . . qui furta luit . . viscere fœtó . . dedit et docuit . . condere vires . . arte Prometheus . . dedit et tenui . . sulfure tectos . . Mulciber ignes . . Et vivaces . . fulgura flammæ . . De cognato . . Phaetonte tuli . ."—Senec., *Medea,* act iv., sc. 2.

[†] Apollon., *Rhod. Argonaut.,* lib. iii.

guished by means of vinegar.* Joinville enters
into a curious detail upon the use of this fire, which
the Saracens darted forth upon the Crusaders.†
The Arabs have, at all times, made a great use of
inflamed darts for the attack and the defense of
places; so that the Sheik of Barnou, who derived
his knowledge from this people, was much astonished to learn that the English had never employed this method of destruction in war.‡

Manuel Comnenus§ employed the Greek fire
upon the galleys which he had armed to oppose
Roger of Sicily; and the historian observes that
he restored the use of it, after it had been given
up for a *long time*.‖ Alexius Comnenus had employed it, however, against the Pisans. Upon the
prow of his vessels were *lions* of bronze, which
vomited flame in every direction where it was intended to fall.¶ Anna Comnenus** speaks of fire
that the soldiers, armed with tubes resembling our
fusees, shot forth upon the enemy. But, accord-

* Millot, *Histoire littéraire des Troubadours*, tome i., p. 380;
tome ii., pp. 393, 394.

† *Mémoires de Joinville*, fol. edit., 1761, p. 44.

‡ *Voyages of Denham, Oudney, and Clapperton*, vol. i., pp. 115,
238.

§ Manuel Comnenus, although the second son of John Comnenus, yet ascended the throne after the death of his father, in
1143. His reign, of thirty years, was filled with the vicissitudes
of military enterprises against the Christians, the Saracens, and
the scarcely civilized nations beyond the Danube. He believed
in astrology, and the professors of that mystical art had promised
him many years of glory, even when his death was approaching;
but not feeling any confidence in their predictions, he requested
to have the habit of a monk brought to him, and, substituting it
for the royal robe, he expired.—ED.

‖ " Ignis Græcus qui longo jam tempore abditus latuerat."

¶ Ann. Comnen., *Hist.*, lib. xi., cap. ix. Alexius Comnenus
commenced his reign in 1081. His daughter Anna endeavored
to immortalize his memory in the Alexiad, or the history of his
reign. If her narrative can be depended upon, it would almost
induce the belief that the use of gunpowder was then understood
and employed instead of the Greek fire; or that gunpowder was
that fire.—ED.   ** *Ibid.*, lib. xii. cap. ix.

ing to her, they prepared their fire with a mixture of sulphur and resin reduced into powder. This account, however, is not worthy of credit; for such a composition would have melted before igniting, and would not have shot forth with an explosion.

Here three observations present themselves : 1st. The *lions* in bronze, employed by Alexius Comnenus, recall to our remembrance the *fire-vomiting bulls* manufactured in bronze by Vulcan—they are evidently the same description of weapon. 2d. Sixty years had scarcely elapsed between the maritime expedition of Alexius and that of Manuel Comnenus; in so short a space of time had the Greek fire been almost entirely forgotten! How many other processes of occult science may have perished by a more prolonged disuse. 3d. The delusive process which Anna Comnenus gives for the composition of the Greek fire is another proof of the care with which the ancients then concealed these processes beneath a double veil of mystery and of falsehood.

Constantine Porphyrogenitus,* indeed, recommends his son never to disclose to the barbarians the secret of the composition of the Greek fire; but to say to them that it was brought from heaven by an angel, and that it would be sacrilegious to

---

* He was the son of Leo, and, although clothed with the imperial purple, yet he was of a retired habit, and dedicated much of his time to the cultivation of literature and science. He drew many learned men to his court, and himself became an author. He delineated what he regarded as a perfect image of royalty, in the life of his grandfather, Basil; he also wrote a treatise, intended to instruct his son in the practice of government; and another entitled *Theurata,* in which a detailed account of the empire is given. Such a monarch was likely to inquire into the nature of the Greek fire; and, knowing it, to secure its influence for his people. Water only increased its burning; it was only extinguished by stifling it under a heap of dust.—ED.

II.   N

reveal it to them.*   Leon, the philosopher,† ordered brass tubes to be placed upon the vessels, and
tubes of smaller dimensions to be put in the hands
of the soldiers.   Both shot forth fire upon the enemy, with a noise similar to that of thunder; but
the emperor alone directed the fabrication of that
fire.

. ˜ It is said that Callinicus, of Heliopolis, in Syria,
invented the Greek fire in the seventh century of
our era; but he only restored or divulged a process, the origin of which, like many others, was
lost in the obscurity of initiations.   The initiated,
who were discovered and punished at Rome in the
year 186 B.C., possessed the secret; they plunged
their lighted torches into water without extinguishing them, " because," says Livy, " the composition
consisted of lime and sulphur;‡ but they most
probably added a bitumen, such as naphtha or
petroleum, to the other ingredients."

Callinicus and the initiated must have borrowed
their unextinguishable fire from some Asiatic initiation.   The Persians possessed the secret, but
they reserved the use of it for combats.   " They
composed an oil with which they rubbed the darts,
which, when thrown with a moderate force, carried with them, wherever they fixed themselves, devouring flames,§ increased and strengthened by
water, and only extinguishable by dust."

* Constantin. Pophyr., *De administ. imper.*
† Léon le philosophe, *Institutions militaires*, *inst.* xix., vol. ii.,
p. 139.
‡ Tit. Liv., lib. xxix., cap. xxiii.
§ Ammian. Marcell., lib. xxiii., cap. vi.   Pliny (*Hist. Nat.*, lib.
ii., cap. civ.) describes the effects of a substance called *maltha*, of
which the inhabitants of Samosate made use against the soldiers
of Lucullus.   The *maltha* was drawn from a neighboring pond
situated near the town.   Naphtha, or petroleum, doubtless formed
the basis of it.   Besieged by Lucullus, the defenders of Tigrano-
certa shot out inflamed naphtha upon their enemies. (Dio Cass.
--Xiphilin in *Pompeio.*)

Traditions almost always lead us back toward
Hindostan, when we are desirous of discovering
the inventors of ancient arts.

Among the numerous writers who have transformed the history of Alexander into romance,
some relate that the Macedonian, when in India,
opposed to the elephants of his enemies machines
of bronze, or of iron, which vomited fire, and
which secured his conquest.* Others, on the contrary, describe "the large flashes of flame that
Alexander beheld as showered upon his army, on
the burning plains of India."† These conflicting
recitals have a common foundation, and the tradition
only relates that, in India, a composition analogous
to the Greek fire was employed as an engine of
warfare. It was a composition similar to that which
a sorcerer and a sorceress shot forth from inflamed
jets, mentioned in one of the marvelous narrations
of Hindoo origin. The spectators of the combat,
and the combatants themselves, experienced the
bad effects of it.‡ Fictions of this kind generally
originate in reality. The *fire which burns and
crackles on the bosom of the waves*, instead of being
extinguished, denotes that the Greek fire was
anciently known in Hindostan, under the name of
the fire of *Barrawa*.§ It was employed against
besieged towns. On the banks of the Hyphasis,
an oil was composed, and inclosed in pots of
earth; and, on being shot out against the wood-
works, or the gates of a city, kindled with an un-

* J. Vactrius, *Vit. Alexand.* (discovered and published by M.
Maï), *Biblioth. Univ. Littérature*, vol. vii., pp. 225, 226. Extract
from the romance of *Alexander the Great*, from a Persian manu-
script, &c.—*Bibliothèque des Romans*, Octobre, 1775, tome i.
† This tradition, given in an apocryphal letter of *Alexander to
Aristotle*, has been adopted by Dante, *Inferno*, cant. xiv.
‡ *The Arabian Nights' Entertainments*, 55th night, vol. i., pp.
320–322.
§ *Sacountala ou l'Anneau fatal*, act. iii., sc. 2.

extinguishable flame. The fabrication of this dangerous substance was left to the king; no other person had permission to prepare even a drop of it."[*] This recital by Ctesias has been rejected, because what the historian adds, as to the manner of composing this unextinguishable oil, is thought improbable. He has been assured that it was drawn from a very dangerous *water serpent*. This circumstance does not appear absolutely destitute of truth. Philostratus[†] says that the unextinguishable oil was extracted from a *fresh water* animal, resembling a worm. In Japan, the *inari*, an aquatic lizard, black and venomous, furnishes an oil, which is burned in the temples.[‡] Nothing interferes with the supposition that, in India, the element of the unextinguishable fire—an animal grease or oil—is united to the naphtha for giving more body to the incendiary projectile, and a longer duration to its action. In supposing, moreover, that Ctesias had incorrectly translated and misunderstood the account he received, or that an erroneous account purposely had been given to him, the fact itself does not remain less probable. We again repeat, that we are too apt to accuse the recitals of the ancients of absurdity. To confirm what they had said of the Greek fire, Cardan has indicated the method of preparing fireworks endowed with similar properties.[§] Prompt to refute Cardan, Scaliger,[||] a man more erudite

---

[*] Ctesias in *Indic.*—Ælian, *De Nat. Animal.*, lib. v., cap. iii.

[†] Philostrat., *Vit. Apollon.*, lib. iii., cap. i.—Ælian (*De Nat. Animal.*, lib. v., cap. iii.), quoting Ctesias, also uses the expression $\Sigma\kappa\omega\lambda\eta\xi$, worm; but this worm, which lives in the river Indus, is seven cubits long and of proportionate breadth. From the expression of Ælian it may be inferred that the oil thus prepared is kindled without fire, and by the contact alone of a combustible body.   [‡] Koempfer, *Histoire du Japan*, liv. iii., chap. v., p. 53.

[§] H. Cardan, *De Subtilitate*, lib. ii.

[||] J. C. Scaliger, *Exoteric. ad. Cardan*, xiii , no. 3.

than able, and more presumptuous than erudite, boldly ridiculed those who professed that they could produce physical compositions which, exposed to the rays of the sun, or sprinkled with water, would ignite.   A student of chemistry would ridicule Scaliger for such an opinion, and work, before his eyes, two apparent miracles, which he had declared to be impossible.

CHAPTER X.

Compositions similar to Gunpowder.—Mines worked by it under Herod; by the Christian Priests under the Emperor Julian at Jerusalem; in Syria under the Caliph Motassem; and by the Priests of Delphi, in order to repulse the Persians and Gauls.— Antiquity of the Invention of Gunpowder; its probable Origin in Hindostan; it has been known from Time immemorial in China.—Tartar Army repelled by Artillery.—Priests of India employed the same Means to hurl Thunder upon their Enemies.— The Thunder of Jupiter compared to our Firearms.—Many assumed Miracles explained by the Use of these Arms.—Gunpowder was known in the latter Empire, probably until the Twelfth Century.

PHYSICAL phenomena, and the services that science extracts from them, link the one to the other.   The examination of the brilliant apparent miracles effected by spontaneous inflammations leads us to a discussion of the resources that the Thaumaturgists employed in war to turn fire into an offensive or defensive weapon.   From the facts which we have already quoted, we may presume that very anciently they were in possession of some inflammable composition more or less similar to gunpowder,* and that those tubes which threw out a brilliant fire, with a noise like that of thun-

---

* Dutens (p. 194) supposes that they were actually acquainted with gunpowder.—ED.

der, may have been the first rough delineations of
our cannons and firearms.* We could not then
have been accused of romancing, if we had said
that the ancients possessed, by these means, the
power of imitating the most formidable scourges ;
whether by shaking the earth by mines they saw
it open in chasms at their enemies' feet, or by
sending from afar bolts as burning, speedy, and
inevitably fatal as lightning.

Herod descended into the monument of David
in the hope of finding treasure there. His cupidity
not being satisfied with what he had already found,
he extended his researches, and caused the vaults
in which the remains of David and Solomon were
laid to be opened. A fierce flame suddenly burst
out ; two of the king's guards, suffocated and burned by it, perished.† Michaelis attributes this prodigy to the gas, which, escaping from the vault, was
kindled by the torches destined to light the workmen who were employed in clearing an entrance.‡
But if such had been the case, these latter would
have been the first victims, as the expansion of the
gas must have taken place as soon as an opening
had been effected in the vault. We should rather
think that the priests, who had more than one motive
for hating Herod, and who looked upon the treas
ures inclosed in David's monument as the property
of the theocratic government, being justly indignant at the sacrilegious pillage which the Idumean
prince was committing, sought, by stimulating his
cupidity, to attract him into the interior vault, where
they had prepared the certain means for his de-

---

* Bacon is inclined to think that the Macedonians had a kind
of *magic powder*, in its effects approaching to those of gunpowder.
(*Encyclop. méthod Philosophie*, vol. i., p. 341, col. 1.
    † Josephus, *Ant. Jud.*, lib. xvi., cap. iii.
    ‡ *Magasin Scientifique de Göttingue*, 3e année, 6e cahier, 1783.

struction, if, as they expected, he should be the first to enter it.[*]

Michaelis[†] explains, in the same manner, by the inflammation of subterraneous gas, the miracle which interrupted the works ordered by the Emperor Julian for the restoration of the Temple of Jerusalem, and at which the Christians rejoiced so exceedingly that they were suspected to have been the authors of it. This explanation seems to us even less plausible than the former. If in the globes of fire which shot out from the midst of the rubbish, wounding and putting the workmen to flight—if in the shaking of the ground, and the overthrow of several buildings, we are not to recognize the springing of a mine—we ask, what are the signs by which the springing of a mine is to be recognized?[‡]

* The conjecture of Michaelis is much more probable than the explanation of our author. In long shut up vaults and caverns, carbureted hydrogen gas, fire-damp, as it is termed by miners, frequently form in large quantities, and is instantly fired on coming into contact with a torch or any burning body. Now, as the torches must have been in the hands of the soldiers, not in those of the workmen who preceded them, the gas would pass uninflamed over the workmen and be ignited only when it reached those who held the torches.—Ed.

† *Magasin Scientifique de Göttingue*, loc. cit.

‡ This opinion, so confidently advanced by our author, is not authorized by the account of Ammianus Marcellinus, who witnessed the event, and who, being inimical to the Christians, was not likely to conceal the opinion, if it existed, that the explosions and emissions of fire, which defeated the intention of Julian to rebuild the Jewish temple, were the result of art. The Jews, also, who were eager for the restoration of the temple, would have searched out the artifice and exposed it, had any existed; beside, had the cause which forced Alypius to discontinue the work, been a mine which was sprung, although it might have overthrown the buildings and killed the laborers, yet, it would not have been constantly repeated in the manner described by the historian, who, indeed, evidently ascribes the event to the elements in these expressions : " Hocque modo elemento obstinatius repellente."[*] And also by his statement that " the victorious ele-

* *Ammianus Marcellinus*, lib. xxxiii., cap. i.

We may observe, that neither the Jews of Jerusalem, the Emperor Julian, nor Ammianus Marcellinus, who has transmitted the account of it to us, were converted to Christianity by this miracle.

ments continuing in this manner obstinately and resolutely bent in driving them (the workmen) to a distance, Alypius thought proper to abandon the enterprise." Had the materials for springing several mines been placed in a limited space, and the eruptions confined to one spot, the destruction caused by the first explosion would have rendered any after-attempts to produce the same ineffective. Again, were we to admit that new explosive materials were employed in the subsequent explosions, new excavations must have been made; but any attempts to effect such a purpose could not have been carried on unknown to the Jews and pagans assembled on the spot; yet the eruptions were constantly renewed as soon as the labor was resumed, until they effectually constrained the abandonment of the enterprise. The Editor has no hesitation in saying, that if these explosions and earthquakes were not a real miracle, as he firmly believes they were, there are no data whatever for asserting that they were produced by human art, as our author would imply; and, consequently, although they may ever remain otherwise unexplained, yet they certainly can not be regarded as the result of the springing of a mine. In favor of their being a real miracle, the prohibition of our Savior with regard to the restoration of the temple required to be fulfilled, and it has been accomplished up to the present time: hence we see a purpose which the miracle was intended to fulfill; and, in the event, the operation of a power adequate to the effect. To borrow the language of Dr. Thomas Brown, " the possibility of the occasional direct operation of the power which formed the world, in varying the usual course of its events, it would be in the highest degree unphilosophical to deny; nor even, we presume, to estimate the degree of its probability, since, in many cases, of the wide bearings of which on human happiness we must be ignorant, it might be the result of the same benevolent motives which we must suppose to have influenced the Divine Mind in the original act of creation itself."* Such is also the firm belief of the Editor; and, in the events detailed, he perceives no law of nature violated, and certainly no reason to withhold our faith in the testimony of the historian of the event; on the contrary, we may rationally suppose that the statement given of it by Ammianus was in opposition to his personal interest. The phenomena presented no violation of nature; but, as in every real miracle, it was an extraordinary event, the result of new and peculiar circumstances, and a display intended to sanction the revelations of that Being by whom the universe itself was called into existence. —ED.

---

* *An Inquiry into the Relation of Cause and Effect*, p. 500, notes

If we consult the annals of Greece, we shall find that the priests of Apollo at Delphi, after having announced by the voice of the oracle, that their god knew well how to save his temple, did, in fact, preserve it from the invasion of the Persians, and then from that of the Gauls, by the explosion of mines placed in the rocks that surrounded it. The assailants were crushed by the fall of innumerable blocks of stone, which, in the midst of devouring flames, were rained upon them by an invisible hand.*

Pausanias, who attributes the defeat of the Gauls to an earthquake and a miraculous storm, thus describes their effects: "The lightning not only killed those who were struck by it, but an inflammable exhalation was communicated to those who were near, and reduced them to powder."†

The explosion, however, of many mines, as violent as we could imagine, could not have produced that total destruction of the assailants depicted by the historians. On the contrary, we hear of the same Gauls immediately afterward making a successful incursion into Asia. They had been repulsed, not exterminated, at Delphi.

With regard to the cause assigned for their repulsion, would not the construction, it may be argued, of considerable mines, hollowed in the rocks of Delphi, have required the aid of too many cooperators for the secret to have been so long kept? To this argument it may be answered, that the more simple and toilsome details must have been confided to rude workmen, who could neither dream, guess, nor divulge the intention of them; and that these excavations were probably commenced long beforehand, as in the defensive works

* Herodot., lib. viii., cap. xxxvii.–xxxix.—Justin., lib. xxiv., cap. viii.   † Pausanias, *Phoc.*, cap. xxiii.

of modern strong places, and merely required the fulminating composition to be deposited in them when needed. Historical tradition furnishes us, however, with a more decisive answer. Every Greek, from Delphi to Thermopylæ, was initiated in the mysteries of the temple of Delphi.* Their secrecy, upon every point where silence was commanded, was guarantied, therefore, by a fear of the evils threatened to a perjured revelation, and by a general confession required from each aspirant to this initiation : a confession which rather caused them to fear the indiscretion of the priests than to give the latter occasion to doubt theirs.

We may finally remark, that the god of Delphi, so powerful in protecting his temple from strangers, made no attempt to rescue its wealth from the hands of the Phocians. When these latter drained its resources, in order to defend their country against the hypocritical ambition of Philip, they had probably either obtained or compelled the acquiescence of the priests, and no longer feared a destructive apparent miracle, which could hardly be effected without the consent or the aid of their chiefs.

So customary is it to deem the use of gunpowder of a very modern date, that these remarkable facts have remained unnoticed, or, at least, have merely led to the supposition that ancient nations were acquainted with some composition almost as deadly.† "All that has been written," says M. Na-

---

* Plutarch, *De Oracul. Defect.*

† Various explosive substances are as destructive as gunpowder, and some of them might have been known to the ancients. When a solution of gold in aqua regia is precipitated by ammonia, and the product washed and dried without heat, it becomes fulminating gold. It is exploded by the slightest friction, and even can not be put into a bottle with a glass stopper without the greatest danger. It explodes with a loud noise.
When nitrate of silver is acted upon by nitric acid and alcohol

pione, " by Egidio Colonna,* on instruments of war employed at the end of the thirteenth century, gives rise to a suspicion that the invention of gunpowder is of much more ancient date than we are accustomed to believe, and that this formidable composition was perhaps nothing more than a modification or perfection of the Greek fire, known many centuries before gunpowder was invented in Europe."

We have established the fact, that the invention of the Greek fire belongs to a remote antiquity; and we think that Langles was right in placing that of gunpowder in an equally distant period. The following is the substance of the facts by which he supports his opinion.† The Moors in Spain made use of gunpowder at the commencement of the fourteenth century. From the year 1292, a poet

at the same time, a gray powder is procured, which, being washed and dried, is fulminating silver. The explosive force of this powder is great; it detonates with a tremendous noise on being touched with a glass rod dipped in sulphuric acid.

When mercury is dissolved in nitric acid, and afterward alcohol added, effervescence takes place, and a precipitate is thrown down, which, after being washed and dried with a very gentle heat, forms detonating mercury. It explodes with the least friction.

A mixture of chlorate of potassa and sulphur detonates with friction, and even evolves flame. The noise caused by the explosion of a few grains is equal to that of a musket.

The chloride of nitrogen, which was discovered by M. Dulong, in 1812, is one of the most violent of all detonating substances. It is procured in the form of an oil, and requires the utmost caution both to make it and to preserve it. If a small globule of it be thrown into olive oil, the most violent explosion takes place; and this also happens when it is brought into contact with phosphorus, naphtha, volatile oils, and many other matters.

All these compounds may have been unknown to the ancients; but they are mentioned to show the probability of our ancestors having an acquaintance with many detonating powders beside those which we possess.—ED.

* A Roman monk, who had a share in the education of Philip-le-Bel.—*Memorie della reale Academia delle Scienze di Torino*, tome xxix.—*Revue Encyclopédique*, tome xxx., p. 42.

† Dissertation inserted in the *Magasin Encyclopédique*, fourth year, tome i., pp. 333–338.

of Grenada celebrated this means of destruction
in his verses.   There is also some reason for believing that the Arabs had made use of it against the
fleet of the Crusaders in the time of St. Louis; and
in 690 they employed it in the siege of Mecca.
Missionaries have undeniably proved that gunpowder has been known in China from time immemorial.   It was also known in Thibet and in Hindostan, where fireworks and *fireballs* have been always
used in war, and in public rejoicings.   In districts
of that vast country, where neither Mussulmans nor
Europeans had ever penetrated, iron fusees, attached to a dart, which carried them into the
enemy's ranks by the violence of the powder, have
been found.   The laws collected in the code of the
Gentoos, the antiquity of which is lost in the obscurity of the times, forbid the use of firearms (a
prohibition which, no doubt, prevented them from
becoming common).

These laws make a distinction between *darts of
fire* and those bolts that killed a hundred men at
once: the latter remind us of the effects of our
own cannon.   The Hindoos, though unacquainted
with mortars, hollowed out holes in the rocks, and,
filling them with powder, rained down stones upon
their enemies, precisely like the hail which the
priest of Delphi sent down upon the Persians and
Gauls.   Finally, a commentator of the *Vedas* attributes the invention of gunpowder to *Visvacarma,**
the artist god, who is said to have manufactured
arrows which the gods made use of when fighting
against the evil genii.

From this feature of the Hindoo mythology,
learned from travelers, is it not likely, we may ask,

---

* If this name has, as we are tempted to believe, furnished the
etymology of a French word (*vacarme*), but little known, it would
be inaptly translated " burning power."

that Milton derived the idea of attributing to the
rebel angels the invention of gunpowder and firearms ? Langles has omitted to notice this resemblance ; and, doubtless, the right of poets to invent
appeared to him to weaken very much the authority of their narrations. It was, nevertheless, easy
for him to find, in unexceptionable authorities on
physical facts, the confirmation of his conjectures.
He might have observed that, in China and in
Hindostan, the soil is so impregnated with saltpeter that this salt frequently effloresces on the
surface of the earth : a phenomenon which must
have early suggested and facilitated the confection
of pyrotechnical compositions; and, at the same
time, have rendered the knowledge of them common, in spite of their importance as a part of the
sacred and occult sciences. It is this, also, that
has given to the Asiatic pyrotechnics so great a
preponderance over the European, and a superiority scarcely yet controverted. Both the one and
the other advantages have often excited our incredulity, and prevented us from confessing that others
may be able to perform feats of which we know
nothing. Fontenelle says that in China, according
to the annals of that empire, " thousands of stars
are seen to fall at once from the heavens into the
sea, with a great noise, or to dissolve away into
rain. One star went bursting toward the east,
like a *fusee*, and always with a great noise."[*]
How came it that the ingenious philosopher did
not recognize the effects of fusees and firework
bombs[†] in this description ? It was well known

* Fontenelle, *De la Pluralité des Mondes, sixième soir* (vers. la
fin).

† " A very brilliant meteor, as large as the moon, was seen
finally splitting into sparks, and illuminating the whole valley."
—Ross's *Second Voyage to the North Pole*, chap. xlviii. We might
have thought that the Chinese tradition related to some fact

that the Chinese excelled in composing both ; but Fontenelle preferred jesting on the pretended astronomical science of the Chinese.

With more reason has a remarkable passage from the voyages of Plancarpinus been turned into ridicule.   The Tartars informed this monk that Prester-John, King of Great India (probably a chief of Thibet, or of some nation professing the *Lamish* religion), when attacked by Tossuch, son of Tchinggis-Khan, led against his assailants figures of bronze mounted on horseback. In the interior of these figures was fire, and behind each a man, who *threw within them something* which immediately produced an immense smoke, and enabled the enemies of the Tartars to massacre them.*   It is difficult to believe that an intense smoke would be sufficient to put to flight the companions in arms of Tchinggis.

It is less repugnant to one's prejudices to suppose that these bronze figures might be either small swivel guns, or cannon similar to those used in China, which, by being taken to pieces, could be easily transported about on horses†—pieces of artillery, in short, that most certainly emitted something else beside smoke.   Tossuch's soldiers, unacquainted with these arms, and having in their flight abandoned their dead and wounded, could only tell Plancarpinus of the flames and smoke they had seen ; but we can recognize the real cause of their defeat, which was neither difficult to understand nor miraculous.   We know the intercourse that Thibet, and the nations following the religion of the Lamas, have always held with China.

similar to that which Ross had observed ; but no European had seen such meteors in China, and every traveler boasts of the fireworks of that country.
* *Voyage de Plancarpinus*, art. v., p. 42.
† P. Maffei, *Hist. Indic.*, lib. vi., p. 256.

Now, a grandson of Tchinggis-Khan, in 1245, had in his army a body of Chinese matrosses; and, from the tenth century, they had in China thunder chariots (*chars à foudre*), producing, from the same causes, the same effects as our cannon.[*] Being unable to fix the period when the use of gunpowder, firearms, and artillery was commenced in that empire, national tradition has ascribed the invention to the first king of the country.[†] Now, as this prince was *much versed in magic arts*,[‡] it was not without some reason that we ranked the discovery, of which he has the honor, among the means employed for working apparent miracles.

These affinities strengthen, instead of affecting the opinion of Langles, which ascribed the invention of gunpowder to the Hindoos, from whom China, no doubt, received her civilization and arts, as well as her popular religion.

The Greeks were not ignorant of the formidable power of the weapons which were prepared in India by a secret process. Philostratus describes the sages who dwelt between the Hyphasis and the Ganges, as lanching forth with redoubled fury lightning upon their enemies, and thus repelling the aggressions of Bacchus and the Egyptian Hercules.[§]

We may recall to remembrance the particular arrows with which the gods of Hindostan armed themselves against the evil genii. In the Greek mythology, distantly, but decidedly derived from the Hindoo, the gods are described as fighting

---

[*] Abel Remusat's *Memoirs upon the Political Relations of the Kings of France to the Mongol Emperors.*—*Asiatic Journal*, vol. i., p. 137.

[†] P. Maffei, *Hist. Indic.*, loc. cit.

[‡] Linschott's *Travels in China*, 3d edit., p. 53.

[§] Philostrat,, *Vit. Apollon.*, lib. ii., cap. xiv. ; lib. iii., cap. iii.—Themist., *Orat.* xxvii.

against the rebellious Titans, and securing their
victory by similar terrible arms. The numerous
points of resemblance, indeed, in the details of
these battles assimilate the weapons of the king of
the gods and men to modern artillery. " The Cyclops," says the historian Castor,* "assisted Jupiter
against the Titans with dazzling lightnings and
thunder." In the war of the gods against the
giants, Vulcan, according to Apollodorus, killed
Clytius,† by sending fiery stones against him.
Typhon, brought forth by the earth to avenge the
giants, sent *fiery stones* flying against the heavens,
while from his mouth issued flames of fire. " The
brothers of Saturn," says Hesiod,‡ "freed from
their bonds by Jupiter, gave to him the thunder,
the dazzling lightnings, and thunderbolt, *which
had been inclosed in the center of the earth ;* and by
these weapons secured to this god his empire over
men and immortals."

It is from the bosom of the earth that saltpeter,
sulphur, and bitumen, which most probably composed the fulminating substance of the ancients, are
taken. Minerva alone, of all the divinities, knew
where the thunder§ was kept; the Cyclops alone
understood the manufacture of it; and Jupiter
severely punished Apollo for having attempted the
life of these invaluable artists. Now, if we set
aside the mythological ideas attached to these
names and recitals, we shall fancy that we are
reading the history of a prince, to whom some individual, from gratitude, had imparted the secret
of fabricating gunpowder, and who was as jealous

* Euseb., *Chronic. Canon.*, lib. i., cap. xiii., note. This im-
portant passage is only found in the Armenian version published
by Zorhab and Maï.
† Apollodor., *Bibliothec.*, lib. i., cap. v.
‡ Hesiod, *Theogon.*, vers. 502–507.
§ Æschyl., *Eumenid.*, vers. 829–831.

of the exclusive possession of it, as the Byzantine emperors were of reserving to themselves the secret of the Greek fire.

The resemblance between the effects of thunder and those of the inflammable compound we have noticed is so striking, that it has been recorded in all the historical and mythological narrations : nor did it escape the observation of the natives of the continent discovered by Christopher Columbus, and conquered by Cortes and Pizarro. These unfortunate people took their conquerors for gods armed with thunder, until they obtained the knowledge for which they had paid dearly, namely, the right of knowing in their persecutors only malevolent spirits and enemies to humanity.

This resemblance explains a passage which Pliny probably borrowed from some ancient poet, and which has been the torment of his commentators. In treating of the origin of magic, Pliny expresses his surprise that this art had been dispersed over Thessaly from the time of the siege of Troy, before which time Mars alone directed the thunder (*solo Marte fulminante*). Is there not a visible allusion to the power possessed by the sacred science, and which magic, originating in the temples, aimed at arrogating to itself, the power of producing lightning, as well as that of arming itself with it in battle, and of producing explosions equaling claps of thunder ?

Finally, it explains the death of Alexander's soldiers, who, having penetrated into the temple of the Cabira, near Thebes, perished there, struck by lightning and thunder :* and also the story of Porsenna† killing, with one stroke of lightning, a monster which ravaged the lands of his subjects.

* Pausanias, *Bætic.*, cap. **xxv.**
† Plin., *Hist. Nat.*, lib. ii., cap. liii.

II.   O

In addition to these, we may mention the presumption of the Etruscan magicians who, when Rome was threatened with a siege from Alaric, offered to repel the enemy, by sending down upon him lightning and thunder; boasting that they had effected this miracle at Narnia, a town which did not, in fact, fall into the power of the Gothic king.[*]

But, it may be asked, how came an art which was known to the Christians of the fourth century, to the Etruscan magicians at the end of the fifth, and preserved until the ninth century in Syria, to fall into oblivion? And why, for instance, did the historian Ducas describe the *falconets* used against Amurat II., by the defenders of Belgrade,[†] as a novel invention, utterly unknown to his countrymen? In reply, I may inquire, how have so many other arts perished which were more widely dispersed and more immediately useful than those referred to? And, beside, the secret imposed by severe laws against revealing the composition of the Greek fire may have existed as strictly with respect to other important compositions.

I may, nevertheless, venture to affirm that this art was not lost until a more recent period in the latter empire. In the fifth century, Claudian describes in verse fireworks, and particularly the *burning suns*.[‡] Anthemus of Tralles, the architect, who, under Justinian, traced out the designs and

---

[*] Sozomen, *Hist. Eccles.*, lib. ix., cap. vi. If we may believe Zozimus (*Hist. Rom.*, lib. v.) the Bishop of Rome had consented that the magicians should attempt the fulfillment of their promises; but they were sent away, on account of the repugnance of the people to their proposal, and the town capitulated.

[†] Ducas, *Hist. Imp. Joann, &c.*, cap. xxx.

[‡]   Inque chori speciem spargentes ardua flammas
       Scena rotet: varios effingat Mulciber orbes,
       Per tabulas impunè vagus; pictæque citato
       Ludent igne trabes; et non permissa morari,
       Fida per innocuas errent incendia turres.
          Claudian, *De Mall. Theodos. consulat.*, vers. 325–329.

directed the construction of the church of St. Sophia,* is reported to have sent lightning and thunder upon the house adjoining his own.† Another learned man points out a process for the manufacture of fire to be sent against the enemy, which reminds us of the composition of our gunpowder.‡ In short, the same composition for making it, and in the proportions used in the present day, is described by Marcus Græcus,§ who certainly did not live later than the twelfth century, and has been thought by some to have existed before the ninth. It would, no doubt, be curious to trace out these inventions from the period when they still existed in the latter empire to that in which they became spread over Europe. One obstacle, difficult to overcome, is opposed to this investigation, namely, that ignorance which, disdaining the simple truth, and eager after the marvelous, first treated as miracles, and then rejected as fabulous, the very histories that might have instructed us.

CHAPTER XI.

The Thaumaturgists might have worked pretended Miracles with the Air-gun, the Power of Steam, and the Magnet.—The Compass was probably known to the Phocians, as well as the Phœnician Navigators.—The Finns have a Compass of their own; and in China the Compass had been used since the Foundation of the Empire.—Other Means of working pretended Miracles.—Galvanic Phenomena.—Action of Vinegar upon Lime.—Amusements of Physics.—Lachryma Batavica, &c.

WE approach the termination of our career. Brilliant as may have been the promises we placed

* Procop., *De Ædific. Justiniani*, lib. i., cap. xxii.
† Agathias, *De Rebus Justiniani*, lib. v., cap. iv.
‡ Julius Africanus, cap. xliv.—Veter. Mathem., edit. Paris p. 303.
§ Marcus Græcus, *Liber Ignium ad comburendos hostes*, edit. de La Porte du Theil, Paris, 1804.

in the mouth of the Thaumaturgist, we believe we have proved that it would not have been impossible for him to accomplish many of them.

The subject is not yet, however, wholly exhausted. We might draw upon the knowledge possessed by the ancients, as affording more than one means of accounting for many marvels.

In speaking of missile weapons, we have not included those set in motion by the elasticity of compressed air. Even in the present day, the display of an air-gun, sending out some deadly projectile, without noise or explosion, would present a miraculous appearance to men who were indifferently educated.   Philo, of Byzantium,* who must have flourished in the third century before our era, has left an exact description of the air-gun.   He does not claim the invention ; and no one would dare to decide how far it may or may not have been of ancient date.†

Many historians speak of poisoned needles, projected through a tube by the breath ;‡ and in the

* *Revue Encyclopédique*, tome xxiii., p. 529. Philo was an architect, and built a dock at Athens.—Ed.

† The air-gun expels the ball by the sudden expansion of strongly condensed air, in a hollow ball screwed on to the barrel of the gun immediately under the lock.   The bullet is charged with the air by means of a condensing syringe before it is screwed on the barrel.   When it is to be used, the ball is introduced into the empty barrel ; and the trigger being pulled, opens a valve which admits the condensed air to rush from the hollow ball, and, acting upon the bullet, to impel it to the distance of sixty or seventy yards, according to the degree of condensation of the discharged air.   If the condensation be twenty times that of atmospheric air, the velocity of the bullet will be equal to one seventh of that caused by gunpowder, the elasticity of the gas formed by the inflammation of which is equal to one thousand times that of common air.   No noise accompanies the expulsion of the bullet: hence the astonishment in the mind of a person wholly ignorant of the nature of the air-gun would be greatly increased.—Ed.

‡ Some of the tribes in South America, and on the coast of Africa, impel small poisoned arrows through long tubes in this manner, and thus kill their prey, or victims, at a considerable distance.—Ed.

abridgment of Dion Cassius,* we find two instances of this crime having been committed with
impunity.   The rapidity with which the poison of
these needles acts must, in particular cases, have
rendered their effects more marvelous.   Some
Frenchmen employed in the service of Hyder Ali
and Tippoo Saib saw the prick of poisoned needles
cause death in less than two minutes, neither am-
putation nor any other means being of the least
use in preventing the fatal event.   The ancients
were acquainted with poisons no less rapid.†   We
repeat once more, therefore, what we have frequently had occasion to say, namely, that with such
a secret, how easy must it have been to work apparent miracles !

The expansive power of water, when converted
into steam, is an agent, by the use of which, in the
present day, the aspect of the mechanical arts has
been completely changed ; and which, engrafting
upon them an ever increasing progress, has prepared for future generations an aid to industry, the
results of which we are unable to predict.   We
may inquire, was this agent absolutely unknown
to the ancients ?   Did not Aristotle and Seneca,
when they attributed earthquakes to the action of
water, suddenly vaporized by subterranean heat,
point out a principle, the application of which
alone remained to be tried ?   And did not Hero,
of Alexandria, a hundred and twenty years before
our era, demonstrate how steam might be used for
giving to a hollow sphere a rotatory movement ?‡

* Xiphilin in *Domitian* . . . . in *Commod.*
† The Gauls impregnated their arrows with so powerful a poison, that the hunters made great haste to cut from the animal
they had hit that part touched by the arrow, lest the venomous
substances should infect and corrupt the entire mass of flesh.
‡ Arago, *Notice sur les Machines à Vapeur.—Almanach du Bu-
reau des Longitudes*, 1829, pp. 147–151.

We shall quote, in conclusion, two remarkable facts, one of which belongs to Anthemus of Tralles, a learned man of the latter empire, to whom we have already referred. It is related by Agathias, his cotemporary, that, in order to revenge himself upon the inhabitant of the house next his own, he filled several vessels with water, upon which he fixed copper tubes, very narrow at the upper end, but sufficiently large at the lower extremities to cover the vases to which they were hermetically sealed. He applied the upper openings to the rafters supporting the roof of the house which was the object of his anger; then, causing the water to boil, the steam soon rose in the tubes, expanded, and affected the rafters opposing its escape with violent movement.* The coppers, it may be said, would have burst a hundred times before one rafter would have been lightly shaken. True,— but, we may ask, were these tubes really copper? And might not the philosopher of Tralles encourage such an erroneous opinion, in order to conceal and to preserve to himself the secret of this proceeding? Strange, therefore, as is the explanation related by the credulous Agathias, it clearly indicates that Anthemus was acquainted with the gigantic powers of steam.†

Another example conducts us to the banks of the Weser, where *Busterich* received the homage of the Teutons. His image was of metal, and hollow; it was filled with water, and the orifices,

* Agathias, *De Rebus Justiniani*, lib. v., cap. iv.
† The same historian has also adopted (loc. cit.) an erroneous explanation of the marvel quoted by us at the conclusion of the preceding chapter. According to him, Anthemus had managed it by means of burning-machines and a concave mirror, the movement of which made the dazzling reflections of the sun to fly here and there. So slight an artifice would not have persuaded a man, who was, like Anthemus's enemy, a little instructed, that they were sending the lightning against his dwelling.

or openings for the eyes and the mouth, were closed
with wooden wedges. When burning coals were
placed upon its head, the steam forced out the
wedges with an explosion, and escaped in torrents
of vapors from within*—a most certain sign of
the god's anger in the minds of his rude adorers.

If, passing from a nation a little civilized, we
look into the very infancy of society, we shall observe a similarity between the miraculous image
of the Teutonic god and the missile weapons used
by the natives of New Guinea, the explosion of
which, although they were not muskets,† was accompanied by smoke; a fact which seems to indicate their impelling power to have been analogous
to steam. It would be curious to investigate this
matter!

Are we also certain that we know how far the
ancient Thaumaturgists made use of the magnet?
Its attractive property was so far understood by
them, that it was employed, it is said, for suspending a statue from the vault of a temple.‡ This

* *Tollii Epistolæ Itinerariæ*, pp. 34, 35.
† *Nouvelles Annales des Voyages*, tome i., p. 73.
‡ Vitruvius (*De Archit.*, lib. iv.) and Pliny (*Hist. Nat.*, lib. xxiv.)
say that this marvel was projected, but not executed. Suidas,
Cassiodorus, Isidore of Seville, and Ausonius, speak positively
of its existence. According to Ausonius (*Eidyllium x., Mosella,*
vers. 314–320), Dinochares, by this means, elevated to the vault of
the temple the image of Arsinoe, the wife and sister of Ptolemy
Philadelphus: an iron hidden from sight by the hair of the statue
being attached to a magnet in the summit of the vault. Suidas
(verbo Μάγνης) speaks of a statue of Serapis, which, he says, was
of brass (probably plate copper), and supported by the same artifice. Cassiodorus (*Variar.*, lib. i., p. 45) and Isodorus (*Origin.*, lib.
xvi., cap. 4) say that, suspended to the vault of one of the temples
of Diana, was an iron statue (doubtless of very thin iron plate),
which, according to the first of these writers, was a statue of Cu-
pid. Isidorus says that it was held there by the power of the
magnet, a particular and important feature in the narrative, which
Cassiodorus passed over in silence. Vitruvius and Pliny, being
more ancient, may have been better informed than the writers of
the latter empire: but in order to show that these may not have

tradition, whether true or false, shows that the ancients may probably have taken advantage of magnetic attraction in working pretended miracles.

· The attractive power of the magnet was not unknown to the ancients ; but, following the custom adopted for increasing the veil of mystery, they affirmed, and attempted to make it generally believed, that this property belonged to one species of magnet only, namely, that of Ethiopia.* We are well aware, in the present day, of the effects displayed by magnetic attraction and repulsion in the exhibitions of experimental philosophy ; and let us remember that, in the temples, such performances would have been looked upon as miracles.

Modern Europe claims the discovery of the principle that regulates the compass ;† but this preten-

sinned against probability, it will be only sufficient to state that the statue may have been hollow and light, and the magnet very strong.

The fable, which is extensively known, touching the coffin of Mohammed, which is said to be suspended to the vault of a mosque, furnishes an example of the inclination which men have of naturalizing among themselves wonders borrowed from a foreign country and religion ; nevertheless, a gross counterfeit does not destroy the possibility of a fact, however much it may bear the appearance of improbability.

* Isid., *Hispal. Origin.*, lib. xvi., cap. iv.

† For the sake of some of our readers, it may be necessary to state that the compass consists of a flat bar of steel, which, being repeatedly rubbed with a magnet, and fixed upon a delicate pivot, takes a direction nearly corresponding to the meridian. When used for marine purposes, the needle is placed on a steel pivot, which works in an agate socket let into the center of the magnetized bar. A circular card is divided into thirty-two parts, or points, and these subdivided, so as to form three hundred and sixty points at the circumference. It is attached to the needle, with its point to the North Pole, marked usually by a kind of *fleur-de-lis*. The whole apparatus is fixed in a circular box, in such a manner that the card and needle are always level, and move freely, and yet so as not to be deranged by sudden concussions. As far as regards Europe, the compass was first used at sea by Seig. B. Givaia, of Naples, in the thirteenth century.—ED.

sion may be contested.   A remarkable passage in the Odyssey has inspired an English scholar with a very ingenious conjecture on this point. Alcinous* tells Ulysses that the Phocian vessels are regulated and guided by a spirit.   Unlike common boats, they require, says he, no helmsman or pilot; and, in spite of the profound darkness of the night and the haze, they traverse the ocean with the greatest rapidity, running no risk of being wrecked.   Mr. William Cook† explains this passage, by supposing that the Phocians understood the use of the compass, and that they had learned it from the Phœnicians.

Upon this conjecture we shall offer some observations :

1st. His author might rely upon what Homer several times‡ says of the swift sailing of the Phocian vessels.   Directed at large by the compass, their speed must, in fact, have appeared prodigious to navigators accustomed and forced to coast, from the fear of losing sight of land for too long a period.

2d. The figurative style characterizing the passage quoted belongs to a secret which the poet knew only by its results.   Homer thus transforms a natural fact into a miracle ; and, when he relates that Neptune, unwilling that the Phocians should save more strangers from the perils of the sea, had changed into a rock the vessel which brought back Ulysses to his country, adopts this opinion, the origin of which we have already pointed out,§ in order to explain that the art which had rendered

---

* Homer, *Odyss.*, lib. viii., vers. 553–563.
† William Cook, *An Inquiry into the Patriarchal and Druidical Religion, &c.*, in 4to., London, 1754, p. 22.
‡ Homer, *Odyss.*, lib. vii., viii., et xiii.
§ Refer to chap. iii., vol. i.

navigation so secure was lost from among the subjects of Alcinous.

3d. That the Phœnicians should have understood
the use of the compass it is not difficult to believe,
particularly when we remember the frequent voyages their navigators made to the British Isles: but
there is nothing to prove that they communicated
this secret to the inhabitants of Corcyra. Homer,
who is so exact in collecting all traditions relative
to the communication between the ancient Greeks
and the East, is silent upon this point. But he informs us that the Phocians dwelt for a long time
near the Cyclops, and had but recently separated
from them; and, at the same time, he terms the
Cyclops *very ingenious men :** an appropriate expression when applied to artists learned in the do-
cimasic and pyrotechnic arts, and who, for more
than thirty centuries, have left their names on
the gigantic monuments of architecture in Italy,
Greece, and Asia. We have elsewhere established,† and, perhaps, with some probability, that the
Cyclops, like the Curetes, belonged to a learned
tribe, who had come from Asia to civilize and
govern some of the Pelasgian nations of Greece.
It is not surprising that the Phocians should have
profited by the instructions of this caste, before becoming so tired of its despotism as to have separated from it forever. We can even discern why
their good fortune or skill in their voyages ceased
soon after this separation. The father of Alcinous
had decided upon it, and under the reign of Alcinous the Phocians renounced navigation. Might
it not have been because the instruments obtained
from the liberality of their ancient masters had

* Homer, *Odyss.*, lib. vii., vers. 4-8.
† *Historical and Philosophical Essay upon the Names of Men,
Nations, and Places*, § 81, vol. ii., pp. 161-172.

been destroyed, and that they were ignorant how to reconstruct others?

It remains only to prove that the Cyclops did possess so valuable a knowledge—a proof which is nearly impossible.

We only know that they came from Lycia* into Asia; but they might have only crossed Lycia, and have come from some more interior country of Asia, like the hyperborean Olen, when, with hymns and a religious faith, he brought the elements of civilization into Greece.

It was from the extremities of Asia also that there came into Greece and Italy that northern or Scythian Abaris, said to be endowed by the god he worshiped with an arrow, by the assistance of which he could overrun the universe. It has been poetically said, and repeated by Suidas and Iamblichus, that, by the virtue of this precious gift, Abaris *traversed the winds*.† This expression has been taken in its strictest sense; but Iamblichus adds, immediately afterward, that "Pythagoras deprived Abaris of *the golden arrow with which he steered his course* (*qua se gubernabat*); that, having thus robbed him, and having hidden the arrow, without which he was unable to discover the track he should follow, Pythagoras compelled him to explain its nature.‡ If, instead of the pretended arrow, we substitute a magnetic needle of the same form and large dimensions, gilded to preserve it from rust, instead of an absurd fable, we shall have in the narration of Iamblichus a real fact, related by a man who had not penetrated its scientific mystery.

---

* Lycia was a Pelasgian settlement.—ED.

† Suidas, verbo *Abaris*.—Iamblich., *Vit. Pythagor.*, cap. **xxviii.** —See also Herodot., lib. iv., § 36.—Diod. Sic., lib. iii., cap. **xi.**

‡ Iamblich., loc. cit.

All this, nevertheless, offers us only conjectures more or less probable. Let us quote a fact. The Finns possess a compass which could not possibly have been given to them by Europeans, and the use of which among them can be traced to ages unknown. It presents this peculiarity: it describes the rising and setting of the sun in summer and winter, in a manner that could only agree with the latitude of 49° 20'.[*] This latitude crosses in Asia the whole of Tartary, the Scythia of the ancients. It is that under which Bailly was led to place the nation which might be called " inventors of the sciences;"[†] and that, too, in which, as Volney[‡] has remarked, the *Boundehesch*, or fundamental book of religion of Zoroaster, was written. If we follow it, we are conducted in the East to that portion of Tartary, the population of which—sometimes conquerors, sometimes subjects—were yet intimately connected with the Chinese Empire. Now, the ancient existence of the compass in China has been denied by no one;[§] and we can not regard as false the tradition,[||] according to which a Chinese hero, a long time before our era, successfully made use of the magnet to guide his march in the midst of darkness.

As the compass was known at the same time

---

* *Nouvelles Annales des Voyages*, tome xvii., p. 414.

† Bailly, *Lettres sur l'Origine des Sciences.—Lettres sur l'Atlantide.*

‡ Volney, *Œuvres Complètes*, tome iv., pp. 202, 203.

§ The Chinese trace the use of the compass among themselves to the reign of Hoang-ti 2600 B.C. There is mention made of magnetic chariots, or bearers of compasses, in the historical memoirs of Szu-ma-thsian, 1110 B.C.—J. Klaproth, *Letter upon the Origin of the Compass.—Bulletin of the Geographical Society*, second series, vol. ii., p. 221.

|| Abel Remusat, *Memoirs upon the Political Relations between the Kings of France and the Mongol Emperors.—Asiatic Journal*, vol. i., p. 137. The Hindoos made use of the compass, and there is nothing to prove that they received it from the Europeans.

among the Chinese and the Finns, it is but natural to recollect that the use of family names, unknown in Europe for so long a period, but existing from antiquity in China, seems to have passed from the latter country to the Samoyedes, the Bashkirs, and the Laplanders.* This extension in the dark ages of so useful and popular an institution, points out to us the route which the disciples of the learned caste, the possessors of a secret capable of displaying miracles, apparent, useful, and brilliant, might possibly have taken in emigrating westward. It renders probable an opinion, which at first might seem chimerical, that the knowledge of the magnet came from the latitude beneath which the religion of Zoroaster sprang,† into those western countries of Asia Minor where this religion was already established, and where it had naturalized the practice of working apparent miracles peculiar to the worshipers of fire.‡

* Eusèbe Salverte, *Essai Historique et Philosophique sur les Noms d'Hommes, de Peuples, et de Lieux,* § 21, tome i., pp. 35–44.

† Isidore de Seville (*Origin.*, lib. xvi., cap. iv.) says that the magnet was first found in India, and consequently received the name of *lapis indicus*; but this isolated and vague fact does not seem a sufficient reason for us to seek for the origin of the compass in Hindostan.

‡ The idea suggested by the author, that the knowledge of the magnet, consequently of the compass, came from the East, is ingenious, and most probably correct. Both, assuredly, were known in China, Japan, and India, from a period of high antiquity, although they were unknown to European nations until the twelfth century. It does not, however, appear that, although the Chinese had long before employed the compass on land, it was not used by them for maritime purposes until the dynasty of Tsin, which existed in A.D. 419; at least there is no direct proof that such was the case. It is stated in the great dictionary, Poi-wen-yeu-fou, that "there were then ships directed to the South by the needle." That it was generally known as a guide at sea, to the Asiatic nations, may be inferred from the following passage, contained in a MS. written in 1242, by Baiiak Kibdjaki, and quoted in the *Penny Cyclopædia* (art. *History of the Compass*): " The captains who navigate the Syrian Sea, when the night is so dark as to conceal from view the stars which might direct their

We must hasten to add, in order to forestall objections, in which a natural partiality would be
mingled with a just love of truth, that the existence
of particular knowledge in antiquity, and among

course according to the position of the four cardinal points, take
a basin full of water, which they shelter from the wind by
placing it in the interior of the vessel; they then drive a needle
into a wooden peg or a cornstalk, so as to form the shape of a
cross, and throw it into the basin of water, on the surface of
which it floats. They afterward take a loadstone, of sufficien
size to fill the palm of the hand, or even smaller, bring it to the
surface of the water, give to their hands a rotatory motion toward
the right, so that the needle turns on the surface of the water';
they then suddenly withdraw this hand and the magnet, when
the two points of the needle face north and south. They gave
me ocular demonstration of this process during our voyage from
Syria to Alexandria in the year 640 (of the Hegira)." The use
made of it on land by the Chinese, formerly referred to, is founded
on the following story, connected with the history of a Chinese
hero named Tehi-yeou, the truth of which is admitted to be undoubted :—

" Tehi-yeou bore the name of Kiann; he was related to the
emperors Yan-ti. He delighted in war and turmoil. He made
swords, lances, and large crossbows, to oppress and devastate
the empire. He called and brought together the chiefs of provinces; his grasping disposition and avarice exceeded all bounds.
Yan-ti-wang, unable any longer to keep him in check, ordered
him to withdraw himself to Chae-hao, in order that he might
detain him in the west. Tehi-yeou, nevertheless, persisted more
and more in his perverse conduct. He crossed the river Yang-
choui, ascended the Kieounae, and gave battle to the Emperor
Yang-ti at Khoung-sang. Yan-ti was Hinan-yuan, the proper
name of the emperor. Houang-ti then collected the forces of the
vassals of the empire, and attacked Tehi-yeou in the plains of
Tehou-lou. The latter raised a thick fog, in order that, by
means of the darkness, he might spread confusion in the enemy's
army. But Hinan-yuan constructed a chariot *for indicating the
South, in order to distinguish the four cardinal points,* by means
of which he pursued Tehi-yeou and took him prisoner."* It
appears also that the Chinese used the compass for maritime
purposes in the third century of the Christian era; it was also, as
stated above, employed on the coast of Syria before it came into
general use in Europe; and although the Syrian compass was
of a very rude construction, yet it was sufficient for navigating
their vessels at night. Vasco de Gama, when he doubled the
cape of Good Hope, found the Indian pilots expert in the use of
the compass.—Ed.

* Davies's *Early History of the Mariner's Compass.—British Annual,*
1837.

nations long unknown to us, does not prove that
the Europeans did not in modern times really invent the arts and sciences, the discovery of which
they claim, and which they have undoubtedly rediscovered. The art of typography is as ancient in
Thibet and China as the histories of these countries; but it is less than four centuries ago since
Faust, Schöeffer, and Guttenberg enriched European civilization with it. It is sixteen or seventeen lusters since the progress of science has enabled us to recognize in the narrations of antiquity
the art of conducting lightning, rediscovered by
Franklin. The learned, perplexed in determining
the precise period of the reinvention of the compass and of gunpowder, have no less difficulty in
stating that the use of either has been known over
Europe for not more than five or six hundred
years. The secrets of thaumaturgy must have
been very numerous, since the learned caste studied the physical sciences only with the view of
finding in them, almost with every new discovery,
a fresh means of astonishing, alarming, and govern-
ing the multitude. If, then, many of these secrets
have irrecoverably perished with the priests and
the temples, there may be others, the .memory of
which, entombed in some ancient documents beneath a fabulous covering, will some day emerge
from their graves, awakened by fortunate events;
in effecting the disinterment of which, without
doing less honor to the human mind, their authors
will nevertheless be but reinventors.

We might proffer some specimens of this kind.
Chance revealed to Cotugno the first phenomena
of galvanism, as accident also afterward revealed
them to Galvani, who has merited the title of the
discoverer, from having brought to perfection, by
reasoning and investigation, a knowledge at first

fortuitous. If chance had enriched some ancient
Thaumaturgist with the same discovery, with what
apparent miracles would he not have electrified
his admirers, even although he had merely limited
himself to the first principles of galvanism, and to
the experiments which they might place in his
power upon the bodies of animals recently deprived of life.* Even in the eighteenth century
we have witnessed men who pretended from some

---

* Galvanism is a modification of electricity, which is capable
of producing on bodies effects not usually obtained from ordinary
electrical excitation. The first display of its power was noticed
by Subzer, a German, who found that when a disk of lead is
placed under the tongue, and one of silver over the tongue, and
the edges of both metals are brought into contact, a peculiar
taste is perceived ;* but he pursued the inquiry no further.
Other fortuitous incidents afterward might have led to the discovery, but, for the reason stated in the text, Galvani, professor
of anatomy at Bologna, is justly regarded as its discoverer. It is
unnecessary, here, to enter upon the general phenomena produced, both on organic and inorganic matter, by galvanism ; but,
in order to demonstrate how it might be employed to excite
astonishment and even terror, and, consequently, become an instrument of power over the ignorant and the superstitious, in
periods of less general intellectual cultivation than the present, I
will only mention a few of its physiological effects. If a piece
of tinfoil, attached to the extremity of a wire connected with one
pole of a galvanic pile, be placed on the tongue, and the bent extremity of another wire from the opposite pole be pressed upon
the inner corner of the eye, a flash of light and a sensation of a
blow on the eye will be immediately perceived by the person
thus treated. When a current of galvanism is passed along a
nerve to any muscles of voluntary motion, these muscles are
thrown into convulsive contraction, even if the animal has been
dead for a short time, as long as the muscles retain their irri-
tability. Aldini operated on the body of a criminal executed at
Newgate : the convulsive movements were such as might have
excited a belief that the dead man was restored to the power of
sensation ; and, from the terrific expressions of human passion
and agony, that he was enduring the most intense suffering. I
may again repeat, what extent of power would such experiments
have, placed in the hands of those who aimed to deceive the
credulous into the conviction that the whole was the result of
supernatural agency ; a deception easily effected were the instru
ment concealed, and the wires only brought into view.—Ed.

* *Theorie des Plaisirs*, p. 115.

internal feeling, or by the aid of a divining rod, to discover the springs concealed in the earth at depths more or less considerable.* Edrisi relates that a caravan traversing Northern Africa was nearly perishing from thirst upon a barren and sandy soil, when one of the travelers, a black Berberi man, taking a little of the earth up and smelling it, pointed out a spot where they might dig and find a spring of water.† His prediction was instantly verified. Place a charlatan in such a situation, he would pride himself upon having performed a miracle, and the gratitude of his companions in danger would support his pretensions.

In the month of August, 1808, an egg was found upon the altar of the Patriarchal Church at Lisbon, bearing upon its shell the sentence of death of all the French, although there did not appear to be traces of the writing being the production of the hand of man. This apparent miracle caused much anxious excitement among the Portuguese, until the French distributed throughout the town, and had placed in all the churches, an immense number of eggs, upon the shells of which the contradiction of this lie was written; at the same time proclamations were everywhere posted up, ex-

---

* The divining rod is a forked branch of hazel, or even any tree, which, if carried slowly along, loosely suspended in the hand, is said to dip toward the ground when brought over the spot where a mine or a spring is situated. Compared with other divinations, this rod is of recent introduction, and demonstrates that superstitious credence and impudent imposture are not confined to any age; and humanity is humbled in beholding men with considerable pretensions to science believers in the powers ascribed to the divining rod. Thevenot published a memoir on the relation of the phenomena of this rod to those of electricity and magnetism; and Pryce, our countryman, in his work entitled *Mineralogia Cambriensis*, published in 1778, has collected accounts of many successful experiments which he affirms were performed by it.—Ed.

† Edrisi (*traduction Française*), lib. i , cap. xxii.

plaining the secret of the supposed miracle, which consisted in writing upon the shell, when covered with an oily substance, and then plunging and re-taining the egg for some time in an acid.*

By the same method, letters or hieroglyphics can be engraved, either grooved or in relief, upon a tablo of calcareous stone, leaving behind no traces of a mortal hand. Now, the ancients were acquainted with the strong action of vinegar upon such stones, although they have somewhat exaggerated it, by adopting the story which they have recorded in history of the passage of the Alps by Hannibal.†

The area of the base of a vessel compared with its height, whatever may be its form, is the measure of the pressure of the liquid it contains. This principle, which explains the powerful action of the hydrostatic press, may possibly have been known in the ancient temples; and how easy would it not have rendered the execution of many apparent miracles? Indeed, is it not very closely resembling a miracle, when the effect produced appears so greatly disproportioned to its actual cause? What more wonderful than the enormous pressure which the small quantity of liquid necessary to produce it causes?‡

* P. Thiebault, *Relation de l'Expédition de Portugal*, pp. 170, 171.

† Plin., *Hist. Nat.*, lib. xxxiii., cap. i. et ii.—Dion. Cass., lib. xxxvii., cap. viii. Might not the story this refers to have its origin in some manœuver employed by Hannibal to restore to his troops that courage which the multiplicity of the obstacles they had to overcome were depriving them of?

‡ Without entering into any explanation of the nature of this machine, some idea of its power may be given by simply stating the fact that, in a machine the area of the section of the piston of which is sixty-four inches, that of the valve admitting the water into the cylinder is an eighth of an inch, and the power of the pump applied to it is one tun, the pressure effected by it will be four thousand and ninety-six tuns!—Ed.

Let us descend, however, to the amusements of experimental philosophy. Let us suppose that the ancient Thaumaturgists were acquainted with inventions, the singular effects of which will always astonish the vulgar—the Lachryma Batavica,* for instance, or the Bologna matrasses ;† even the games of children, such as the kaleidóscope,‡ or those little dolls which, when placed upon musical tables or instruments, move in time, and turn one another round, as in waltzing.§ If it be possible to effect wonders by such insignificant means, are we not right in concluding that an immense number of the assumed miracles of antiquity proceeded from similar causes ? The means are lost, but the remembrance of the effects remain.

We might multiply such suppositions, but we think we have said enough to attain our object.

* Tears of glass, which may be struck by a hammer upon their spherical surface without breaking, but which fall into powder as soon as the thread which forms the tail of the tear is broken.

† Little pear-shaped bottles of unannealed white glass, within which balls of marble or of ivory may be rolled, without injuring them ; but if a fragment of flint, although no larger than a grain of hemp seed, fall into them, they break in the hand into five or six pieces. These matrasses and Batavian tears are truly interesting to curiosity. They are now seldom manufactured; and when the time arrives, long after they shall have ceased to be made, the account of them will appear a fable, and we shall refuse to believe in their wonderful properties.

‡ The kaleidoscope is a small instrument invented by Sir David Brewster. It consists of a cylindrical tube, containing two reflecting surfaces inclined to each other at any angle which is an aliquot part of 360°, and having their edges in contact, so as to have the form of a half-opened book. When any object is placed in the tube, so as to be reflected by the above surfaces, and the other end of the tube is applied to the eye, and turned round, an ever varying succession of splendid tints and beautiful symmetrical forms are perceived ; sometimes vanishing from the center, sometimes emerging from it, and sometimes playing around it in double and opposite oscillations in the most pleasing manner.—ED.

§ This game was known, when invented, under the name of *danso-musicomanes.*

Setting aside every thing belonging to sleight of hand, to imposture, or the illusions of the imagination, there are none of the ancient apparent miracles that may not be reproduced by any person well versed in the modern science, either immediately, or by applying himself to penetrate the mystery, and discover the causes. Modern science also affords facility for operating other apparent miracles, not less numerous nor less brilliant than those contained in history.

The observation of what modern jugglers are able to effect, tends, in a great degree, to explain many of the magical operations of the ancients.

CHAPTER XII.

Conclusion.—Principles followed in the Course of the Discussion.—Reply to the Objection that the scientific Acquirements of the Ancients are lost.—Democritus alone, among them, occupied himself with Observations on Experimental Philosophy.—This Philosopher perceived, in the Operations of Magic, the scientific Application of the Laws of Nature.—Utility of studying the apparent Miracles of the Ancients in this Point of View.—The Thaumaturgists did not connect together their learned Conceptions by any Theory, which is a Proof that they had received them from a prior Period.—The first Thaumaturgists can not be accused of Imposition; but it would be dangerous, in this day, to attempt to subjugate a People by apparent Miracles.—Voluntary Obedience to the Laws is a certain Consequence of the Happiness which just Legislation procures to Men.

WE have undertaken to restore to ancient history that grandeur of which an apparent mixture of puerile fables robbed it; and to demonstrate that the apparent miracles and the magical operations of the ancients were the result of real scientific knowledge, more or less advanced, which the Thaumaturgists, for the most part, had secretly transmitted from one period to another; at the same time, with the greatest care, concealing that knowledge from all other men.

Two principles have regulated our conclusions :·

1st. We consider it absurd to wonder at, or to refuse to believe, what appears supernatural, when it can be naturally explained.

2d. We regard it reasonable to admit that the physical knowledge proper for the working of apparent miracles was possessed by some men, at the time and in the country where historical tradition has placed the miracles.

There must, we maintain, be a plausible motive for denying what has often been attested by many authors, and repeated at divers times : that motive no longer exists ; and the apparent miracle reënters the class of historical facts, when an explanation, deduced from the nature of things, has dispelled the supernatural appearance that caused it to be regarded as chimerical.

But, again, how is it that conceptions of such high interests have never descended to us ? Histories have been lost over all the world connected with the greatest parts of past times ; and also much knowledge of every kind, the possession of which by the ancients can not be disputed. To the general causes of destruction which have occasioned these immense gaps in the domain of human intelligence are joined two in particular, the power of which we have described: the one is the mystery with which religious and political interests endeavored to envelop free ideas ; the other is the want of a systematic connection, which alone could have established between them an accurate theory, a connection without which facts were successively lost. There was also no possibility remaining for those which survived to recover those which sank gradually into the abyss of oblivion, from the lapse of time, from negligence, fear, superstition, and ignorance.

We must not judge ancient conceptions by our own. Experimental chemistry, considered as a science, dates from the last century. It only existed before as a capricious empiricism, directed by chance, misled by the dreams of the alchemist. More anciently, the Romans had copied the writings of the Greeks, who themselves, without attempting more experiments, copied what they found in the most ancient books, or in the recitals of foreign authors, whom they did not always understand. Democritus* alone seems to have felt the necessity of observing, of learning, and of knowing for himself.† He passed his life in making

---

* Democritus was born at Abdera, in Thrace, in the year 460 B.C. He received his first instructions partly from some Magi that were left by Xerxes at Abdera, partly from Leucippus, a celebrated philosopher of Elea. He traveled into Egypt, in order to acquire geometry from the Egyptian priests; and also visited Persia and Athens for the purpose of obtaining knowledge, in the pursuit of which he expended all his patrimony, and returned to Abdera in a state of indigence. This rendered him liable to a law which denied funereal rites in the state to any native who had spent his patrimony; but having read one of his works, the *Diascosmus*, aloud to his fellow-citizens, he not only acquired an exemption from this law, but received a present of, it is said, five hundred talents; and, at his death, was buried at the public expense.

Democritus loved retirement and study; and the tradition runs, that he put out his eyes that he might not be disturbed from meditation by external objects. He was, perhaps, on this account accused of insanity; but Hippocrates declared that his accusers, not Democritus, were mad. His doctrines were of a very singular character. Thus, he contended for the eternity of the universe; that every thing, even mind, was material; and that the latter was only different from material bodies by the arrangements of its component atoms. In morals, he contended that the only thing needful was a cheerful spirit; and as he took every opportunity of laughing at the follies of mankind, he acquired the appellation of the *Laughing Philosopher*. From the extent of his acquirements, he was regarded by the ignorant as a magician, especially in the close of his life, which extended to one hundred and four years. He died in the year 357 B.C.—ED.

† *Encyclop. Méthod. Philosophie Ancienne et Moderne*, tome i., p. 319.

experiments, in noting down in a book, which *treats
of nature*, facts that he had verified.* We may
ask, to what point had he conducted his researches, in pursuing which he had probably no theory
to serve him as a guide ? It is difficult to conjecture, his works having long since perished. It is
at least certain, that in the general opinion they
had acquired very great authority. So great was
the weight of his testimony in physics and in natural history, that works published under his name,
but not written by him, circulated widely, although
filled with ridiculous fables upon the properties of
minerals, animals, and plants.† Pliny, who often
quotes these pretended works of Democritus, believed in their authenticity; but Aulus Gellius has
unveiled the impositions, and is justly indignant at
the outrage made on the memory of so great a man.

In a passage, unfortunately too concise, Solinus‡
seems to present Democritus as engaged in a frequent contest against the Magi, and opposing to
their impostures phenomena prodigious in appearance, but nevertheless natural, to show them how
far the power of the hidden properties of bodies
can extend. "Democritus," says Lucian,§ "believed in no miracle, persuaded that those which
were effected owed their success to deception ; and
he applied himself to discover the method by
which they could deceive : in a word, his philosophy brought him to this conclusion, that magic
(an art well known by him, since the Magi‖ were

* Petron., *Satyric.*—Vitruv., *De Architect.*, lib. ix., cap. iii.
† Aul. Gell., *Noct. Attic.*, lib. x., cap. xii.—Columell, *De Re
Rustica*, lib. vii., cap. v.—Diogen. Laert. in *Democrit. vit.*, sub.
finem.
‡ "*Accepimus Democritum Abderitem, ostentatione scrupuli hujus*
(catochitis lapidis) *frequenter usum, ad probandam occultam naturæ
potentiam, in certaminibus quæ contrà magos habuit.*" (Solin., cap.
ix.) § Lucian, *Philopseud.* ‖ Diogen. Laert. in *Democrit. vit.*

its institutors), *was entirely confined to the application and the imitation of the laws and the works of
nature.*"

This opinion, professed by the first acknowledged
philosopher of antiquity who studied science as it
ought to be, is precisely that which we have
striven to establish. If we have not labored in
vain, we may be allowed to deduce from this theo-
rem some consequences upon the possible advances of the knowledge of nature, in reference to the
history of mankind and the principles of civilization.

1st. The ancients, until an epoch which we have
not presumed to trace back, were so much occupied with particular facts, that they did not seek
to arrange and connect them. The moderns, perhaps, fall into the opposite excess. Do they not
neglect too much to take advantage of isolated
facts deposited in books, and reproduced even in
the laboratories, but which, otherwise, do not direct
our researches to any immediate application, nor
display either any affinity or any opposition to the
existing theories ?

We have seen that much may be gained to natural history by the examination and the discussion
of the prodigies related by the ancients : and we
contend that the study of their apparent miracles
and their magical operations would not be without
advantage to physics and to chemistry. In attempting to arrive at the same results as the Thaumaturgists (and at which they have allowed us to
glance), or that can be supposed to have emanated
from them, curious,. even useful discoveries, in
application to the arts, would be obtained ; and a
great service thus rendered to the history of the
human mind, as the important sciences lost sight
of would be recovered. The loss of these among

the Romans and the Greeks was owing to, or, at least, was accelerated by, the absolute defect of method and of theory.

2d. The inevitable consequence of this failure is, that the magicians and the Thaumaturgists have never been separable from their books, and have been merely the slaves of their formularies—truly apprentices; and indeed, they were only mechanically acquainted with the processes of their art, without even distinguishing how far superstition, or the intention of imposing it, had mingled with superfluous ceremonies. The most ancient, as well as the most recent, present this characteristic trait. If they did not, then, invent any thing, from whom, it may be asked, did they procure their secrets, their formularies, their books, and their entire art? We have to investigate this branch of knowledge, as every other, precipitated into indeterminate times, when the sciences were either invented or perfected. They afterward fell into decay, and only were kept in view by incoherent lights, shed upon the minds of men who retained the employment of them without understanding their nature. We are here thrown back into that antiquity which history points out confusedly, but which is anterior to history.

3d. In attempting to penetrate, by the aid of some probable conjectures, into that darkness which the course of time renders progressively more profound, a remarkable trait has struck us: namely, that the opinion which ascribed a celestial origin to miracles and to magic was not, in the main, the consequence of an imposition, but was born of that piety which desired that every kind of excellence should emanate from the Divinity.*

* As far as respects real miracles, no other opinion can be formed; for what idea can be formed of a miracle if not that published

It was maintained by the *figurative style*, which
naturally amalgamated itself with religious sentiments.   Thus, among the legislators, who have had
recourse to this venerated agent for giving stabil-
ity to their operations, the most ancient, at least,
are not supported by falsehood; they have not professed that execrable doctrine, *that it is necessary
to deceive men*.   It was in good faith that they declared themselves inspired, and that they offered
their marvelous works as proofs of their mission,
because they humbly ascribed their knowledge,
their virtues, their sublime views, and their conceptions above the vulgar, to the Divinity.

These great men, were they now alive, would
adopt a very different method.   He who would
seek, in the present day, in the art of working apparent miracles, an instrument for acting
upon civilization, would soon fail, because he would
knowingly deceive : his dishonesty, contrary to
morality, would be contrary to the spirit of *pro-
gressive civilization*, which ever tends to draw aside
the veil behind which nature and truth are often
concealed.

Must it then be concluded that, deprived of this
powerful lever, legislation must be powerless over
the minds of men, and that to direct their actions
it has need of a perpetual coercive force ?   We
reply, certainly not!   Whatever may be said of
our own times, it is not necessary to deceive men
when it is intended to conduct them to happiness.
The man who deceives thinks less of serving
those whom he deceives than of upholding his
own pride, securing his personal ambition, or satis-

by Dr. Thomas Reid, namely, that it is "an effect that indicates
a power of a higher order than the powers which we are accustomed directly to trace in phenomena more familiar to us, but a
Power whose continued and ever present existence it is Atheism
only that denies."—ED.

fying his cupidity. The desire of being governed is natural to men, when they become members of the social state; it increases among nations in the ratio of their knowledge and well-being, and in proportion to the reasonable desire of enjoying undisturbed the advantages that they possess. It is with this sentiment that the politician whose intentions are upright will find ‑a foundation to build upon, not less solid than that which he would acquire from an assumed intervention of Divinity— a foundation which will never give way, nor leave him exposed to the inconveniences nor to the serious consequences that religious fiction leads to, and which will never threaten to overthrow what is founded upon reason, and upon the progress of natural perceptions.

"Kings! reign for your people!" and then to the astonished observer, who shall ask to what illusions their obedience and your power are due, you can reply, " Here is all our magic ; here is the source of all our apparent miraculous power."

ILLUSTRATIONS.

UPON DRAGONS AND MONSTROUS SERPENTS, MENTIONED IN
A GREAT MANY FABULOUS OR HISTORICAL NARRATIONS.

THERE are, perhaps, in the empire of the marvelous no
narrations that occur more frequently than those which describe some winged dragon, or serpent of monstrous dimensions, devouring men and animals, until, by the force of heroic valor or some miraculous power, the country which is
exposed to its ravages is delivered. Dupuis[*] and M. Alex.
Lenoir[†] have imagined these narrations to be the figurative expressions of the astronomical themes of Perseus, the
liberator of Andromeda, threatened by a sea monster; of
Orion, the vanquisher of a serpent, emblems in themselves
of the victory of virtue over vice, the principle of good over
the principle of evil. They regard it also, when divested of
every allegorical veil, as intimating the victory of the spring
sun over the winter sun, and of light over darkness.

It is under a different aspect that we propose to treat of
the same subject: we shall inquire how it is that an astronomical emblem has been so frequently converted into a
positive subject of history; what are the causes which have,
in different places, introduced such remarkable variations
into the legend; and, finally, why other myths or other facts
have been added or united to this legend, which originally
were unconnected with it?

§ I.

OF REPTILES ATTAINING UNCOMMON GROWTH, WHICH HAVE EX-
ISTED, AND GIVEN RISE TO, OR CONFIRMED, MANY OF THESE
NARRATIONS.

We may inquire whether there ever existed reptiles of
a proportion extraordinary enough, or animals of a form monstrous enough, to have given a natural origin to the legends
now under discussion?

---

[*] Dupuis, *Origine de tous les cultes.*
[†] A. Lenoir, *Du Dragon de Metz, appelé* Graouilly, &c. *Mémoires de
l'Académie Celtique*, tome ii., p. 1-20.

Finding, from traditions, that dragons abounded in the department of Finisterre, and were overcome by supernatural power, an observer* has conjectured that these monsters, the subjects of so many legends, might have been the crocodiles that formerly infested the rivers of France, and the bones of which have been found in several parts. The thing is not impossible.

In 1815 a crocodile was killed near Calcutta, which measured from seventeen to eighteen English feet in length, armed with enormous claws. "At the place where the head and body joined was a swelling, from which rose four bony projections ; and upon the back were three other rows of similar projections, and four more diverged from the tail, the end of which formed a kind of saw, being, indeed, the continuation of these projecting files."† These *swellings* and these *bony projections* were looked upon as defensive weapons ; and similar projections were also found upon the famous *Tarasque* of *Tarascòn*, and many other dragons or serpents represented in the pictures of different legends. Here, again, the fiction may possibly have originated in the paintings exaggerating a fact actually observed.

It was rumored several years ago, that a monstrous reptile had been killed at the foot of Mount Salevus ; and ravages proportioned to its size were attributed to it. Its carcass was examined by naturalists, first at Geneva, and then at Paris. It proved to be nothing more than an adder of ex traordinary growth, but in no respect prodigious. In a less enlightened age, we may ask, would more have been necessary for furnishing to the mountaineers of Savoy a marvelous narration, which would have been confirmed by tradition, and probably enlarged in each succeeding generation?

History has perpetuated the memory of the serpent which Regulus opposed in Africa with engines of war. It was probably a boa constrictor, which had attained to its greatest degree of growth.‡ Allowing something to exaggera-

---

* M. de Fréminville, *Mémoires de la Société des Antiquaires de France,* tom. xi., p. 8, 9.

† *Bibliothèque Universelle* (Genève) *Sciences*, tome iv., p. 222, 223.

‡ The tradition, as Livy relates it, makes this gigantic Numidian Python one hundred and twenty feet long; and it also stated that, when destroyed, the decomposing carcass of the monster so polluted the air that the Romans were forced to move their camp. The skin was nevertheless secured, and sent in triumph to Rome. This serpent, the African Python, differs in some of its features from the boa of South America, but it resembles that reptile in its bulk, its muscular strength, and the absence of poison fangs. In South America the boa is viewed with horror, on account of a belief that it exercises a certain influence over the destiny of any one who injures it, and, sooner or later, he suffers severely

tion, the natural language of surprise and fear, it becomes easy to reconcile the tradition here with truth and probability.

It is not always necessary to assume much exaggeration. A modern traveler* assures us that in the mountains of *Galese* serpents from thirty to forty feet in length are still to be met with. Ælian† mentions also, in several places, reptiles of an extraordinary size. Let us recollect that an almost religious respect for the lives of certain animals must formerly, particularly in India, have permitted serpents, by growing old, to attain to enormous dimensions. This respect for serpents was seconded by a superstition which, in the temples, consecrated many of the reptiles. Alexander admired in one of the Indian temples a serpent which is recorded to have been seventy cubits in length.‡ We know that sacred dragons were revered at Babylon, at Melita in Egypt, in Phrygia, in Italy, in Epirus,§ in Thessaly,‖ in Bœotia, and in the grotto of Trophonius.¶

Finally, we may remark, that the progress of civilization has expelled these immense reptiles from countries where they formerly lived in peace. There are no longer any boas in Italy. Solinus places them in Calabria, and describes their habits with so much correctness, that we can not suppose he meant to speak of monstrous adders. Pliny confirms this narration, by mentioning a boa in the body of which a child was found. It was killed in the Vatican, in the reign of Claudius, only thirty years, at the utmost, before the period in which Pliny wrote.**

These positive facts would prepare credulity to confound with history every legend in which, for some other reason, these monstrous serpents figured.

for his audacity.* Allowing for exaggeration, it is probable that the Python referred to in Livy was of unusual size, and hence well calculated to strike terror into the minds of those unaccustomed to the sight of enormous serpents. It seized its victim with its teeth, but, like the boa, destroyed it by pressure within the folds of its powerful body. The author of *The Seasons* describes this Python:

> From his dark abode,
> Which e'en Imagination fears to tread,
> At noon, forth issuing, gathers up his train
> In orbs immense.—THOMSON.—ED.

* Paulin de St. Barthélemi, *Voyages, &c.*, tome i., p. 479.
† Ælian, *De Nat. Anim*, passim, et lib. xvi., cap. xxxix.
‡ Ibid., lib. xv., cap. xii.
§ Ibid., lib. xi., cap. xvii.; lib. xii., cap. xxxix.; lib. xi., cap. ccxvi.
‖ Aristotle, *De Mirabil. Auscult.*   ¶ Suidas, *verbo Trophonios.*
** Plin., *Hist. Nat.*, lib. viii., cap. xiv.

* Smith's *Illustrations of South America.*

§ II.

Winged serpents, the true dragons, could never have existed ; and the supposed union of two natures so opposite
must have been originally merely hieroglyphic—an emblem.
But poetry, which lives in figures, did not hesitate to possess
itself of the image as well as the expression. The reptiles
which tore to pieces the sons of Laocoon were called dragons by Q. Calaber ;* Virgil gives them the name of dragons
and serpents by turns.† The two terms seem to have been
synonymous in poetical language ; and the wings with which
dragons have been endowed are only the emblem of the
promptitude with which the serpent pounces upon its prey,
or, in order to seize it, raises itself to the tops of trees.
Here, as in many other circumstances, the figurative expressions have taken place of the reality in the belief of the
vulgar, not less ignorant than eager after the marvelous.

The modern Greek gives the expressive name of *winged*
serpents to the locusts, which, carried on the wind in vast
swarms, devastate his harvests.‡ This metaphor is probably ancient, and may have originated many fables and
narrations respecting the existence of *winged serpents*.

But these explanations and those connected with physical
facts are vague, and sometimes purely local.   They can not
be applied to a precise fact, which is found in every country and in every age, related in the same manner, and with
only slight variations in the principal circumstances.

§ III.

St. Romanus, in 720 or 628, delivered the town of Rouen
from a monstrous dragon. "This miracle," it is said in a
dissertation upon the miracle of St. Romaine and La Gargouille, " is only the emblem of another miracle of St. Romanus, who made the Seine, which had overflowed its banks,

---

* Q. Calaber, *De Bello Trojano*, lib. xiii. A Greek poet, who lived in
the third century, and wrote a poem in fourteen books, as a continuation
of the Iliad.—ED.
　† " *Immensis orbibus*, angues" (vers. 204).
　" Serpens *amplexus uterque*" (vers. 214).
　" *Delubra ad summa* dracones" (vers. 225).
　　　　　　　　　　　　Virgil, *Æneid.*, lib. ii.
　‡ Pouqueville, *Voyage dans la Grèce*, tome iii., p. 562, 563.

and was about to inundate the town, return to its bed. The very name given by the people to this fabulous serpent is another proof of it: gargouille is derived from *gurges*," &c.[*]

In support of his opinion, the author quoted a strophe from the hymn of Santeuil:

" Tangit exundans aqua civitatem;
Voce Romanus jubet efficaci;
Audiunt fluctus, docilisque cedit
Unda jubenti."

In Orleans, also, a town frequently exposed to the ravages of the waters which bathe and fertilize its territories, a ceremony is celebrated similar to that which perpetuates the miracle of St. Romanus at Rouen. Indeed, a great number of traditions might be quoted in support of this conjecture.

The Island of Batz, near St. Pol de Leon, is said to have been desolated by a frightful dragon. St. Pol, who died in 594, by the virtue of his stole and staff precipitated the monster into the sea. Cambry,[†] who relates this tradition, tells us that the only fountain existing in the Island of Batz is alternately either exposed or covered by the tides of the sea. He then relates that, "near the Castle of Roche Maurice and the ancient River of Dordoun, a dragon devoured men and animals."[‡]

It seems but natural to suppose that these two narratives are emblematical of the ravages committed by the sea and the waters of the Dordoun.

St. Julian, first Bishop of Mans, in 59 destroyed a horrible dragon at the village of Artins, near Montoir.[§] This dragon, under the system discussed by us, should represent the inundations of the Loire, which flows in the vicinity. It might be also imaged by a dragon of nine or ten fathoms long, over which, in a cavern by the side of a *fountain*|| near Vendôme,

* *History of the Town of Rouen*, by Servin, 1775, 2 vols. 12mo, vol. ii. p. 147. It is more probable that the fable of the destruction of the serpent is founded on the fact of St. Romanus having destroyed the remnant of idolatry, and leveled with the ground temples of Venus, Jupiter, Apollo, and Mercury, which existed in his diocese. "No traces of this story," says Butler, speaking of the story of the serpent, "are found in any life of this saint, nor in any writings before the end of the fourteenth century. The figure of a serpent, called *Gargouille*, seems here, as in some other towns, originally to have been meant to represent symbolically the devil overcome by Christ."—*Lives of the Fathers, Martyrs, &c.*, October 22.—ED.

† Cambry, *Travels in the Department of Finisterre*, vol. i., p. 147, 148.
‡ Id. ibid., vol. i., p. 57.
§ Moreri, *Historical Dictionary*, art. *St. Julien*. M. Duchemin la Chenaye gives the name of La Roche Turpin to the scene of this victory.— *Mémoires de l'Académie Celtique*, tome iv., p. 311.
|| M. Duchemin la Chenaye, ibid.. pages 308 and following.

Q

the hermit St. *Bié* or *Bienheuré*, toward the end of the fourth century, triumphed. The inundations of the Scarpe might be represented by the dragon who terrified and expelled from an island the holy bishop who had bequeathed his name to the town of St. Amand ;* those of the Moselle, by the Graouilli, the monstrous serpent which St. Clement overcame at Metz ;† and those of Clain by the dragon of Poitiers, which hid itself near this river, and whose death was a benefit conferred by St. Radegonde, toward the middle of the sixth century.‡

In the same manner may be explained by the inundations of the Rhone the history of the monster of Tarascon, which, in the first century, was bound with the garter of St. Martha, who caused its death ; and the representation of which, called Tarasque, is still carried in procession in the town on the morning of the Pentecost.§ The overflowings of the Garonne would be emblemized by the dragon of Bordeaux, yielding, in the eleventh century, to the virtue of the Virgin of St. Martial ; and the dragon of St. Bertrand de Comminge, conquered by the Bishop of St. Bertrand in 1076.‖

Thus, also, the dragon from which St. Marcel delivered Paris,¶ and the winged dragon of the Abbey of Fleury,** offer images of the overflowing of the Seine and Loire.

Thus, also, at Lima, on the fête day of St. Francis of Assisi, if one observes figuring in the procession an ideal monster called Terascon,†† it will recall the fact that Lima, situated near the sea, is watered by a river which supplies every house with water. Thus, M. Champollion explains with probability the hieroglyphic of the two serpents, each with the human head, seen in the Church of St. Laurence at Grenoble, by the proverb " Serpens et draco devorabunt ur-

* M. Bottin, *Traditions des Dragons volans dans le Nord de la France. Mélanges d'Archéologie* (8vo, Paris, 1831), p. 161-164.
† A. Lenoir, *Du Dragon de Metz, &c., Mémoires de l'Académie Celtique,* tome ii., p. 1 and following.
‡ M. Jouyneau-des-Loges. *Mémoires de l'Académie Celtique,* tome v. p. 57.
§ Rouvière, *Voyage du Tour de la France,* 12mo, 1713, p. 401, 402. Dulaure, *Description des principaux Lieux de la France,* tome i., p. 16, art *Tarascon.* Millin, *Voyage dans le Midi de la France,* 4 vols. 8vo, tome iii., p. 451-553. The figure of the Tarasque may be found in the atlas of the Travels, plate 63 ; it is not, however, very correct.
‖ M. Chaudruc, *Mémoires de l'Académie Celtique,* tome iv., p. 313.
¶ *Lives of the Saints for every Day of the Year,* 2 vols. 4to, Paris, 1734 tome ii., p. 84 : *Life of St. Marcel,* 3d of November. Gregor. Turon., *D Gloriâ Confess.,* cap. lxxxix. It is thought St. Marcel occupied the Episcopal throne of Paris toward the end of the fourth century.
** Du Cange, *Glossar.,* verbo *Draco,* 2 ... tome ii., p. 1645.
†† *Description of the actual State of Peru,* extracted from the *Mercurio Peruviano. Annals of Travel,* by M. Malte Brun, vol. i., p. 92.

bem," rendered by the vulgar tongue into these two verses :

> " Lo serpein et lo dragon
> Metront Grenoble en savon,"

alluding to the situation of the town at the mouth of the Drac (Draco), in the Isère, represented by the serpent, whose sinewy writhings are pretty well imitated by the course of this river.[*] The comparison between the windings of a river and the writhings of a serpent are, indeed, as frequently found in common language, and in ordinary names, as in poetical metaphors. Near to Heleno Pole, a town in Bythinia, flows the River Draco (Dragon) ; this name, says Procopius,[†] was given to it from its numerous windings, which obliged travelers to cross it twenty times together. It is doubtless for a similar reason that a river, which rises in Mount Vesuvius and waters the walls of Nuceria (Nocera), received the name of Dragon.[‡]

This explanation is strengthened by a confession, the more remarkable, because the author, with whom it originated, had collected and tendered as positive facts all the popular stories of dragons and monstrous serpents which, at the commencement of the eighteenth century, were broached in the interior of Switzerland. Scheuchzer[§] allows that the name of Drach (Draco) was frequently given to impetuous torrents, which suddenly burst forth like avalanches.

The *dragon*, the multitude would then exclaim, has *made an irruption* (Erupit Draco). The cavity in which the torrent rose, or that in which the waters were absorbed, were consequently naturally called the Dragon's Hole, or the Dragon's Marsh, names which we find in many places celebrated by some one or other of the legends which have occupied our attention. In spite of the probability which many of these affinities present, two grave objections refute the system they are destined to establish.

First. If it is as easy for a supernatural power to arrest the inundations of a river or the sea as to put to death a monstrous serpent, such a comparison can not be applied to the limited strength of an ordinary man. Now, in these legends we shall see figuring chevaliers, soldiers, banished men, and obscure malefactors, whom no celestial grace could

[*] *Dissertation upon a Subterraneous Monument existing in Grenoble*, in 4to, année xii. *Encyclopedical Magazine*, ixth year, vol. v., p. 442, 443.
[†] Procop., *De Ædific. Justin.*, lib. v., cap. ii.
[‡] Id., *Hist. Miscell.*, lib. i, cap. lv.
[§] Scheuchzer, *Itinera per Helvetiæ Alpinas Regiones*, &c., tome iii., p. 377–397. *Vide* p. 396 et p. 383, 384, 389, 390.

have called out to work miracles. And who can be persuaded that a single individual, whatever may be his zeal or his power, would be able to turn back into their beds the Loire and the Garonne, widely inundating the plains with their waters?

Secondly. The multitude of the legends does not allow us to suppose that, in times and places so different, it would have been agreed to represent by the same emblem events which, although similar, yet were peculiar to each period. An emblem always the same, supposes a fact, or rather an allegory, received in all ages and in all places; such as that of the triumph obtained of the principle of *good* and *light* over the principle of *evil* and *darkness* represented by the *serpent*.

§ IV.

THE LEGEND OF THE SERPENT HAS BEEN TRANSPORTED FROM ASTRONOMICAL PICTURES INTO MYTHOLOGY AND HISTORY.

We shall not here retrace, in its details, the astronomical picture of this triumph so frequently renewed. Let us only observe that three accessory objects are grouped almost always with the principal subject: namely, a *virgin*, a *young girl*, or a *woman*; a *precipice*, a *cavern*, or a *grotto*; and the *sea*, a *river*, a *fountain*, or a *well*.* We find one part of this legend put into operation, if I may so express myself, in the manner in which the sacred dragons of Epirus, Phrygia, and Lanuvium received their food. It was carried to them in their *cavern* by a young *girl*, who was exposed to terrible punishment if she was not a virgin.† A *woman*, also, the magician, whom the unfortunate Dido expressed a desire to consult, presented the nourishment to the sacred dragon which guarded the Hesperides.‡

The Greek mythology is rich in legends, the astronomical origin of which is not dubious. Is it necessary to explain why a serpent or a dragon figures so often in the celestial planisphere? In the war of the gods against the giants, an enormous serpent attacked Minerva. The virgin goddess seized the monster and threw it toward the heavens, where it became fixed among the stars.§ Ceres placed in the heavens one of the dragons that drew her chariot. Triopas having offended the same divinity, the goddess punished him

---

* A. Lenoir, *Du Dragon de Metz, &c., Mémoires de l'Académie Celtique*, tome ii., p. 5 et 6.
† Ælian, *De Nat. Animal.*, lib. xi., cap. ii. et xvi. *Propert.*, lib. iv., Eleg. viii.   ‡ Virgil, *Æneid*, lib. iv., vers. 483–485.
§ Hygin, *Poet. Astronom.*, *Serpens.*

first by the torment of an insatiable hunger, and then put him to death by a dragon, which from that time took a place with her in the heavens. According to other mythologists, Phorbas, the son of Triopas, merited this honor for having delivered the Island of Rhodes from a monstrous serpent. Some observe in the constellation of Ophiucus, Hercules upon the borders of the River Sagaris, vanquishing the serpent which Omphalus had commanded him to combat.*

Themis, the heavenly virgin, answered the petitions of mortals at Delphi. Python, the monstrous dragon, approached, and the oracle was deserted ; nor did any one dare to resort to it until Apollo (the sun) had pierced Python with his irresistible arrows.† Let us observe that the tradition in these narrations does not omit the divine nature of the dragon. Apollo, after having destroyed the monster, was obliged to submit himself to a religious aspiration ; and the sacred serpents of the Epirus were supposed to have owed their being to Python.‡

Near the river in Colchis, Jason, assisted by Medea, who was yet a virgin, triumphed over the dragon which guarded the golden fleece. Hercules and Perseus delivered Hesione and Andromeda, virgins who were exposed as prey to the voracity of a sea monster. A *woman* learned in the arts of enchantment saved the inhabitants of Tenos, by destroying a dragon that threatened to depopulate their island.§

According to a legend, preserved by the Christian faith in the figurative sense only, but adopted literally by painters, and which has a host of believers, St. Michael felled to the ground, and pinned down with his lance, a dragon which was vomited forth from the infernal *pit*, and which was the same that, according to Dupuis, in the Apocalypse, pursued the heavenly virgin. Half a mile on the road to Baruth (the ancient Berythe) is to be seen the cavern where dwelt the dragon killed by St. George, at the moment when about to devour the daughter of the king of the country.‖ According to another legend, it was on the borders of a lake, the asylum of this monster, that St. George saved the king's daughter and twelve other virgins, whom an oracle had commanded to be given up to this horrible dragon.¶

---

* Hygin, *Poet. Astronom. Ophiucus.* † Pausanias, *Phocic.*, cap. v.
‡ Ælian, *Var. Hist.*, lib. iii., cap. i. &c. *De Nat. Animal.*, lib. xi., cap.
ii. Plutarch, *De Oracul. Defectu.* § Arist., *De Mirabil. Auscult.*
‖ *Voyages de Villamont* (1613), liv. iii. p. 561. Thévenot, *Relation d'un Voyage fait au Levant*, &c., 4to, Paris, 1663, p. 442.
¶ *Memoirs and Observations made by a Traveler in England* (La Haye, 1698. p. 214-232). This work is attributed to Max. Misson.

Almost all mythologics contain, with some variations, the
same legend ; and, we may add, in how many of the Greek
myths may it not be traced! Hercules, conqueror of the
dragon of the Garden of Hesperides, a monster whose defeat was followed by the discovery of a fountain till then unknown ; again, a dragon dwelt in a gloomy cavern, and
guarded the fountain of Mars until killed by Cadmus, who
was himself afterward transformed into a serpent ; and it
was a dragon from which Diomedes, on his return from Troy,
delivered the Corcyreans.*   Cenchreus was implored by the
inhabitants of Salamis to be their king, as a reward for his
victory over a dragon that had devastated their territories.†

Upon a monument discovered in Thebes, Anubis is represented as St. Michael and St. George are in Christian paintings, armed in a cuirass, and having in his hand a lance,
with which he pierces a monster that has the head and tail
of a serpent.‡

In a succession of narrations, the marvelous portions of
which have been principally borrowed by their compilers from
the ancient mythology of Hindostan, we see some monstrous
figures : now in the form of enormous serpents ;§ then as

As this celebrated religious hero, St. George, is the patron saint of England, it is proper that some account of him should be here given. He
was born in Cappadocia, of noble Christian parents. After the death of
his father he went into Palestine with his mother, who had a considerable estate there, which fell to him. He became a soldier, and after having
served as a tribune, he was raised to the rank of a colonel, and afterward
to higher rank, by the Emperor Dioclesian, as a reward for his courage
and conduct. But, being equally strong in his faith, he threw up all his
well-merited honors when that emperor began his persecutions of Christianity ; an act, in conjunction with his reprobation of the emperor's cruelties, which cost him his life. He was thrown into prison and cruelly
tortured, and on the following day he was beheaded.

St. George became the patron saint of military men ; and, like all the
other saints of the Romish calendar, did many wondrous acts and performed many miracles, both during his life and after his death : hence
churches were erected in honor of him in various parts of Europe. He
was constituted the patron saint of England by our first Norman kings ;
and, under his name, Edward III. instituted the most noble order of
knighthood in Europe. The promulgation of the pretended apparition
of St. George to Richard I. in his Saracenic expedition had such a beneficial effect on the spirits of his troops as insured them victory. He is
usually represented on horseback, slaying a dragon, an emblematical representation of his Christian fortitude in overcoming the Devil, the arch-
dragon. See *Butler's Lives of the Fathers, Martyrs, &c.*—Ed.

  * Heraclides, in *Politiis.*

  † Noël, *Dictionnaire de la Fable,* art. *Cenchreus.*

  ‡ A. Lenoir, *Du Dragon de Metz, &c., Mémoires de l'Académie Celtique,*
tome ii., p. 11, 12.

  § *The Thousand and One Nights,* translation of Ed. Gauthier, 7 vols. 8vo,
Paris, 1822, 1823, vol. v., p. 425, 426.

gigantic dragons, flapping their tails against their scaly
sides ;* and having their voracity yearly satiated by young
virgins, but yielding to the valiant attacks of warriors aided
by supernatural powers, at the very moment when the king's
daughter is about to become their victim.

Chederles, a hero revered among the Turks, we are told,
"killed a monstrous dragon, and saved the life of a young
girl exposed to its fury. After having drunk of the waters
of a river which rendered him immortal, he traversed the
world upon a steed as immortal as himself."† The commencement of this recital recalls to mind the Hindoo myths
and fables of Hercules and Perseus. The termination may
be regarded as an emblem of the Sun, the immortal traveler,
who ceases not his revolutions around the earth.

Among the figures sculptured on a granite block; discovered in the deserted town of Palenqui Viejo, was remarked a serpent, from the throat of which issued the head
of a woman.‡ One is tempted to connect this emblem to
the legends of monstrous dragons. It is, at least, difficult
not to imagine that the legend had passed into the *New
World*. The Caribbees believe that the Supreme Being
made his Son descend from heaven in order to kill a dragon,
which, by its ravages, desolated the nations of Guiana.§
The monster succumbed ; and the Caribbees sprung from
the worms generated in the decomposition of its corpse ; and
on this account they regard all those nations with whom the
cruel monster had formerly waged cruel war as their enemies. At first sight this is but the myth of Python ; but
what are we to think of the strange origin that the Caribbees
attribute to themselves? We can but suppose that they had
formerly received this tradition from a nation superior to
themselves in strength, who wished to humiliate and de-
grade them ; and that they had preserved it from custom,
and to justify their national hatreds and thirst for conquest.
A no less singular belief is to be found among the same
people. The Caribbees of Dominica assert that a monster,
having its retreat in a precipice surrounded by rocks, bore
upon its head a stone as brilliant as a carbuncle, from which
issued so bright a light that the neighboring rocks were il-
lumined by it.‖ Similar legends have for a long time been

* *The Thousand and One Nights*, tome vi., p. 303–305, et tome v., p. 423,
424. † *Dictionnaire de la Fable*, art. *Chéderles.*
‡ *Revue Encyclopédique*, tome xxxi., p. 850.
§ Noël, *Dictionnaire de la Fable*, art. *Cosmogonie Américaine.*
‖ Rochefort, *Histoire Naturelle et Morale des Isles Antilles* (Rotterdam,
1658), p. 21.

received in countries with which it is supposed the Caribbees could not have had any communication.

At some period, which chronologists have had pretensions
enough to fix, St. Margaret overcame a dragon, and from
the head of the monster this virgin, afterward raised to a
heavenly abode, extracted a ruby, or carbuncle, an emblem
of the brilliant star of the *northern crown* (Margarita), placed
in the heavens near the head of the *Serpent*.

In the history of Dieudonné of Gozon, we find mention
also of a stone taken from the head of a dragon killed by this
hero at Rhodes, and preserved, it is said, in his family. It
was the size of an olive, and displayed many brilliant colors.*

Two Helvetian traditions describe a serpent offering to a
man a *precious stone*, as a token of homage and gratitude.†
Faithful to these old superstitions, the popular language of
the Jura still designates, under the name of *vouivre*, a winged
and immortal serpent, the eye of which is a diamond.‡

Pliny, Isidorus, and Solinus§ speaks of the *precious stone
which the dragon carries in its head.* An Eastern story-teller,∥
who describes a miraculous stone, the real carbuncle that
shines in darkness, states that it is only to be found in the
head of the. dragon, the hideous inhabitant of the Island of
Serendib (Ceylon). Philostratus also assures us that in India a precious stone, concealed in the heads of dragons, was
endowed with a powerful brilliancy and wonderful magical
virtues.¶

That error which, by transforming an astronomical allegory into a physical fact, decorated the heads of serpents
with a brilliant stone, had its rise in a great antiquity. " Although the serpent has a ruby in its head, it is, nevertheless,
injurious," says a Hindoo philosopher, who has collected
into his proverbs the precepts of the most ancient times.**
This legend, arising from the figurative expressions of the
relative positions the constellations of Perseus, the Whale,
the Crown, and the Serpent occupy in the heavens, has been,
we have seen, first connected with the victory of the spring
sun over winter, and of light over darkness. The carbuncle,

* *Dictionnaire de Moréri*, art. *Gozon* (Dieudonné). Gozon died in 1353
† Scheuchzer, *Itinerar. per Helvet. Alp. Reg.*, tome iii., p. 381–383.
‡ *Mémoires de la Société des Antiquaires*, tome vi., p. 217.
§ Plin., *Hist. Nat.*, lib. xxxvii., cap. x. Isidor., *Hispal. Origin.*, lib. xvi.,
cap. xiii. Solin., cap. xxxiii.
∥ *Stories of Cheikh el Mohdy*, translated from the Arabian by J. J. Mar-
cel, 1833. ¶ Philostrat., *De Vit. Apollon.*, lib. iii., cap. ii.
** *Proverbs of Barthoveri*, &c., inserted in the work of Abraham Roger.
*The Theater of Idolatry ; or, the Door Opened, &c.: a French translation,
1 vol. 4to (1760), p. 322.

or ruby, which there held its place, and with which Ovid decorated the palace of the sun,* was, in fact, consecrated to that orb from its color of flaming red.†

§ V.

THE SAME LEGEND CREPT INTO CHRISTIANITY, ESPECIALLY AMONG THE PEOPLE OF THE WEST.

As long as oppressed Christianity strove in secret against polytheism, its worship, no less austere than its code of morals, only admitted in its ceremonies, still concealed by the aid of mystery, simple rights unencumbered by material representation. The researches and cruelties of persecutors could only tear from the faithful their holy books and sacred vases ; they had few or no images.‡

But public worship could ill dispense with remarkable outward and visible signs ; for, in the midst of a large assembly, words could hardly be conveyed to the ears of all the audience, but the images would speak to the eyes of all ; they could awaken the most natural, the most universal inclinations. The multitude, therefore, delight in the magnificence of religious acts, and think that it can not multiply too many images.

This would necessarily happen, even to Christianity, when (on the ruins of polytheism) it publicly established its temples and worship. The progress was much more rapid, because the religion of Christ succeeded a religion rich in pomp and emblems ; and it feared to repulse, by too rigid a simplicity, men accustomed to see and to touch what they believed in and worshiped.

Hence, as it was difficult to destroy and utterly to proscribe the former objects of veneration, the Christians often preferred appropriating them to their own faith. More than one temple was changed into a church ; more than the name of one god was honored as the name of a saint ; and an

<hr>

* Flammasque imitante pyropo.
Ovid. *Metamorph.,* lib. ii., ver. 2.

† The Cardinal Dailly and Albertus Magnus, bishop of Ratisbon, said Cartaut of La Villate, distributed the planets among the different religions. The sun fell to the lot of the Christian religion. It is for that reason we have always held the sun in singular veneration ; that the town of Rome is called the *solar town :* and that the cardinals who reside there are habited in *red,* the color of the sun.—*Critical Thoughts on Mathematics,* 1 vol. 12mo, Paris, 1752 ; with permission and approbation.

In India an idea universally prevails that a stone exists in the head of serpents ; and the snake charmers pretend to extract it from the head of the cobra di capella.—ED.

‡ *Encyclop. Method. Théologie,* art. *Images.*

immense number of images and legends passed without difficulty into the new faith, and were preserved by the ancient
respect of the new believers.

The legend of a heavenly being overcoming a serpent, the
principle of evil, was conformable to the language, the spirit,
and the origin of Christianity. It was received, therefore,
and reproduced in the religious paintings and ceremonies of
the early Christians. St. Michael, the first of the archangels,
was presented to the eyes of the faithful, piercing the infernal dragon, the enemy of the human race.*

In the fifth century in France,† and rather later in the
West, were established the processions known by the name
of *Rogations*.‡ For three days the image of a dragon and
winged serpent were presented to the observation of the
faithful; and his defeat was depicted by the ignominious
manner in which he was borne about on the third day.§

The celebration of the Rogation varied according to the
dioceses, from the first days of Ascension week to the last
days of the week of Pentecost. It corresponds to the time

* This mode of representing the triumph of the faithful over the evil
principle was general over every Christian country in the Middle Ages.
The serpent, or dragon, was usually placed in the painting or the sculpture,
under the feet of the saint; but the populace could not understand the
allegory; and as it was the interest of the monks to nourish their credulity, a fable or legend was attached to these representations, detailing the
victory of the saint over a true dragon or a real serpent. Thus, the
allegorical representation of the patron saint of England, St. George,
destroying the dragon, is still extensively believed by the multitude as
the record of a real victory over a material dragon; and to prove how
eager the monks were to maintain the belief, "the monks in Mount St.
Michael, in France, did not hesitate to exhibit, as pious relics, the sword
and shield with which St. Michael the archangel combated the dragon of
the Revelations."*—Ed.

† St. Mammert, bishop of Vienne, in Dauphiny, instituted the *Rogations*
in 468 or 474.—*Encyclop. Méthod. Théologie.* art. *Rogations.*

‡ The fasts termed *Rogations* were established by St. Mammertus on
the occasion of an assumed miracle, said to have been performed through
the influence of his prayers. A terrible fire broke out and raged in the
city of Vienne, in Dauphiny, where he was archbishop, in spite of every
effort to extinguish it; but suddenly went out in consequence of the
prayers of the saint: and the same result followed his supplications on
the occurrence of a second great fire, which alarmed the city more than
the first. The worthy prelate then formed the design of instituting an
annual fast and supplication of three days to appease the Divine wrath,
by fasting, prayers, tears, and the confessions of sins.† This fast gradually extended to other churches; hence we find the *Rogations* kept in
many other parts besides Vienne; but why the procession of the dragon
was ingrafted upon those of the *Rogations* does not appear.—Ed.

§ Guill. Durant. *Rationale Divinorum Officiorum*, fol. 1479, folio 226
recto.

in which, the first half of the spring being passed, the victory
of the sun over winter is fully achieved, even in our cold and
rainy climate.   It is difficult not to perceive an intimate connection between the legends of the allegorical dragon and
that period in which its appearance was each year renewed.

Other circumstances increase the strength of this argument.   In the sixth century, St. Gregory the Great ordered
that St. Mark's day, 25th of April, should be annually celebrated by a procession similar to that of the Rogation.   The
origin of this ceremony was as follows : Rome was desolated by an extraordinary inundation.   The Tiber rose like
an immense sea to the upper windows of the temples.   Innumerable serpents, it is said, had emerged from the overflowing waters of the river, and finally an immense dragon,*
a new Python, was born of this new deluge.†   Its breath
infected the air and engendered a pestilential disease,‡ by
which the inhabitants were cut off by thousands.   An annual procession perpetuated the remembrance of the scourge
and of its cessation, obtained by the prayers of the pope and
his flock.   The date of the 25th of April, less distant than
that of the Rogations from the equinox, is suitable to a country in which the spring is always more forward than in Gaul.

Whether by chance or by calculation, those people who
transported to Lima under a southern hemisphere the *Tarasque*, the dragon of a Northern nation, have fixed it on the
7th of October, the fête day of St. Francis of Assisi.   This
period approaches still nearer to the equinox of the spring.
But in equatorial countries, as under the moderate climate
of Lima, the victory of the sun is not so long undetermined
as in our northern regions, where the first weeks of spring
seem but a prolongation of winter.

Pliny has spoken of a mysterious egg,§ to the possession
of which the Druids attributed great virtues, and which was
formed by the concurrence of all the serpents of a country.
The inhabitants of Sologne, the echo of the Druids after
two thousand years have passed, assert, without doubting
the antiquity of the myth they repeat, that all the serpents
of the country assemble to produce an enormous diamond,

* Guill. Durant, fol. 225 verso. *Siffredi Presbiteri Mimensis.   Epitome*,
lib. i., *De Miro Prodigio.*
† " *Ut Noe Diluvium renovatum crederetur.*"—Platina, *De Vitis Mac
Pontific.* in *Pelag. II.*
‡ " *Pestis inguinaria seu inflatura inguinum.*"   These are the expressions made use of by the author of the *Rationale* (loco citato); he adds,
that the Pope Pelagius II., successor to St. Gregory the Great, suddenly
died of the same disease, with seventy other persons, while in the midst
of a procession.   ,   § Plin., *Hist. Nat.*, lib. xxix., cap. 3.

which, superior to the stone of Rhodes, reflects the liveliest colors of the rainbow. The day assigned for their miraculous production is the 13th of May,* a day belonging to the second half of the spring, like the days when the serpent of the Rogations was paraded. The epoch of this apparition furnishes us with a remark which is not devoid of interest. Its fixedness alone proves contrary to what we have hitherto advanced, that the dragon was not the emblem of inundations, of overflowings of rivers, which could not every where have taken place on the same day. How then, it may be asked. came such an opinion to be established ! When the original emblem was lost, the attention would naturally be arrested by a circumstance occurring in all the legends which reproduced it, namely, that the scene of action was always upon the shore of the sea or banks of a river. The idea of the cessation of the ravages of the water must have appeared the more probable, from the procession of the dragon being regularly celebrated at a period of the year when the rivers, which had been swelled by the fall of snow, or the equinoctial rains, returned to their usual course.

§ VI.

ALLEGORICAL EXPLANATIONS OF EMBLEMS IN WHICH THE FIG-
URE OF THE SERPENT OCCURRED.

Every church had its dragon. The emulation of exterior piety had, in these representations, the effect of making them excel in a desire to excite in the spectators sensations of admiration, astonishment, and fright. The visible part of the worship became soon the most important part of the religion to men who were solely attentive to that which struck their senses ; the dragon in the Rogation processions was too remarkable not to attract the attention of the populace, and to usurp a prominent place in their belief. Each dragon had soon its peculiar legend, and these legends were multiplied without end. To those who would throw a doubt upon the probability of this cause we shall answer by one fact, that among the lives of the saints revered by the Christians of the East, who did not adopt the institution of the Rogations, the victory achieved by a heavenly being over a serpent is rarely to be found.

The word dragon, contracted to that of *Drac*, designated a demon, a malevolent spirit, whom the credulous Provençal

* Légier (du Loiret), *Traditions et Usages de la Sologne, Mémoire de l'Académie Celtique*, tome ii, p. 215, 216.

supposed to exist beneath the waters of the Rhone, and to feed upon the flesh of men. To act the *drac* was a term synonymous with doing as much evil[*] as the devil himself could be supposed to desire. Persons bitten by serpents were cured as soon as they approached the tomb of St. Phocas, owing to the victory which this Christian hero, by undergoing martyrdom, achieved over the devil, the old serpent.[†] When, in the eighth century, it was related that an enormous serpent had been found in the tomb of Charles Martel,[‡] was any thing else meant but the insinuation, that the demon had taken possession of this warrior, who, though he saved France, and probably Europe, from the Mussulman yoke, had had the misfortune to thwart the ambition of the heads of the Church, and the cupidity of the monks!

It seems, then, reasonable to believe, as the author of the Rationale[§] expressly teaches, that the serpent, or dragon, carried in the processions of the Rogations was the emblem of the infernal spirit, whose overthrow was supplicated from heaven; and that this defeat was attributed to the saint more particularly revered by the faithful in each diocese and parish. This kind of explanation has been reproduced under different forms by sensible Christians, who could not believe, in a physical sense, recitals too often renewed ever to have been true.

The demon is vice personified; victories achieved over vice may then have been figured by the same emblem. At Genoa, upon a small spot near the Church of St. Cyr, is to be seen an ancient *well*, which, it is stated, formerly concealed a dragon, the breath of which was destructive to men and flocks. St. Cyr exorcised the monster, and forced him to come out of the well and to throw himself into the *sea*.[‖] This miracle is still represented in pictures, and is allegorically interpreted by the erudite as the victory achieved by this holy preacher over impiety and libertinism. The same interpretation might be applied to the triumph of St. Marcel over the serpent that ravaged Paris, since they say, "This serpent first appeared outside the town, near the tomb of a woman of quality who had lived an irregular life."[¶]

* Du Cange. *Glossar.*, verbo *Dracus.* Millin. *Travels in the Interior of France*, vol. iii. p. 450, 451.
† Gregor. Turon. *De Miracul.*, lib. i. cap. 99.
‡ Mézérai. *Abrégé Chronologique de l'Histoire de France*, année 741.
§ Guill. Durant. *Rationale Divinorum Officiorum*, folio 235 recto.
‖ *Description of the Beauties of Genoa.* 8vo. Genoa. 1781, p. 39–41. Millin. *Travels in Savoy and Piedmont*, vol. ii. p. 239.
¶ *Lives of the Saints for every Day in the Year*, vol. ii. p. 84.

M. Dulaure,[*] nevertheless, is of opinion that this and many other legends were emblematical of the triumph of the Christian faith over the Roman and Druidical rituals. Incredulity is, in fact, the worst of all vices in the eyes of the heads of any faith. The retreat of the dragon which was vanquished by St. Julian[†] was near a temple of Jupiter; its fall may have figured that of polytheism, when, at the voice of the apostle of Mans, its worshipers overthrew the altars of the dethroned god, and left his temple desolate. Upon the site of Epidaurus is to be seen a cavern, which tradition has sometimes designated as the retreat of Cadmus when metamorphosed into a serpent, but more frequently as the abode of the serpent of Esculapius. When St. Jerome related that at Epidaurus St. Hilary triumphed over a devastating serpent concealed in that cavern, the learned seemed to have some reason for supposing the recital to be emblematical of the victory of the preacher of the Gospel over the worship of Esculapius.[‡] A similar allegory also explains the miracle that rendered St. Donat, bishop of Corinth, the vanquisher of a serpent so enormous that eight yoke of oxen could scarcely drag along its corpse.[§] The date of the miracle, in the year 399, is also the period in which paganism fell irrevocably beneath the blow struck against it by the command of the two sons of Theodosius.

A monstrous dragon desolated the neighborhood of Theil, near Roche aux Fées (Rock of the Fairies), in the department of the Isle and Vilaine. St. Arnel, the apostle of that country, led it with his stole to the summit of a mountain, and then commanded it to precipitate itself into the River Seiche. M. Noual de la Houssaye is of opinion that this miracle is emblematical of the victory which this saint achieved over the remains of the Druidical religion, the ceremonies of which had, till then, been perpetuated on the Rock of the Fairies. He explains in the same way the repetition of a similar miracle in the legend of St. Efflam, and in that of other saints.[‖] His conjecture may be easily extended to the works of a thaumaturgist, who, before a stone, most probably druidical and still honored by superstitious rites, overcame a dragon which had ravaged the territory of

---

[*] Dulaure, *Physical, Moral, and Civil History of Paris*, 1st edit., p. 161, 162, and 185, 186.

[†] *Mémoires de l'Académie Celtique*, tome iv., p. 311.

[‡] Appendini, *Notizie Istorico-critiche sulle Antichità, &c., de' Ragusea*, tome i., p. 30. Pouqueville, *Voyage dans la Grèce*, tome i., p. 24, 25.

[§] Sigeberti, *Chronicon*, anno 399.

[‖] *Mémoires de l'Académie Celtique*, tome v., p. 377.

Neuilly Saint Front skirting Chateau Thierry.* On a leaden medal, struck at Amiens in 1552 (doubtless from so ne more ancient type), St. Martin is represented as piercing with a lance the body of a dragon which he tramples under foot. This was intended to designate the victories of the saint over the pagan divinities.†

Constantine, the overthrower of paganism, loved to have himself painted armed with a cross, and striking with his lance a formidable dragon.‡ Thirty years ago, in a town of Normandy, might be seen an old picture which served as a sign to a hotel; the costume and figure were those of Louis XIV., the new St. Michael leveling to the earth the infernal dragon. It was, I presume, as a commemoration of the revocation of the Edict of Nantes.

Heresy, indeed, not less than false religion, is reputed to be the work of the spirit of darkness.§ The bronze dragon, therefore, which, until 1728, the monks of St. Loup, at Troyes, carried in the procession of Rogation,‖ passed for the emblem of the victory of St. Loup over the Pelagian heresy.

§ VII.

MULTIPLICITY OF FACTS OF THIS NATURE ADOPTED AS REAL FACTS.

Allegories are beyond the comprehension of the ignorant multitude, who are accustomed to believe whatever they are told. The serpent paraded on Rogation day was generally regarded as the representation of a real serpent, to the existence of which they assigned a certain date. In vain was the meaning of the allegory revealed to the superstitious; in vain they were shown, for instance, a picture of St. Veran loading the evil spirit with chains; they persisted in believing, and in relating that the territory of Arles was formerly delivered by St. Veran from the ravages of a monstrous serpent; and a picture perpetuates the remembrance of this victory,¶ which, according to the legend, was obtained at the entrance of a grotto near a fountain.

* *Mémoires de la Société des Antiquaires de France*, tome i, p. 426. 427.
† *Mémoires de l'Académie du Département de la Somme*, tome i, p. 699.
‡ Euseb. Pamph., *De Vitâ Constantini*, lib. iii, cap. iii.
§ The Emperor Sigismond instituted the order of the *Vanquished Dragon*, in celebration of the anathema denounced by the Council of Constance against the doctrines of John Huss and Jerome of Prague. The dragon signified heresy overcome.
‖ Grosley, *Éphémérides*, 3e partie, chap. xci, tome ii, p. 222, 225.
¶ I saw these pictures in 1813, in Majore Laa Church, in Arles.

Every parish had its dragon ; and still, in all the parishes
in Spain, the image of the serpent (Taras) is carried in procession on Corpus Christi day.   The history of the monster
varies still more than its forms, as imagination and credulity
attributed to it supernatural deeds.   From dread they passed
to respect.   The dragon of Poitiers* was piously surnamed
the *good St. Vermine*; they prayed to it, and they were
eager to obtain chaplets touched by it.   It is difficult to say
whether, as a monument, it remained what it had formerly
been, an idol, or that it became so by degrees among a superstitious people.

More commonly the emblem was surrounded by signs of
hatred and horror.   Its legendary history justified these sentiments.   It had been the curse of the country in which its
image was paraded.   Its venom had poisoned the springs,
and its breath infected the air with contagious diseases.   It
devoured the flocks, killed men, and chose young girls, virgins consecrated to the Lord, for its victims, while children
disappeared ingulfed in the abyss of its terrible jaws.   The
Bailla, a figure of a dragon that was paraded at Rheims
every Easter day, had probably this origin.   The gilded
dragon that figured in the processions of the Rogation, in
the parish of St. James of Douai, was the emblem of the demon that had devoured the corn in the ear, and destroyed
the harvest to punish the cultivators of it for having refused
to pay the tithes.†

At Provençe, until 1761, in the parishes of Nôtre Dame
and St. Quiriace, there was carried in the former, in the processions of the Rogation, a winged dragon, and in the latter
a monster termed a lizard, two animals which had formerly
desolated the town and its environs.‡   St. Florence went,
we are told, by the command of God, to establish himself in
a grotto, or cavern, situated on the left bank of the Loire, and
to expel from it serpents with which it was filled.   Soon
afterward he delivered the inhabitants of *Mur*, now Saumur,
from an enormous serpent which devoured men and animals,
and hid itself in a wood upon the banks of the Vienne.§

At Tonnerre, the holy Abbot Johan overcame a basilisk
which infected the waters of a fountain.‖   The *Vivre* of
Larré, to which a Burgundian proverb likened any woman

* Notes of the *Society of the Antiquaries of France*, vol. i., p. 464.   Notes
of the *Celtic Academy*, vol. v., p. 54, 55.
† Bottin, *Traditions des Dragons volants, &c.*, p. 157, and 160, 161.
‡ Ch. Opoix, *Histoire et Description des Provins*, p. 435, 436.
§ J. J. Bodin, *Recherches Historiques sur Saumur et le Haut-Anjou*, tome
I., p. 117-122.   ‖ Greg. Turon., *De Glorid Confessor.*, cap. lxxxvii.

accused of beshrewing,* was a serpent hidden near a fountain in the vicinity of a priory of the order of St. Benoit, and long an object of public terror. At Aix, in Provençe, the procession of the Rogations deposits upon a rock, called the Rock of the Dragon, and near a chapel dedicated to St. Andrew, the figure of a dragon, killed by the intercession of this holy apostle.† No less the source of succor than St. Andrew and St. George, St. Victor at Marseilles overcame a monstrous reptile.‡ St. Theodore trampled a serpent under foot ;§ and St. Second, patron of Asti, is represented on horseback piercing a dragon with his lance.‖ We might quote many other similar legends without pretending to exhaust the subject. Knowing the common origin of all, and the causes which, since the fifth century, multiplied them in the East, we are far from being astonished at their number ; on the contrary, we are surprised that more do not exist.

§ VIII.

VARIATIONS IN THE CIRCUMSTANCES AND DATES OF THE NARRATIONS ; NEW VESTIGES OF THE ASTRONOMICAL LEGEND.

The custom of bearing the image of the serpent in the ceremonies of the Rogations ceased very gradually ; and it may be said, this emblem of the *Prince of Darkness* yielded but slowly to the advancement of the light of truth. Several churches in France did not abandon the use of it until the eighteenth century ; in 1771, Grosley found it kept up in full force in all the Catholic churches of the Low Countries.§ During so long a lapse of time the narrations must necessarily have varied, and, consequently, the explanations of them.

To overcome the Gargouille, the dragon of Rouen, St. Romans caused himself to be accompanied by a criminal condemned to death, whose pardon was obtained by the miracle of the saint.

The clergy willingly gave credit to these kinds of tales. They augmented their power by obtaining for the heads of

* La Monnoye, *Noel Borguignon*, 12mo, 1720, p. 399, 400. *Vivre, vouivre*, or *guivre*, viper, serpent. The word *guivre* has still this sense in the heraldic vocabulary.

† Fauris Saint Vincent, *Memoire sur l'Ancienne Cité d'Aix. Magasin Encyclopedique*, year 1812, vol. vi., p. 267.

‡ In the Abbey of St. Victor at Marseilles.

§ Dorbessan, *Essay upon Sacred Serpents, Historical and Critical Miscellanies*, vol. ii., p. 132.

‖ Millin, *Travels in Savoy and Piedmont*, vol. i., p. 121.

¶ Grosley, *Travels in Holland. Unpublished Works of Grosley*, 3 vols 8vo, Paris, 1815, vol. iii., p. 300.

R

their order the right of pardoning, or, at least, as at Rouen, that of giving liberty to prisoners. It was regarded as not granting too much to the memory of a miracle, of which, by the will of God, a condemned criminal became the instrument.

Still more willingly did the vulgar receive this variation of the universal legend ; according to them, no man could have resolved to undertake so perilous a combat, unless with the fear of some infamous and cruel death before him. In this manner, a criminal condemned to death robbed St. Radegonde of the honor of having vanquished the *Grand'gucule*, the terrible dragon of Poitiers, which, issuing every day from its cavern on the banks of the River Clain, devoured the virgins of the Lord, the nuns of the Convent of St. Croix.* Another doomed man was said to have delivered the parish of Villiers, near Vendôme, from the ravages of a serpent.† A third killed a dragon, or a crocodile, which, hidden beneath the waters of the Rhone, was the scourge of the sailors and the inhabitants of the country.‡ A deserted soldier, in order to obtain his pardon, fought with a dragon that spread terror into the environs of Niort.§ He triumphed but lost his life in the struggle.

In discussing the history of this pretended soldier,‖ M. Eloi-Johanneau remarks how suspicious it is rendered by one of the names given to him signifying the vanquisher of a *beast* or a *monster*, and particularly by its date, 1589 or 1692, a date much too recent for history not to have recorded the fact. The date assigned by D. Calmet to the appearance of the serpent of Luneville is still more modern. He places it a century from the time in which he wrote.¶ Of all the variations which popular traditions are subject to in the course of time, the most common are those which relate to date. For such stories there exist no archives ; and it is in the nature of man to be forever endeavoring to appropriate to himself recollections bequeathed to him by the past. Too long an interval between them and the time present wearies his imagination, unable to fill up the gap ; he therefore endeavors to narrow it in proportion as the lapse of time may demand. Thus, the dragon of Niort has been successively placed in 1589 and in 1692. That of the Grand'gucule of

---

* *Mémoires de l'Académie Celtique*, tome v., p. 52, 53, 55. *Mémoires de la Société des Antiquaires de France*, tome L, p. 464, 465.
† *Mémoires de l'Académie Celtique*, tome iv., p. 311.
‡ *Id. ibid.*, tome v., p. 111.   § *Id. ibid.*, p. 58, 60, 132, 134.
‖ *Id. ibid.*, p. 59, and 134, 135.
¶ *Journal of Verdun*, June, 1751, p. 430

Poitiers, when attributed to a condemned criminal, was placed at so great a distance from the period in which St. Radegonde lived, that in 1280 the apparition of the flying dragon was also attributed to that town.* Although St. Jerome has described the combat of St. Hilary against the serpent of Epidaurus, the caverns and remains of which are still shown to travelers, its defeat has been attributed to himself.✛ The tradition which attributes the destruction of the Tarasque to St. Martha is modern compared to that which gave the honor to sixteen brave men, eight of whom perished victims to their courage ; the others founded the towns of Beaucaire and Tarascon.‡

We might instance several other dates that time has also disarranged and modernized. It is, nevertheless, for a different cause that the death of the heroes of Tarascon and the soldier of Niort deserve to be remembered. In those myths which describe the struggle of the principle of light over the principle of darkness, the former frequently paid for its victory with its life. It is thus related of Osiris, of Bacchus, of Atys, and of Adonis. In the Scandinavian mythology, likewise, at that terrible day when the world is to be destroyed and renewed, the god Thor, after having exterminated the great serpent, engendered by the principle of evil, is to perish himself, stifled by the venomous breath emitted by the monster. We are not astonished at finding another vestige of the solar legend, or in seeing several vanquishers of enormous serpents falling in the midst of their triumphs, or unable to survive them.

Ancient Greece offers an example of such generous devotion. The town of Thespia, by the command of a miracle, offered every year a youth to a homicidal dragon. Cleostrates was destined by fate for this horrible sacrifice. His friend, Menestrates, took his place ; and clothed in a cuirass, each scale of which bore a hook with the point turned uppermost, he delivered himself to the monster, whose death he caused, although he himself perished.§

Toward the end of the fifteenth century, or, according to a more ancient tradition, in 1273 (for here the date is varied that it may be brought nearer to our times), the mountains of Neufchâtel were ravaged by a serpent, the recollection of

* *Mémoires de l'Académie Celtique*, tome v., p. 61, 62.
† Pouqueville, *Voyage dans la Grèce*, tome i., p. 24, 25.
‡ *Mémoires de la Société des Antiquaires de France*, tome i., p. 423. The foundation of Tarascon (or, more properly, the establishment of the Marseillaise in this town) appears previous to the war of Cæsar against Pompey.   § Pausanias, *Bœotica*, cap. xxvi.

which is still maintained by the names of several places in the environs of the village of Sully.* Raymond of Sully fought with the monster, killed it, and died two days afterward.

Such was also the fate of Belzunce, who delivered Bayonne from a dragon with several heads ; he perished, suffocated by the flames and smoke vomited by the monster.†

Patriotism celebrates with enthusiasm the name of Arnold Strouthan of Winkelried, who, at the battle of Sampach in 1386, devoted himself for the safety of his countrymen. The name of one of his ancestors has a less authentic, but not less popular title to immortality. Upon the banks of the River Melch, near Alpenach, in the canton of Underwald, there appeared in 1250 a dragon, the cave of which is still shown. Struth de Winkelried, condemned to banishment for having fought a duel, determined to regain the right of re-entering his country by delivering it from this scourge ; he succeeded, but died of his wounds the day after his victory.‡ Petermann Eterlin (who in truth wrote two hundred and fifty years later§) has recorded this fact in his chronicles. The hand of the artist has sketched it upon the walls of a chapel near the scene of the encounter ; the place has preserved the name of the *Marsh of the Dragon* (Drakenried ;) and the cavern that of the Dragon's Hole (Drakenlok). These commemorative names, and those of the same kind existing near Sulpy, indicate, perhaps, like that of the *Rock of the Dragon* at Aix, the places where the procession of Rogations stopped, and where the image of the allegorical dragon was momentarily deposited.‖ Perhaps they may also have related, as we have already suspected, to the course of some devastating torrent.

§ IX.

THIS LEGEND HAS BEEN APPLIED TO CELEBRATED PERSONAGES, AND HISTORY HAS BEEN ALTERED THAT IT MIGHT SEEM TO RELATE THE EVENTS.

Eterlin, the biographer of Struth of Winkelried, has trans-

---

* *Roche à la Vuirra; Combe à la Vuirra; Fontaine à la Vuivra (vivra, vivre, guivre, serpent).* *Description des Montagnes de Neufchâtel,* Neufchâtel, 1776, 12mo, p. 34–37. † *Mercure de France,* March 29th, 1817, p. 585

‡ *Le Conservateur Suisse,* 7 vols. 12mo, Lausanne, 1813–1815, tome vi., p. 440, 441. Mayer, *Travels in Switzerland,* vol. i., p. 251, seems to attribute this adventure to Arnold of Winkelried, and places the dragon's cavern near Stanz. § W. Coxe, *Letters on Switzerland,* vol. i., p. 160.

‖ The mountain nearest to Cologne is called Rocks of the Dragons.— *Mémoires de la Société des Antiquaires de France,* tome ii., p. 139, 140

ferred to William Tell the adventure of the apple,* which
Saxo Grammaticus, who wrote more than a century before
the birth of Tell, had already related of a Danish archer
named Toko ;† an adventure borrowed, with precisely the
same circumstances, from a still more ancient tradition of
Egil, father of the clever smith Wailland, and himself an ex
pert archer.‡ Eterlin seems to have taken pains to impress
with an historical character the religious myths and fables
imported from other countries into his own. He wrote down
all popular beliefs ; and nothing is more usual with the vulgar than to apply the histories and fables composing their
documents to personages well known to them. Winkelried
and Tell are to the Swiss peasants what Alexander was,
and still is, in the East. To the name of the King of Macedonia the Asiatics attached a thousand recollections, some
of them anterior to his existence, and evidently borrowing
from mythology. The traditions of a devastating dragon,
over which Alexander triumphed, was in the twelfth century still preserved in an island of Western Africa.§ The
Paladine Roland enjoyed the same honor in the West ; and
this is still attested by the names of several places.‖ Ari-
osto, when singing of Roland, the vanquisher of the Orca,
a sea monster about to devour a young girl,¶ probably did
no more than copy and embellish a tradition of preceding
ages, as in a thousand other passages of his poem.

An individual whose existence and fame are in no respect
fabulous has, nevertheless, become, like Roland, the hero of
a fable which renders him a rival of Hercules and Perseus.
The importance which the remembrance of him had acquired
in a country which was so long his abode has doubtlessly
gained this honor for him. Petrarch was following Laura
in the chase ; they arrived near a cavern where a dragon,
the terror of the country, was concealed. Less ravenous

---

* W. Coxe, *Letters on Switzerland*, vol. i., p. 160. See a writing, entitled
William Tell, a Danish Fable, by Uriel Freudenberger, a work published
at Berne in 1760, by Haller, Jun., 1 vol. 8vo. Uriel Freudenberger, pastor
of Glarisse, Canton of Berne, died in 1768.

† Saxo Gramm., *Hist. Danic.*, lib. x., folio, Francofurti, 1576, p. 166–168.
Saxo died in 1204. Harold, who plays in history the same part as Gesler,
fell beneath the blows of Toko in 981. The fable of the apple being much
more ancient, it was renewed by the public hatred under the name of
Harold, as it has since been reproduced in Switzerland under the odious
name of Gesler.

‡ *Mémoires de la Société des Antiquaires de France*, tome v., p. 229.
§ L'île de Mostachiin, *Géographie d'Edrisi*, tome i., p. 198–200.
‖ La *Baume Roland*, near Marseilles ; la *Brèche Roland*, in the Pyrenees ;
il *C . . . , d'Orlando*, three miles from Rimini, &c.
¶ *Orlando Furioso*, canto xi.

than amorous, the dragon pursued Laura. Petrarch flew to the assistance of his mistress, fought with, and stabbed the monster. The sovereign pontiff, however, would not allow the picture of the triumph of love to be placed in any sacred building. Simon of Sienna, the friend of the poet, evaded this prohibition by painting this adventure under the portal of the Church of Notre Dame du Don, at Avignon. Laura is depicted in the attitude of a suppliant virgin, and Petrarch in the costume of St. George, armed with a poniard instead of a lance. Time, though it has lowered the estimation in which this work was held, has not weakened the tradition which it perpetuates, and which has been repeated to me as a real historical fact.*

In the examination of traditions, sufficient attention has not always been paid to that inclination which induces the ignorant man to find in every thing the myths occupying the first place in his belief. To arrive at such a result, he perverts his recollections, either by attributing to some individual events that have never happened to him, or by introducing into history the incredible parts of a fable. The story in which Petrarch figures is an example of the first kind of alteration; we shall find one of the second kind without diverging from our subject.

A Swedish prince† had nurtured up near his daughter, named Thora, two serpents to be the guardians of her virginity. Grown to an immense size, these monsters spread terror and death around them, chiefly by their pestilential breath. The king, in despair, promised the hand of his daughter to the hero who should kill the serpents. Regner Lodbrog, a prince, a scald, and a warrior, achieved this perilous adventure, and became the husband of the beautiful Thora. That is the fable; but, according to the Ragnara Lodbrog's Saga,‡ the history is as follows. It was not to two serpents, but to one of his vassals, the possessor of a strong castle, that the king had confided the charge of his daughter; the guardian becoming enamored of the princess, refused to restore her; and the king, after vain attempts to compel him, promised that Thora should espouse her liberator. Regner Lodbrog was this happy individual.

* In 1813. I observed that in recitals concerning Laura at Avignon or at Vaucluse, she is always respectfully called *Madame Laura.*

† Saxo Grammat., *Hist. Dan.*, lib. ix., p. 153. Olaus Magnus, *Hist. Sept. Gentium Brev.*, lib. v., cap. 17.

‡ Quoted in the work of Biorner, entitled *Kæmpedater* (Stockholm, 1737), and by Graberg of Hemsöe, *Saggio Istorico Sugli Caldi,* 8vo, Pisa, 1811, p. 217.

In an incursion upon the coasts of Northumberland, however, Regner was conquered, made prisoner, and thrown into a subterranean dungeon filled with serpents : their bites proved fatal. This is said to have occurred about the year 866. The story is related by every historian ;* perpetuated, also, in the Dirge which has been attributed to Regner himself. I, nevertheless, suspect that, in the nature of his punishment, an attempt was made to connect it with the legend of which this hero was already the object. The same spirit which had altered the history of his hymeneals, so as to recall or emblemize the struggle in which the principle of good triumphed over the principle of evil, intended, perhaps, that this tragical end should also recall the death suffered by the principle of good in the allegorical combats. The name of the vanquisher, *Regna Hella*, favors this supposition ; the Scandinavians can discern in it the name of Héla, goddess of Death, like the *great serpent*, the offspring of the principle of evil. What sanctions my conjecture, is the great importance accorded in Scandinavian mythology to the *great serpent ;* it is never described as perishing, except it draws after it, into annihilation, the god with whom it fought. In this manner, serpents and dragons reappear more than once in the Scandinavian annals. I find that, both before and after Regner, the general myth is interwoven, in two different places, into the individual history. Frotho I., ninth king of Denmark,† requiring money to pay his soldiers, attacked, in a desert isle, a dragon, the guardian of a treasure, and killed it at the very entrance of its cavern. Harold,‡ exiled from Norway, took refuge in Byzance. Having been guilty of homicide, he was exposed to the fury of a monstrous dragon. More fortunate than Regner, he overcame it, and returned to occupy the throne of Norway, and to annoy the nephew of Canute the Great, who was then seated upon the throne of Denmark.

---

* Saxo Grammat., *Hist. Dan.*, lib. ix., p. 159. *Olaus Magnus*, loc. cit. Ragnara Lodbrog's *Saga.*

† 761 years before Christ. Saxo Grammat., *Hist. Dan.*, lib. ii., p. 18, 19.

‡ In the 11th century. Saxo Grammat., *Hist. Dan.*, lib. ii., p. 185, 186. I translate the word *antrum* into *cavern.* The ditch in which Regner Lodbrog perished seems to me to correspond with the caverns of almost all the legends quoted.

◊ X.

PHYSICAL OBJECTS AND MONUMENTS, IN WHICH THE VULGAR FIND AGAIN THE PICTURE OF THE DESTRUCTION OF A MONSTROUS SERPENT.

That which daily strikes the senses has an influence upon the belief of uneducated men, at least as much as the recollections which are engraved on the memory; physical objects, paintings, and sculpture, like history, aid the imagination to discover every where legends that favor credulity.

In the Abbey of St. Victor, at Marseilles, in the Hospital of Lyons,* and in a church at Ragusa, the skin of a crocodile is shown to travelers. It is pointed out as the skin of a monster, the hero of legends, belonging to these different places; and, nevertheless, at Ragusa, for example, it is not unknown that it is a skin which was brought from Egypt by Ragusan sailors.† These kind of relics, intended for keeping up and confirming faith, when they do not originate it, have never appeared misplaced in our temples, into which, probably, they were first introduced in the quality of votive offerings. This was the opinion passed by Millin‡ upon the skin of a cayman,◊ suspended from the roof of a church at Cimiers, in the province of Nice. It did not appear that any history was attached to it; whether it was from the lapse of time the legend has fallen into oblivion, or that the *ex voto* was too recent to presume to apply any legend to it.

Another monument of this kind, the existence of which, however, is less certain, is the head of the dragon which was so miraculously conquered by Dieudonné of Gozon. It was preserved at Rhodes. The Turks, when they became masters of Rhodes, respected it. The traveler Thévenot saw it toward the middle of the 17th century, and the description which he gives of it would lead it to be regarded as belonging rather to a hippopotamus than to a serpent.‖ Will it be considered too bold to think that this head, like the cayman of Cimiers, like the crocodiles of Ragusa, of Lyons, and of Marseilles, was first exposed by public piety

---

* *Mémoires de l'Académie Celtique*, vol. v., p. 111.

† Pouqueville, *Voyage dans la Grèce*, tome i., p. 24, 25.

‡ Millin, *Voyage en Savoie, en Piémont, à Nices, à Gênes*, tome ii., p. 124.

◊ The cayman, *Crocodilus Palpebrosus* (Cuvier), is a native of Surinam and Guiana. It does not attain to as large a size as the other species of crocodiles; nor will it attack a man either on land or in the water, as long as he keeps his legs and arms in motion. This species of crocodile has never been found in the old continent; hence it is not to be seen in any of the ancient temples.—ED.

‖ Thévenot, *Relation d'un Voyage fait au Levant, &c.*, p. 223.

or by interest ; and that, constantly attracting the observations of the multitude, it furnished an occasion for applying, at a later period, the legend of the hero who conquered the dragon to a celebrated cavalier, a *grand-master of the order* ?

At Wasmes, near Mons, on Pentecost Tuesday, and on Trinity day, the head of a crocodile is carried in procession. In the eyes of a credulous population, it represents the head of the dragon which, in the 12th century, ravaged the environs of Wasmes, and which, when about to devour a young *girl* in his *cavern*, fell under the blows of Gilles, lord of Chin.* A tradition, carefully preserved in the country, attributes to the father of Chin, who died in 1137, the most striking traits of an exploit, the honor of which, two centuries later, was given to Dieudonné of Gozon, namely, the difficulty of obtaining permission to combat the dragon, the care with which a figure resembling it was manufactured a long time previously, for the purpose of training the horses and the dogs gradually to attack it fearlessly, and the precaution of being followed by devoted servants to the place of combat. Here is another example of the facility with which they applied to persons known at one period and in one country the myths borrowed from another country, and from an anterior epoch.

A direct interest is not always requisite for changing an astronomical myth into local history. There is at Clagenfurt, placed upon a fountain, an antique group, found at Saal or Zolfeld, the ancient *Colonia Solvensis*, representing a dragon of a prodigious size, and a Hercules armed with a club. The people believe it to be a poor peasant who had formerly delivered the country from the ravages of a dragon, the image of which they conceive is properly placed by the side of his own.†

Upon a cross in the cemetery of Dommarie, a commune of the department of the Meurthe (of which the forest of Thorey is a dependence), is sculptured the figure of a winged dragon. Calmet, deceived by this emblem, has related that a winged dragon was formerly the terror of this country.‡

The inhabitants of Trebizonde relate, that in 1204 Alexis Comnenes overthrew with his own hands a monstrous dragon. In memory of this exploit, he caused a fountain, which he called the *Fountain of the Dragon*, to be constructed in the

* *Recherches Historiques sur Gilles, Seigneur de Chin, et le Dragon*, Mons, 1825. *Revue Encyclopédique*, vol. xxviii., p. 192, 193. M. Bottin, *Traditions des Dragons Volants*, &c., p. 165, 173.
† Ed. Brown, *Narrative of many Voyages.*
‡ Bottin, *Traditions*, &c., p. 156, 157. *Journal de Verdun, Juin*, 1751, p. 454.

town. This monument remains ; the mouth of the pipe, whence the water issues, representing the head of the fabulous animal.* This figure of the spout has given to the fountain the name which it bears, and, consequently, is the origin of the legend.

Augustus Cæsar, wishing to immortalize the remembrance of his conquest, and the submission of Egypt, gave as a type for the medals of a colony which he had just founded in Gaul, a *crocodile* tied to a *palm-tree*. The town in which the colony settled had for several centuries recognized Nemausus, whose name it bore, and who was its founder, as its local divinity ; and this name could not fail to figure upon its medals. Very soon, and notwithstanding that the *palm-tree* never grew on the soil of Nismes (the ancient Nemausus), the *crocodile* became one of those monsters in all the different legends, which stated that the imitators of Hercules, holy men, or those worthy of being regarded as such, had overcome. This terrible animal poisoned the waters of a fountain, and desolated the country. The hero had triumphed over it ; and he thus received, and transmitted to the town which he founded near the fountain, the name of Nemausus, which still recalls that he alone had performed *what none had dared to attempt.*†

Here, at least, a *real* representation, although badly interpreted, had attracted observation and excused the error. According to a received tradition at Pisa, Nino Orlandi, in 1109, succeeded in confining an enormous and dangerous serpent in an iron cage, and paraded it thus into the middle of the town. How can we doubt of the truth of the fact ? A bas-relievo, placed in the *Campo Santo*, represented it ; an inscription attested it. Observant eyes have, in our time, examined these two monuments ; the inscription was placed in 1777 ; the bas-relief, a fragment in Paros marble, does not portray a single object that can relate to Orlandi's pretended victory.‡

* Prottiers, *Itinéraire de Tiflis à Constantinople* (Brussels, 1829), p. 206.
† *Nemo Ausus.* M. l'Abbé Simil, *Mémoires sur la Maison carrée. Notices sur les travaux de l'Académie du Gard* of 1812-1822, 1st part, p. 329, 330. Eusebè Salverte, *Essai sur les Noms d'Hommes, de Peuples et de Lieux,* tome ii., p. 279, 280.
‡ See the *Moniteur Universel* of Monday, July 2, 1812.

§ XI.

COATS OF ARMS AND MILITARY ENSIGNS GIVE PLACE TO NEW APPLICATIONS OF THE ASTRONOMICAL LEGEND.

Greedy of glory and of power, it was natural for the nobles and the warriors to wish to share with the demi-gods of paganism, with the favored of heaven, the honor of those triumphs which would secure immortal claims on the gratitude of the people. After the Scandinavian heroes, after Struth of Winkelried, Belzunce, and Dieudonné of Gozon, we can refer to a young noble who accompanied St. Pol when he wished to destroy the dragon of the Isle of Batz ;* and also St. Bertrand, the conqueror of the dragon of Comminges, a bishop who belonged to an illustrious race ; for he was the son of a Count of Toulouse.†

We might also quote the pretended origin of the prænomen of the *Nompar* of Caumont. Reviving for themselves the fabulous history of the founder of Nismes, they relate that this prænomen was transmitted to them by one of their ancestors, who, in fact, showed himself *sans pair* (*non par*) in giving death to a monstrous dragon whose ravages desolated his territory.

But to avoid tedious repetitions, we shall confine ourselves to remarking how much this pretension on the part of the nobles was favored by the figures with which each of them ornamented his helmet or his shield, and which, from them, have passed into coats of arms.

Ubert was the first who, among the Milanese, fulfilled the functions delegated to the *Counts* (*Comites*) of the Lower Empire, and of the Empire of Charlemagne. He adopted, in consequence, the surname of *viscount*, which he transmitted to his descendants. At Milan, in that place where the very ancient Church of St. Denis rears itself, there was a deep cavern, the dwelling of an ever-hungry dragon, whose breath spread death to a great distance. Ubert fought it and killed it ; and he wished its image to figure in the coats of arms of the Visconti.‡ According to Paul Jove, Othon, one of the first viscounts, distinguished himself in the army of Godfrey of Bouillon : a Saracen chief, whom he slew in single combat, bore upon his helmet the figure of a serpent devouring an infant ; the conqueror placed it in his coat of arms, and left to his posterity this monument of his

---

* Cambry, *Voyage dans le Département du Finisterre*, tome i., p. 147, 148.
† *Dictionnaire de Moréri*, art. *Saint Bertrand*.
‡ Carlo Torre, *Ritratto di Milano.* p. 273.

glory.* The recital of Paul Jove, if it is not as true as the other, is at least as probable.

Aymon, count of Corbeil, bore upon his shield a dragon with two heads. In a street of Corbeil there may be seen a covered drain, which terminates at the River of Etampes : according to popular tradition, this was formerly the den of a dragon with two heads, the terror of the country ; the Count Aymon had the honor of conquering it.†

The family *Dragon* of Ramillies had as its arms a gold dragon in an azure field. This family traces the origin of its name, and of its *coat of arms*, to a victory obtained by *John*, lord of Ramillies, over a dragon which desolated the neighboring territory of Escaut, and which the intrepid baron combated even in the cavern into which the monster enticed its victims.‡

The lion, being the symbol of strength, generally decorated the tombs of the knights. Upon the tomb of Gouffier of Lascours a serpent is added to it, as the symbol of prudence. In these representations one may perceive an evident allusion to a marvelous adventure related by the chronicles, in which this warrior had delivered a lion from an enormous dragon by which it was pursued. The grateful animal attached himself to his benefactor, and followed him every where like a faithful dog.§ We may observe that this is precisely the adventure that the author of the *Morgante* ascribes to Renaud of Montauban.‖ But the invention does not belong to him ; the same story is found again in the poetical romance of Chrestein of Troyes, entitled the Knight of the Lion.¶

Similar recitals have arisen from similar causes, before the invention of chivalrous emblems and coats of arms.

A warrior always desires to present to his adversaries objects capable of striking them with terror. The serpent is the emblem of a prudent and dangerous enemy ; the winged serpent, or dragon, is the presage of rapid and inevitable destruction. These signs found their place upon the banners, as well as upon the face of the shields, and upon the tops of the helmets. The dragon figured also among the military ensigns of the Assyrians ; and Cyrus, the conqueror of the Assyrians, caused it to be adopted by the Per-

* Paul Jove, in *Vit. duod. Vicecom. Mediol. Princip., Præfatio.*
† Millin, *Antiquités Nationales,* tome ii., art. *Saint Spire de Corbeil.*
‡ Bottin, *Traditions, &c.,* p. 164, 165.
§ N. Dallou. *Monumens des différens Ages observés dans le Département de la Haute Vienne,* p. 359.   ‖ *Morgante,* Cont. iv., ottav. 7, et seq.
¶ *Manuscr. de la Bibliothèque du Roi,* No. 7535, folio 16 verso, colonne 2.

sians and by the Medes.* Under the Roman emperors, and under the emperors of Byzantium, every *cohort*, or *centurion*, bore a dragon as its ensign.† Grosley affirms (but without bearing out his assertion by decisive proofs) that the dragons, from being military ensigns, which were the objects of the worship of the Roman soldier, passed into the churches, and figured in the processions of the Rogations as trophies acquired by the conquests of religion.‡

We must admit, also, that similar signs have more than once recalled the remembrance of astronomic myths; and when it is known that in religious ceremonies the image of the dragon was carried by the side of that of St. George, before the Emperor of Constantinople,§ we are tempted to believe that St. George owes to this custom the legend which has placed him in the same rank as St. Michael.

Uther, the first king of England, the father of the famous King Arthur, imitated in battle the example of the Assyrians and the Persians, and hoisted a dragon with a golden head as an ensign. In consequence of this transaction, he received the surname of *Pen-dragon* (Dragon-head), a surname which gave rise to many marvelous recitals. For instance, it is related that he saw in the skies a star which had the form of a fiery dragon, and which foretold his elevation to the throne.‖ The astronomical origin of the primitive legend had not been forgotten.

§ XII.

ANCIENT MYTHOLOGY ALTERED FOR THE PURPOSE OF FINDING IN IT THE LEGEND OF THE SERPENT.

After having corrupted history; after having mistaken the origin of physical representations; forgotten the signification of monuments; and even having read and seen upon them what had never existed, the desire of discovering every where a myth which had been familiarized required but one step more: it only remained to sacrifice objects of ancient credulity, and to disfigure a *preceding* mythology, in order to bend it to the recitals of a *new* mythology. The following is a fact of this species, which, without being positive, is not

* Georg. Codin, *Curop. de Official. Palat. Constant.* . . . . . *Feria quæ in Palatio solent, &c.*

† Modestus, *De Vocabul. Rei Milit.* Flav. Veget., *De Re Militari*, lib. ii., cap. 13. Georg. Codin, *Curop.* loc. cit.

‡ Grosley, *Ephémérides*, iiie. partie, chap. ix., tome ii., p. 222–225.

§ Georg. Codin, *Curop. de Official. Palat. Cons.*, loc. cit. " *Cantata igitur liturgiâ . . . aliud* (Flammeolum) *quod fert* sanctum Georgium equitem, *aliud* draconteum." &c.   ‖ Ducange, *Glossar.*, verbo *Draco*.

devoid of probability. It is attached to a memorial sufficiently famous to render excusable the details upon which
we are forced to enter.

In explaining a medal which appeared to belong to the
fifteenth century, and which, on the reverse of the head of
Geoffrey of Lusignan, says, *Geoffrey à la grand'dent*, displayed the head of a fantastic monster. Millin* relates that
Geoffrey was invited to combat a monster which had already devoured an English knight. When prepared to at
tempt the adventure, Geoffrey died of sickness. The head
drawn upon the medal is, he adds, that of the monster,
"which Geoffrey would certainly have conquered, had not
death prevented him." But a medal would never have been
struck out to immortalize what had never occurred : it must
then have been that tradition in the family of Lusignan, to
which Millin attributes the manufacture of the medal, and
which related that the brave count, like so many saints and
heroes who have passed in review before us, was the vanquisher of the monster.

Let us remember, first, that Geoffrey was the son, or,
rather, the descendant of the famous Mellusine or Merlusine,† Melesendis, who transformed herself every Saturday
into a serpent ; secondly, that the Sassenages, who con-

* *Voyage au Midi de la France*, tome iv., p. 707, 708. Geoffrey *à la grand'dent* died about the year 1250.

† I shall not contest with M. Mazet, quoted by Millin (*Voyage au Midi de la France*, tome iv., p. 706), whether the mother of Geoffrey was entitled Melicendis, Melesindis (Melisende), and that this name may have
been confounded with that of *Mellusine*. But, far from admitting that it
has produced it, it is my opinion that the confusion arose because the
name of Mellusine was already celebrated. Still less easily shall I adopt
another etymology, according to which the Lady of *Melle*, bearing this
lordship as her dower to the Sieur de Lusignan, the two names united
and formed that of *Mellusine*.—(*Mémoires de la Société des Antiquaires de
France*, tome iii., p. 279, 280). At the commencement of the thirteenth
century women did not join their names to that of their husband's do
minions. I do not even think that they commonly bore the name of
their own possessions. In pronouncing it Merlusin with Brantome (*Vie
des Hommes Illustres, &c.*, tome viii., p. 322) and with the people, more
certain guides than the learned upon the pronunciation of names hande'
down in ancient stories, I draw near to the orthography of the family
name of Geoffrey, thus written upon the medal before mentioned, Gode-
fridus de Lusinem. You have only to place mère (mater) before the last
word to reproduce the name of Merlusine, and to prove that it was nothing more than the simple title of Mother of Lusignan (Mère des Lusignan),
applied by the people to the woman-serpent, to the fairy from whom this
family claimed or adduced their descent. Our etymology is the less
probable from the fact that Jean d'Arras, the first author who compiled
the history of Merluzine, wrote in the reign of Jean, in the fourteenth century, when the family name of the Lusignans had been long fixed and
become celebrated.

sidered Geoffrey of the great tooth (à la grand'dent) as among their ancestors, had sculptured upon the exterior door of their castle a figure Mellusine,[*] that is to say, half woman, half serpent.

Merlusine was a benevolent fairy ; it seemed, therefore, natural to rank one of her descendants among the number of hero-destroyers of the deadly serpent, and when applying to him the universal and common legend, to ascribe to him a victory perpetuated by the medal, of which an explanation has been attempted by Millin.

But where, in the marshes of Poitou, could a being half woman, half serpent, or alternately the one or the other, have originated ?

A tradition, preserved to the present day, informs us that Merlusine transformed herself into a fish, and not into a serpent.[†] This is the key to the enigma, which belongs to a high antiquity. The image of the mermaid, which the moderns deemed a siren, although all the ancient writings and monuments depict the sirens as *bird* and woman,[‡] this image, so common in the time of Horace, that the poet cited it as the type of absurdity[§]—this image, that the Greeks applied to Eurynome, one of the wives of the God of the

---

[*] Millin, *Magasin Encyclopédique*, 1811, tome vi., p. 108–112.

[†] *Mémoires de la Société des Antiquaires de France*, tome iii., p. 320. Scarron was not ignorant of this tradition, for in his third satire he makes a fop declare that he will make

> "The infant Mellusine ;
> The heroine will be half woman, half fish,"

appear on the stage.

Let us observe, the most generally received tradition very nearly approaches this in placing Mellusine in an immense basin, the blows of her tail forcing the water up to the vaulted roof of the chamber.—*Bulletin de la Société d'Agriculture de Poitiers*, 1823, p. 214, 215.

[‡] In a wall of the interior court of the Museum of Paris is incrusted an ancient alto-relievo of white marble, a bird-woman, a siren. Mountfaucon saw similar figures of sirens in red marble in the town of Aldobrandino (*Diarium Italicum*, 170, p. 190, 191). At Stymphales, upon the borders of Argolis and Arcadia, marble statues represent young girls having the legs of birds (Pausanias, *Arcad.*, cap. xxii). In the ruins of the ancient temples of the Island of Java, several figures of birds having the heads of girls have been discovered, and one was remarked as having the head of an aged man (*Description of Java*, by Marchal, 4to, Brussels, 1824) This proves the antiquity of the myth relative to the siren, but does not indicate the origin of it. Plato, assisted, perhaps, by the traditions of ancient India, placed a siren on each of the eight circles of the heavens, who sung while following the periodical revolution (Plat., *De Repub.*, lib. x.) Menephylle, in Plutarch, rejects this idea, because the sirens, he says are malevolent genii ; but Ammonius justifies Plato.

[§] Turpiter atrum
Desinit in piscem mulier formosa superne.
Horat., *De Art. Poet*

Sea, is that under which the Syrians and Phœnicians invoked Astarte, or Atergatis, the Celestial Virgin.[*] It may be found in the Egyptian planisphere, where it represents the sign of the fishes united to that of the Virgin. It is perpetuated in the religions of Japan[†] and Hindostan,[‡] and preserved in the ancient mythology of the Island of Java.[§]

It has even penetrated into Kamtschatka, doubtless with the Lamich religion. In the Iortes (iourtes) of the northern Kamtschatdales one sees the idol Khan-tai represented with a human body as far as the chest, the remainder resembling the tail of a fish. A fresh image is fabricated every year, and the number of these point out the number of years the Iourt had been constructed.[||] This peculiarity proves that the idol Khan-tai, like the mermaid of the Egyptian planisphere, is of an astronomical origin, since it has remained the symbol of the renewal of the year.

We are not able to speak so decidedly of the *Mother of the Water*, a malevolent divinity half fish, half woman, who, according to the natives of Guiana, delights in attracting the fishermen to the open sea, and then sinking their frail vessels. This fable, it is said, was spread over America before the arrival of the Europeans.[¶]

Could a symbol so frequently reproduced reach Gaul? Could time modify it sufficiently to have changed the extremity of a fish into that of a serpent?

1. To the first question I answer, that this symbol still exists in one of the most ancient towns of France, namely, at Marseilles. Upon an angle of the Fort St. John can be distinguished the gigantic figure of a monster half woman, half fish. If it has been thus reproduced in the construction of Fort St. John, it was most probably because it existed long before as a national monument. Its name, the same as that of the town, Marseilles, indicates that it represented the local divinity, the town itself deified. The Phocians, in adopting a symbol so suitable for characterizing a large maritime city, would not have had occasion to borrow from Tyre, Sidon, or Carthage. They had founded their colony under the auspices of the Great Diana of Ephesus, the heavenly virgin who was adored in this form not only in Asia, but even in Greece; for the statue, half woman, half fish, hon-

---

[*] According to the scholiast of Germanicus (*Aratæa Phenomena Virgo*), the celestial virgin is identical with Atergatis. Hyginus recognizes Venus in the sign Pisces.   [†] Canon, *Japanese Divinity.*
  [‡] *Third Arater of Vishnu.*   [§] *Description of Java.*
  [||] Krachéninnikow, *Description of Kamtschatka*, first part, chap. iv
  [¶] Barbé Marbois, *Journal d'un Déporté*, tome ii., p. 134.

ored at Phigalia, was frequently regarded as a statue of Diana.*

2. Almost all the Tartar princes trace their genealogy to a celestial virgin, impregnated by a sunbeam or some equally marvelous means.† In other language, the mythology which serves as the starting-point of their annals belongs to the age in which the sign of the Virgin was used for denoting the summer solstice.

The Greeks deduced the origin of the Scythians from a virgin, half woman, half serpent, who had intercourse with Jupiter or Hercules,‡ both emblems of the generating sun. If, as it is allowable to suppose, the two origins are synonymous, the Greeks, in the image of the national divinity of the Celestial Virgin, from whom the Scythians and Tartars pretended to derive their descent, will have mistaken or not recognized the form of the lower part, but in place of the extremity of a fish have seen that of a serpent. Now, in order to fix upon the banks of the Sevre both the ancient symbol and the alteration by which it has been disfigured, I need not refer to the Druids, who honored a virgin who was to bring forth children—the Celestial Virgin, who, every year shining in the highest heavens, should at midnight restore to the earth the child-god, the sun, born of the winter solstice. It does not appear that the Druids ever offered physical representations to the veneration of our ancestors, or, at least, not until the times when communication with other nations induced them, by degrees, to imitate their idolatry. But Pytheas, who had coasted along the western shores of Gaul, could not assuredly have been the only one among the Marseillaise navigators ;§ nor could the Phœnicians and Carthaginians, in their researches after tin in the Cassiterides islands, have omitted landing upon the coasts

* Pausanias, *Arcad.*, cap. 41. A priestess of Diana, at Ephesus, had followed the Phoceans to Marseilles, bearing with her a statue of the divinity, and these latter instituted the worship of Diana, as they had received it from their ancestors, in every town they founded in Gaul, as, for instance, at Agde.—*Strabo*, lib. iv.

† Eulogium of Moukden, p. 13, and 221-225. Alankava, or Alancoüa, a Mongol princess, experienced three times successively that a celestial light had penetrated her bosom, and she confidently announced that she should bring forth to the world three male children. Her prediction was verified. Of her three sons, called children of the light, one became the father of the Kap-Giaks Tartars ; another the ancestor of the Selgink, or Selgionkrdes ; and from the third Genghis and Tamerlane were descended.—Petis de la Croix, *History of Genghis Khan*, p. 11-13. D'Herbelot, *Biblioth. Orientale*, art. *Alankava.*

‡ Herodot., lib. iv., cap. 9.—Diod. Sic., lib. ii., cap. 20.

§ The Marseillaise established the worship of Diana of Ephesus in every town they founded.—*Strabo*, lib. iv.

S

of Brittany and Poictiers.   One of these nations may have brought the worship of the mermaid into Western Gaul ; for under the name of Onvana or Anvana, the Gauls adored the figure of a woman, having the tail of a fish.*   A Gallic chief, as jealous as the Tartars of ascribing to himself a supernatural origin, may have pretended to have been descended from this divinity, and would therefore select the image as his distinctive emblem.   The progress of Christianity would have the effect of making the goddess regarded as a woman only, yet endowed like a fairy with supernatural powers, but not of abolishing her memory or effacing her image.   Time and the imperfection of sculpture would, rather later, occasion an error similar to that which the Greeks had already committed ; the tail of a fish would pass for the extremity of a serpent.   Founded upon this mistake, the new tradition would prevail with greater ease, because, as we have already seen, from the fifth to the fifteenth century, serpents held a prominent part in the popular superstitions of the West ; and thus the form given to Merlusine, and the exploit attributed to her descendant, would be the consequences of the sacrifice of an ancient belief to one more recently and generally adopted.

§ XIII.

RECAPITULATION, OR SUMMARY.

The discussion of this conjecture, which we submit to the decision of archæologists, has not caused us to diverge from our subject.   We had proposed seeing how a narration, evidently absurd, false, and impossible, could be spread, and, multiplying itself under a thousand different forms, universally meet with an equal and constant credulity.

Metaphorical expressions of real facts may sometimes have given rise to it, but not have the effect of sending it beyond the narrow circle where the one was observed and the other put in practice.

An accident, as local and variable as the overflowing of a river, could not have been universally represented by the

---

* Martin, *Religion of the Gauls*, vol. ii., p. 110.   Toland, *History of the Druids*, p. 137.   Among the descriptions discovered upon the ancient wall at Bourdeaux, the following was remarked :

" *Caius Julius Florus* ONVAVÆ."

(*Mémoire de l'Académie de Bourdeaux*, Meeting of 16th of June, 1829, p. 182, and shelf 3, No. 52.)   I think *onvavæ* is the dative of the same noun as *onvana*, either the inscription may have been copied incorrectly, or the workman may have made a mistake in transcribing a strange name.

same allegory, which elsewhere could be but very imperfectly applied.

The pretended fact is, in its origin, nothing more than the representation of an astronomical picture, adopted by the greater part of the mythologies of antiquity. When the tradition of this dogma of polytheism ceded to the progress of Christianity, an outward ceremony, perpetuated in this religion, created as many repetitions of the original myth as the Western Church could number congregations of the faithful. In vain they attempted to draw the attention of the vulgar to the allegory expressed by the ceremony; their minds and looks remained fixed on the physical representation. Their habits getting the better of their piety, they looked not for their deliveries among the inhabitants of the heavens alone, but recognized them among men, particularly when conformable with a point of the astronomical allegory; the victor was supposed to have lost his life in the bosom of victory. The names of celebrated personages, those of nobles whose power had been feared, or courage admired, were unceasingly reproduced. Historical remains were falsified for this end; every physical representation which might recall it renewed the recital; and it was sought out among emblems and monuments utterly foreign to it, and even in signs invented by glory or military pride. They even went so far (if our last conjecture is not too rash) as to alter the symbols and beliefs of a mythology prior to it, in order to appropriate them to it. Singular progress of an incredulity not only blind and easy, but greedy and insatiable. Does it not merit being signalized by the meditations of a philosopher? The history of credulity is the most extensive branch, and certainly one of the most important in the moral history of the human race.

ON THE STATUE OF MEMNON.

Notices and Inscriptions attesting the Vocal Property of the Statue; some of them mention even the particular Words pronounced.—Explanations pronounced.—Explanations Proposed by various Authors, but little conclusive.—According to Langlès, the Sounds occasionally uttered by the Statue correspond to the Seven Vowels, emblematical of the Seven Planets.—The Oracle delivered by the Statue of Memnon.—Refutation of the System of M. Letronne.—The apparent Miracles most probably the Result of Chicanery.—The Impossibility of arriving at a satisfactory Solution of the Problem.

In the vicinity of the ancient Thebes stood two colossal figures, each consisting of a single stone, the secret inclo sûre of which bore the name of Memnonia. This word, employed in the Egyptian language to signify "a place sacred to the memory of the dead,"* suggested to the memory of the Greeks one of their heroes, celebrated by Homer. With a vanity ever ready to appropriate and attach to their own traditions whatever might be borrowed from the mythology or the history of a people more ancient than themselves, they regarded one of these colossal figures as consecrated to Memnon, and representing the son of Aurora, a warrior who fell in the Trojan war, invested at an earlier period than the remotest date of Grecian history. This was the statue famed for the peculiarity of emitting, on the rising of the sun, sounds which, to the enthusiast, appeared to convey a salutation addressed to Aurora or to the sun.†

The upper part of the statue was broken at a period not correctly ascertained; but the miraculous sounds continued to be heard, appearing to arise from the lower part. M. Letronne believes the colossus to have been restored in the third century of our era, large masses of gray stone being substituted for that part of the original monolithe, the fragments of which covered the ground.

When Juvenal saw this colossus, in the reign of Adrian, it was broken; Lucian, under Marcus Aurelius, and Philostratus, under Servius, describe it as entire. It is true, that Lucian mentions it in a satirical work; but his raillery is directed against the exaggeration of a witness to the assumed miracle, and does not refer to the statue, whether in its mutilated or restored condition. Philostratus, by a palpable anachronism, causes a cotemporary of Domitian to speak of it. This license, which could not be the effect of ignorance, tends to prove that the restoration was not recent; for no one could place an event which had just taken place in a past century.

The witnesses who attested the vocal nature of the statue cease with the reign of Caracalla. We are ignorant at what period and by what means the restored statue was again broken, and equally so as to the time at which its lower part, long silent, ceased to reveal its ancient glory, except by the inscriptions by which it is covered.

Before discussing the various explanations which have been offered of this apparent prodigy, let us call to mind

* M. Letronne, *La Statue Vocale de Memnon*, 1 vol. 4to. We shall have occasion more than once to quote this erudite work, though we do not adopt the system it advocates.

† The sound was said to resemble the snapping asunder of a musical string, when the first beam of the morning sun fell upon it.—ED.

what has been said regarding it by the Greeks and Romans, the only people from whom we derive direct testimony.

The Egyptians accused Cambyses of having broken and overturned the statue of Memnon, with the same impious fury that led him to insult or to destroy other sacred monuments* in the land of Osiris. Their well-founded detestation for the memory of a barbarous conqueror induced them to impute to him the result of a natural catastrophe, if it be true, as related by Strabo, that the fall of the colossus was occasioned by an earthquake, the date of which is given by this writer.

But for what reason, it may be asked, did Cambyses limit the work of destruction to one of these sacred images? This inquiry, which at first sight appears to weaken the generally received tradition, tends, on the contrary, to strengthen it, if we admit that the miraculous sound proceeding from this image only made it the marked object of religious veneration to the natives, while it attracted to it the fanatic hatred of the fire-worshipers.

Manethon, as quoted by Eusebius, by Josephus, and also by St. Jerome, affirms that the colossal statue of Amenophis was identical with the vocal statue of Memnon. Had not its authority been contested, the testimony given by Ptolemy Philadelphus, an Egyptian priest, of great research into the antiquities of his country, would be of much importance.

Dionysius Periegetes† describes in verse "the ancient Thebes, where the sonorous Memnon hails the rising of Aurora." It is generally supposed that the poetical geographer wrote shortly after Egypt had been reduced to the condition of a Roman province; from which it would follow that the miracle, as well as the fabulous condition connected with it by the Greeks and Romans, was at that time, and had long been known and celebrated. But the critic is left at liberty to fix the epoch at which Dionysius flourished: in the reign of Augustus, of Severus, or of Caracalla.

In speaking of Memnon, "There were," says Strabo, "two colossal statues, each composed of a single stone, and standing near one another. One of them remains entire. It is said that the upper part of the other was overturned by an earthquake; and it is also believed that a sound resembling that produced by a slight blow proceeds from the base, and

* Justin., lib. i., cap. 9.
† Dionys. Perieget., vers. 249, 250. This Dionysius was a writer of the Augustan age. He singularly enough wrote a geographical treatise in Greek hexameters; consequently, he occasionally sacrifices truth to his poetical imaginings.—ED.

from that part of the colossus resting on it. I myself, in company with Ælius Gallus, and a number of his soldiers, heard it toward the dawn of day. But whether, in reality, it proceeded from the base or the colossus, or was produced by connivance, I can not decide. In uncertainty of the real cause, it is better to believe any thing, than to admit that a sound can issue from stones similarly disposed."*

During his travels in Egypt, Germanicus was struck with admiration at the stone image of Memnon, which, as soon as the rays of the sun fell upon it, emitted a sound resembling that of a human voice (vocalem sonum). It is thus that Tacitus expresses himself, an historian so much the more worthy of credit, that he had in his youth learned various important details respecting Germanicus from several old men, cotemporaries of that prince.†

".At Thebes," says Pliny, " in the Temple of Serapis, stands the image said to be consecrated to Memnon, which daily is heard to emit a sound when the first rays of the sun fall upon it."‡

Juvenal, who resided in, or was banished to, Upper Egypt, not far from the district which owes its fame to the monuments of Memnonium, notices the statue in these words: " There," said he, " the magic chords of the mutilated Memnon may be heard."§

" I admired this colossus much," says Pausanias.‖ " It is a sitting statue, which appears to represent the sun; many people call it the statue of Memnon, but the Thebans deny this. It was destroyed (literally broken in two) by Cambyses. At the present day, the upper part, from the crown of the head to the middle of the body, lies neglected on the ground. The other part still remains in a sitting posture ; and every day at sunrise it gives out a sound resembling that produced by the strings of a guitar, or of a lyre, when they break at the instant they are screwed up."

From the times of Lucian, the fame of this colossus attracted the curious into Egypt. In the dialogue upon friendship (Toxaris), it is related by Lucian that " the philosopher Demetrius traveled into Egypt in order to see Memnon, having heard that the statue caused its voice to be heard at the rising of the sun (βοᾶν). I set out for Coptos," he caused Eucrete to say, in the Philopseude, " to see Mem-

* Strabo, lib. xvii.
† Tacit., *Annal.*, lib. ii., cap. 61, et lib. iii., cap. 17.
‡ Plin., *Hist. Nat.*, lib. xxxvi., cap. 7, N. Dion Chrysostom (*Orat.* xxxi.) speaks of the statue of Memnon as of the image of a divinity.
§ Juvenal, *Sat.*, xv., verse 5.   ‖ Pausanias, *Attic.*, cap. 42.

non, and to hear the miraculous sound which issues from it at day-dawn. I did hear it, and not, like many others, producing an uncertain sound: Memnon himself, opening his mouth, addressed to me an oracle in seven lines, which, were it not superfluous, I would repeat to you."

Philostratus says, that "the statue of Memnon, which is turned toward the east, is heard to speak as soon as a ray of the sun falls upon its mouth."[*]

At a period when this assumed miracle had undoubtedly ceased, Himerius, a cotemporary of Ammianus Marcellinus, again asserted that the colossus spoke to the sun with a human voice.[†] But on consideration of the dates, we find that his testimony, as well as that of Callistratus,[‡] merely attests the existence of a tradition which these authors notice without further discussion.

Two unedited works of Juvenal, and the erudite Eustathius, inform us of the modifications that the tradition had undergone in subsequent times.

According to the first,[§] "the statue of Memnon, the son of Aurora, was so contrived by mechanical artifice that it addressed a greeting both to the sun and to the king, with a voice apparently human. In order to ascertain the source of the apparent miracle, Cambyses caused the statue to be cut in two: after which it continued to salute the sun, but addressed the king no longer. Thence the poet has adopted the epithet Dimidio (of which there remained only the half)."

The other scholiast strangely alters the generally received tradition.[‖] It says "that a statue in brass, representing Memnon, and holding a guitar, was heard to sing at particular hours of the day. Cambyses caused it to be opened, on the supposition that mechanism was concealed within the statue. But, notwithstanding its mutilation, the statue having received a magical consecration, still produced the same sounds at the customary hours. It is on this account that Juvenal applies to Memnon the epithet *Dimidius*, open, or divided into two parts."

In commenting on verses 249, 250 of Dionysius Periegetes, Eustathius notices, first, that the colossus represented the Day, the son of Aurora. "It was," he adds, "the statue of a man, from which, by means of a particular mechanism, a voice appeared to issue, and seemed to salute the day,

* Philostrat., *De Vit. Apollon.*, lib. vi., cap. 6.
† Himerius, *Orat.* viii. et xvi. Photii, *Bibl. Cod.*, 243.
‡ Callistrat., *Exercit. de Memnon.*
§ Scholiaste inédit de Juvenal, cité par Vandale, Casselius et Douza
‖ Scholiaste inédit cité par Vandale.

and to render it homage from an inward spontaneous emotion."

Numerous Greek and Latin inscriptions engraved upon the colossus testify that various persons, attracted by motives of religion or curiosity, had heard the miraculous voice. Monsieur Letronne* made a collection of them to the number of seventy-two, and has restored and explained them. In preserving his enumeration, I shall quote such of them only as seem to throw some new light on my subject.

Six inscriptions (Nos. x., xii., xvii., xx., xxxvi., and xxxvii.) affirm that it had spoken to the sun twice on the same day. Another, No. xix., that the voice had been heard three times in the presence of the Emperor Adrian, who looked on this miracle as a pledge of the favor of the gods.

The author of the seventeenth asserts that Memnon spoke to him, addressing him in a friendly manner.

The following, according to Jablonski† and several other learned men, is a translation of the twelfth inscription.

"Memnon, the son of Tithon and Aurora, up to this date, had merely permitted us to hear his voice; to-day he greeted us as his allies and friends. I caught the meaning of the words as they issued from the stone. They were inspired by Nature, the creator of all things." M. Letronne thinks that for this last phrase the following should be substituted: "Did Nature, the creator of all things, inspire this stone with a voice and understanding?" Without entering into a discussion on these words, we may observe that in reality the correction is of less importance than at first sight it appears to be.

The marked distinction between the unnecessary sound which generally issued from the statue, and the particular friendly salutation, appears to me to prove that the authors, both of this inscription and of the seventeenth, have heard distinct words, which they entirely believe to proceed from the sacred stone.

On comparing these various testimonies, we find that, toward the dawn of day, a sound similar to that produced by a' lute or copper instrument usually proceeded from the statue (inscr. xix.). This apparent miracle was repeated two and even three times in a day; at last, increasing in proportion to the credulity of the witnesses, the statue arrived at the pronunciation of consecutive words, and the delivery of complete sentences.

This last prodigy calls to remembrance the inscriptions

---

* *La Statue Vocale de Memnon, &c.*   † Jablonski.   •

and traditions preserved by Homer and Philostratus, and in the Philopseude of Lucian, and is apparently the least admissible of any ; yet I believe it to be the most easily explained.

It was not exclusively confined to Memnon : at Daphne, near Antioch, stood the Temple of Apollo, where at noonday the image of that god was heard to chant a melodious hymn to the admiration of his worshipers.*

If the reader bears in mind what has been already said (c. xii.) concerning the vocal statues celebrated by Pindar, the speaking heads, the uses of ventriloquism, and the advantages derived from the science of acoustics by the thaumaturgists, the impossibility of the account disappears ; all depends on the choice of the moment and the absence of inconvenient spectators. We may even conclude, that while believing that he repeated an absurd falsehood, Lucian has related a real fact, an apparent miracle, that under advantageous circumstances might again be performed in the presence of enthusiasts, who are generally as incapable of penetrating an artifice as of conceiving a doubt or raising an objection.

It is not impossible even that we may recover the oracle in seven lines, heard by Philopseude, which he regarded as an inspiration of "Nature, the creator of all things !" The following oracle, composed of a similar number of lines, and transmitted to us by Eusebius,† appears to answer this question :

"Invoke Mercury, the Sun, and in the same manner
The day of the Sun ; and the Moon when her day
Arrives ; and Saturn's ; and Venus' in her turn ;
By means of the ineffable invocations, discovered by the most skillful of the Magi.‡
King of the *seven times resounding*, known to a great number of men ;
* * * * *
And invoke always, much, and in secret the gods of the sevenfold voice."

The text itself indicates that a verse is wanting, as may be concluded by the omission of the names of Mars and of Jupiter ; this verse was the first, the third, or the fourth, rather than the sixth, completing the oracle, both as to the sense and the number of lines. Having no meaning in the position of the sixth, where it was placed by the inadvert-

* Libanius, *Monodia super Daphn. Apollin.*
† Euseb., *Præpar. Evangel.* lib. iv.
‡ This expression does not specify Zoroaster. The Greeks have frequently given the title of Magi to the Chaldean and even to the Egyptian priest ; they signified by it a person consecrated to a particular goddess inspired by her, and superior to other men in science and wisdom.

ence of a copyist, it would have been totally omitted at a later period.

The oracle prescribes the addressing of invocations to planets, as well as the observance of days particularly consecrated to each. Notwithstanding the loss of the line, it is very clear that the invocations must have been seven in number, in accordance with the days of the week and the number of the planets. He who instituted this form of worship was the king (director) of the *seven times resounding*, a name which appears to indicate a machine or statue capable of producing seven intonations. It is subsequently commanded to address continual invocations to the god of the *sevenfold voice*. Compared with the title, *seven times resounding*, it appears that this was the god to whom the machine was consecrated, or of whom the statue was the image ; even the sun, recognized by the ancients as the king of the celestial world. The statue of Memnon was that of the sun, according to Pausanias.

Other observations concur to support our conjecture.

In the earlier ages of Christianity, a religious signification was attached to the seven vowels. Eusebius observes, that, by a wonderful mystery, the ineffable name of God, in the four grammatical modifications to which it submits, comprehends the seven vowels.[*] This religious signification serves, also, to explain an inscription composed of seven lines, each of which presents the seven Greek vowels under a different combination.[†] Gruter and his editor regard the inscription as apocryphal ; but Edward Holten has seen the seven vowels sculptured on a stone in a similar arrangement.[‡] "All the mystery which they contain," says he, "consists in the name of Jehovah, composed of seven letters, and seven times repeated." With sufficient plausibility, he attributes inscriptions of this nature to the Basilidians, who, like many other sectarians in the earlier ages of the Church, were only theurgists, who grafted on Christianity the rites and superstitious initiations of a more ancient religion.

From Egypt was borrowed, among others, this superstition relative to vowels. The Egyptian priests chanted the seven vowels as a hymn addressed to Serapis.[§] In an inscription preserved by Eusebius,[||] Serapis declares to his worshipers :

---

[*] *Præp. Evangel.*, lib. vi., cap. 6.
[†] Jan. Gruter. *Corp. Inscript.*, tome ii., p. 21.   [‡] Ibid., p. 346.
[§] Dionys. Halicarn.
[||] Euseb., *Præp. Evangel.* Scaliger, *Animadvers. Euseb.*, No. 1730. Let us observe that the vowels were retained to a comparatively late period in the mystic allegories relative to the solar system. The modern writers,

"The seven vowels glorify me, the great and immortal God, the unwearied Father of all things." Is it necessary to call to mind that, in divination, Serapis stood as one of the emblems of the solar system, and that Pliny assigns to Serapis the temple with which the statue of Memnon was consecrated?

The mystery attached to this mode of adoration explains the application to the invocations of the epithet *ineffable*, as well as the silence which Eucrates observes respecting the substance of the oracle in seven lines which he pretends to have heard. Thus, in the religion of the Hindoos, of the Parsees, and even of Islam, certain syllables are consecrated, the pronunciation of which is equivalent to a prayer, and whose sacred efficacy must not be revealed.*

Whatever weight we may attach or refuse to these conjectures with regard to particular occasions, it may be readily admitted that, where the operations of the thaumaturgists were unrestrained by enlightened curiosity, the machinery employed for animating an automaton, or perhaps mere ventriloquism, would suffice to produce the words and the oracles attributed to Memnon.

It is not so easy to explain the repetition of the apparent miracle every morning.

The idea of an artifice that might lend its aid to the colossus appears to have struck Strabo. His language is that of a man who is on his guard respecting any deception that might be practiced on him, rather than to admit that the sound could really issue from the stone. Otherwise, he adduces no fact in support of his conjecture.

The term of which Juvenal makes use appears to indicate that, in his opinion, the miracle was the result of magical art, that is to say, of an ingenious and concealed mechanism. Eustathius† positively affirms it, as well as the two

probably more faithful echoes of the ancients, because they do not fully comprehend them, have preserved the tradition that connects the seven vowels with the idea of the planets. In the sixteenth century, Belot, curate of Milmont, asserted in his *Chiromancie* (chap. xviii.) that the seven vowels are consecrated to the seven principal planets.

* The great mystical word in the Hindoo faith is O'M, applied to the Supreme Being. It occurs in many of the hymns in the Vestas; as, for example, in the following passage translated from them by Sir William Jones: "God, who is perfect wisdom and perfect happiness, is the final refuge of the man who has liberally bestowed his wealth, who has been firm in virtue, and who knows and adores that great one!"
      "Remember me, O'M, Thou divine spirit!"—ED.

† Eustathius was archbishop of Thessalonia in the twelfth century. He was a man of great ambition, and distinguished as a commentator on Homer. His annotations abound with historical and philological descriptions.—ED

scholiastes of the Latin satirist. One of them even alludes to a magical consecration of the statue ; but he is in the habit of taking so much license with history and with received tradition that his testimony is almost without value.

The learned Langlès adopted a similar explanation. To render it plausible, he sets out from the supposition that Memnon repeated the seven intonations in the hymn of the Egyptian priests. To produce these required only a succession of hammers, ranged along a key-board, and striking on sonorous stones, such as from time immemorial have served as instruments of music in China.*

If we could credit the assertion of Philostratus, that the colossus, facing the east, emitted a sound on the rays of the sun falling upon it, and at the very moment when they fell on its mouth, we might easily conceive that this miraculous mechanism was put in motion by some secret familiar to the ancients. A strong and sudden heat, produced by the concentration of the solar rays, would be sufficient to expand one or more metallic rods, which, in lengthening, might act on the key-board, the existence of which is presumed by Langlès. Thus would have been derived from the sun itself the power by which the statue greeted the return of the god to whom it was consecrated, and of whom it was emblematical.

But, notwithstanding this plausible explanation, what grounds exist for the supposition that seven successive intonations proceeded habitually from the colossus? If, in certain very rare cases, the skill of the priest was able to produce something similar to this, the historical testimonies, or the inscriptions, attest in general the emission of but one single sound. Moreover, the miracle was discovered long before the restoration of the statue, and at a time when the head, lying in the sand, no longer communicated with the lower part, whence the sounds appeared to proceed ; and again, no researches have been able to discover in the colossus a cavity capable of containing the musical mechanism supposed by Langlès.

This last remark refutes also the conjecture of Vandale, which suggests that in this colossus, as well as in several other statues, a cavity was contrived for the introduction of priests,† whose office it was to lend the assistance of their voice to the divinity.

* Langlès, *Dissertation sur la Statue Vocale de Memnon.* At the end of the *Voyages de Norden*, tome ii., p. 157, 256.
† Vandale, *De Oraculis*, p. 207-209.

The explanation proposed by Dussault is not more admissible. "The statue being hollow," says he, "the air which it contains became affected by the heat of the sun, and in escaping by some passage, produced a sound which could be interpreted as best suited to the interests of the priests."[*] I may ask, what testimony has ever been given that the statue was hollow? and, moreover, has not Dussault ascribed to the elevation of temperature an unnatural consequence? To arrive at the interior air, the sun must have penetrated a layer of stone of great thickness, and that almost instantaneously, and when the disk of the sun was scarcely risen above the horizon.

In the immense apartments constructed entirely of blocks of granite, which are concealed among the ruins of Carnac, the celebrated sounds emitted from the stones have been heard at the rising of the sun by French artists. "The sounds appear to issue from enormous stones which roof in the apartments, and are threatening to fall: the phenomenon undoubtedly proceeds from the sudden change of temperature on the rising of the sun."[†] I am rather inclined to think that the sounds were produced by the creaking of one of these blocks, apparently about to fall. Masses of red granite, when struck by a hammer, sound like a bell.[‡] In short, if we admit this explanation, we must also grant that the statue of Memnon could never have ceased to be sonorous; and we must believe that the ceilings, the walls, the colossal figures, the obelisks of granite, raised in such numbers in Egypt, also rendered sounds at the rising of the sun. Allow this, and the miracle disappears; the sonorous stones claim no more attention than any other simple fact, as common as the course of a stream or the noise of a tempest. But we know that the colossus of Memnon alone enjoys the prerogative; and since that peculiarity has disappeared, its exposure to the sun and the temperature of the climate have not been subjected to the slightest alteration.[§]

The assertion on which this explanation is founded is otherwise destitute of probability. Could the successive change of temperature, such as is supposed, cause a sonorous body to sound? I reply, No. There is no direct experiment on record which can authorize us to credit the assertion. A bell, or tam-tam, would remain silent if exposed to it; no sound proceeds from the æolian harp, though the

* Dussault, *Traduction de Juvenal*, 2e édit, tome ii., p. 452, note 5.
† *Description de l'Égypte*, tome i., p. 234.
‡ *Magasin Encyclop.*, 1816, tome ii., p. 29.
§ *Revue Encyclop.*, 1821, tome ix., p. 532.

coolness of night is succeeded by a temperature very perceptibly higher; and yet the strings of this harp readily procure lengthened chords on meeting with the slightest breath of air.

Sir A. Smith, an English traveler, asserts that he has visited the statue of Memnon, and that, accompanied by a numerous escort, he heard very distinctly, about six o'clock in the morning, the sounds which rendered this image so celebrated in antiquity. He conceives the mysterious sound to issue from the pedestal, not from the statue; and believes it to arise from the percussion of air on the stones of this part, which are so disposed as to produce this singular effect. But what can this *disposition* mean, since the base and lower part of the colossus have always consisted of, and do still form, but one piece? And how could it produce the result indicated? This the traveler does not explain. In conclusion, it may be asked, how he alone, of all modern spectators, should have heard the colossus whose voice has been for centuries silent? How could such an important phenomenon have escaped the observation of the French, who remained several years in Egypt, and who pushed their learned investigations to a great length? In all probability, Sir A. Smith was deceived by a crashing noise similar to that heard by the French artists at Carnac.

Such was the state of the question when M. Letronne attempted to resolve it definitely by a new hypothesis, which he supports with profound erudition and more logical meaning.*

The silence of Herodotus and Diodorus of Sicily respecting the existence of this apparent miracle, and also in reference to the tradition which imputes the destruction of the monument to Cambyses, induces him to reject it; while he fixes the period at which the statue of Memnon was first heard to have been some centuries later. He puts aside, as an interpolation, the important passage from Manethon; and sets out, from the assertion of Strabo, comparing it with the notice by Eusebius, of a great earthquake which caused many disasters in Egypt, twenty-seven years before our era.† This brings him to the conclusion, that at that time the colossus was one among many other monuments that were broken; and that, by its mutilation, it acquired a vocal power, which previously it had not enjoyed.

This new property appeared at first of little importance to the surrounding population. At a subsequent period, the

* *De la Statue Vocale de Memnon, &c.*   † Euseb., *Chronicon.*

Greeks and Romans recognized it as a miracle; but its renown did not become universal or widely spread before the reign of Nero. It was then the traveler commenced to inscribe on the columns the reverential admiration he had experienced. None of these inscriptions are of Egpptian authorship; a proof that it excites in the natives neither enthusiasm nor admiration. Tacitus, in relating the travels of Germanicus in Egypt, has spoken of the statue of Memnon as it is described by Domitian and Trajan : he erred in substituting for the opinions of an earlier century the ideas conceived regarding it in his own times. The fame of the assumed miracle increased continually, and in the reign of Adrian it reached its height. It had suffered no diminution when Septimus Severus* conceived and executed the project of restoring the colossus, by substituting blocks of gray stone for that portion of the original mass which had been broken by the fall. The statue then became mute ; the last inscriptions alluding to its vocal power do not extend after the simultaneous reign of Severus and of Caracalla ; after this reign, also, no writer speaks of the miracle in the character of a witness.

M. Letronne adopts the conjecture, which refers the sounds proceeding from the ruins remaining in their place after the fall of the anterior portion of the statue, to the sudden difference of temperature between night and day. The mass-

---

* Lucius Septimus Severus, who acquired the imperial purple by proclaiming himself emperor when he commanded the Roman forces stationed against the Barbarians on the borders of Illyrium ; to secure his aim, he joined Albinus, who commanded in Britain, as his partner in the empire. His first object was to depose Didius Julianus, who had purchased the government, and who, being soon deserted by his dependents, was assassinated by his own soldiers. At this time, however, another rival for the purple existed in Pesuntius Niger ; but, after many battles, he also was defeated, and Severus left with no other rival than his partner, who, however, soon fell beneath his fortunate sword at the plains of Gaul, and he thus became sole master of the empire.

It was this emperor who built the wall across the northern parts of our island, to defend his territory in Britain from the frequent invasions of the Caledonians.

As a monarch he was tyrannical and cruel ; and having risen by ambition, he maintained his power by severity, and by the unhesitating destruction of every one whom he thought likely, in any manner, to oppose his inclination.

The restoration of the statue of Memnon, mentioned in the text, was attempted during a progress made by Severus into the East with his sons. He was recalled by a revolt in Britain, which he soon reduced ; but his triumph was sullied by an attempt of his son Caracalla to murder him ; an event which so much depressed his spirit, and added so cruelly to his bodily sufferings from gout, that he died at York, A.D. 210, after a reign of less than eighteen years.—ED.

ive blocks with which, at a later period, it was loaded, forced it, by their weight, to resist this influence. This pretended miracle, therefore, thus confined in duration within the limits of two centuries, he considers was not the result of fraud, as the Egyptian priests did not attempt to attach to it a religious importance.

This system is plausible; sufficiently so, indeed, to tempt one, on a cursory glance, to regard the problem as definitively solved: on reflection, however, several grave objections present themselves.

First. The silence of Herodotus and of Diodorus furnish, it is confessed, an argument of apparent weight; but it is one of a negative character only. To make it conclusive, it must be shown that, if the fact were true, these authors could not have avoided making mention of it. But, in exploring a foreign country, some things may escape the attention of the observer; and, still more possibly, some of those things which he has seen or been informed of may be omitted in description. The learned of modern times have had proof of this in Egypt itself, when they visited that country with works of their predecessors in their hands. Further, it was a history, not a description, that was written by Herodotus. This distinction is important: description can not be too complete, while history, passing by even interesting details, gives prominency only to the principal features.

We will not take advantage of the exaggerated accusation with which Josephus stigmatizes Herodotus, as having, through ignorance, disfigured the history of the Egyptians.[*] But Herodotus himself, in his journey to Memphis,[†] to Heliopolis, and to Thebes, mentions that, from what he had been able to learn, he intended merely to notice the names of the divinities. When an author thus fixes beforehand the limits of the information he proposes to give, what argument can be drawn by the critic from his silence respecting facts of which he has declared his determination not to speak?

The plan of Diodorus, being on a still more comprehensive scale than that of Herodotus, allows still less of detail. We may observe, also, that this writer, who flourished in the reign of Augustus, just concludes his work at the period when, according to M. Letronne, the vocal powers of the statue were well attested. He has not, however, spoken of it. Is it fair to conclude, from his silence, something against the reality of a lately ascertained fact, sufficiently singular to attract his attention? Certainly not; as his silence

<hr>

* Joseph. *Adv. Apion.*, lib. 1.　　　† Herodot., lib. ll, cap. 3.

proves nothing against the real existence of the ancient and well-known apparent miracle.

Secondly. M. Letronne looks on the passage from Manethon, quoted by Eusebius, as an interpolation, merely because Josephus has omitted quoting it from the text of the Egyptian priests ;* yet, in a quotation otherwise exact, an incidental phrase is frequently suppressed, if it do not bear on the subject treated of, or if it tend to distract the reader's attention from the point on which it is desirable to fix it. Josephus had no concern in the identity of the statues of Amenophis and of Memnon ; and as irrelevant to the Jewish history, he has passed over these particulars in silence. In fact, he expressly says, at the close of the quotation, that for the sake of brevity he purposely omits many things. This acknowledgment is sufficient to overturn M. Letronne's argument. The passage of Manethon exists as it was quoted by Eusebius, who could have no object in altering it. The vocal powers of the colossus and its form were then facts known in the time of Ptolemy Philadelphus ; thence they might be referred to a much earlier time, even to the reign of Cambyses.

Thirdly. The mutilation of the colossus, falsely ascribed to the Persian king, was, according to Strabo, the effect of an earthquake ; the same which, says M. Letronne, in the twenty-seventh year of our era, overturned the whole of Thebes. The Greek text of Eusebius confirms this opinion ; but the Armenian version corrects the exaggeration of the extent of this disaster, limiting its effects to the suburbs.

An earthquake has at all times been a rare phenomenon in Egypt ; a circumstance proved by the number of ancient edifices that, after the lapse of so many centuries, remain standing in that country. The Egyptians, therefore, were not likely to forget a catastrophe so fatal to their ancient capital, and to a monument which was the object of national veneration. Yet the terms are very vague in which the testimony by Strabo respecting it is addressed. His words are, " It is said that the upper part was overthrown."

The consideration which has been supposed to supplant the theory which I combat, namely, that Strabo must have witnessed the earthquake in the year 27 B.C.,† mentioned by Eusebius, does not make his language the less extraordinary. The expedition of Ælius Gallus into Arabia took place in the year 24 B.C., according to Dion Cassius ; and

* Joseph., *Adv. Apion.*, lib. i.
† The Armenian versions of Eusebius place this event three years later, the year 24 B.C.

II.   T

we must assign the same date to the journey of Strabo when he visited Thebes in company with that general. Would, we may inquire, such a judicious writer have expressed himself so incorrectly respecting a cotemporary event; or one the traces of which must still have been obvious after the interval of only two or three years?

Again, how can we admit that, five hundred years after the death of Cambyses, the mutilation of the colossus could have been attributed to that prince, if it were really the effect of an earthquake, of which all Egypt must have been aware, and must long have retained in their remembrance? Would the cotemporaries of Charles VII. have attributed the fall of an edifice crumbling away before their eyes to the ravages of the Normans, to whom Charles the Simple yielded Neustria? The coincidence between the passages of Eusebius and of Strabo is an hypothesis contrary to all probability, and supported by no certain indication; yet this forms the foundation of M. Letronne's theory.

What, I would ask, is the testimony of Strabo? He visits the statue, hears the miraculous voice, and quits the spot without further research, convinced that it is better to believe any thing, than to admit that stones so disposed were capable of producing sound! This is the language of a witness too prejudiced to allow of consideration for his opinions.

M. Letronne concludes that the vocal statue did not yet bear the name of Memnon, because Strabo does not give it that title. I do not think so absolute a conclusion may be drawn from so simple an omission. It is already answered in the passage from Manethon.

Fifth. M. Letronne believes that he can fix the epoch when the miracle acquires celebrity by the date of the earliest inscriptions engraved on the colossus. We may consent to his rejecting the authority of Dionysius Periegetes, by taking advantage of the uncertainty respecting the time at which the poetical geographer wrote. But we can not go along with him in supposing that an historian such as Tacitus,* a man who, in his youth, had conversed with the cotemporaries of Pison and of Germanicus, would, in relating the travels of that prince, insert facts which could not have been observed till forty years afterward. In order to establish the existence of so strange an inconsistency, it were necessary to produce positive proofs; but none are brought forward by M. Letronne.

Sixth. Shall we conclude, with M. Letronne, that the mi-

* Tacit., *Annal.*, ii., cap. 61, and iii., cap. 16.

raculous sound was not heard by Germanicus, because we do not find the name of that prince inscribed upon the colossus? Ælius Gallus and Strabo both heard it, yet did not engrave their names on the stone as witnesses.

Seventh. M. Letronne has rendered valuable services to science, in collecting and deciphering the existing inscriptions; but does he not go too far in saying that the apparent miracle had no religious interest attached to it, for the natives, owing to the inscriptions being all Greek or Roman, could not decipher them? and again, in supposing that their dates fixed the duration of the sonorous property between the reign of Nero and that of Septimus Severus?

Was it possible that a phenomenon, to say the least of it, surprising in itself, could either have existed for ages or been suddenly discovered within the observation of the most superstitious people in the world, and yet not have been sought out and turned to advantage by those who traded in the credulity of men? This, indeed, would be a miracle without a precedent in history, and, in its own way, no less astonishing than the existence of a speaking stone. We have traced the priest in every country to be the inventor of assumed miracles, or having dignified with this name natural facts often in themselves scarcely extraordinary. Wherever the populace imagined they could discern the work of a god, privileged men were not long in appearing to receive in the name of that god the tributes of admiration and of gratitude. The Egyptian priests were not likely to prove exceptions where so singular a phenomena as the vocal statue invited them to profit by it, even though by the Greeks and Romans it was revered under a name they did not acknowledge, and which did not impart an idea of their own mythology to the credulous stranger. Thanks to the daily apparent miracle, which could be produced in no other temple, they were entitled to receive offerings on their altars and to entertain respect for themselves.

But, it may be argued, they have celebrated it by no inscription. In Egypt, the walls of the temples, and even the bodies of the statues, were loaded with hieroglyphics, the sense of which is as yet imperfectly revealed to us. Can we confidently affirm that none of the mysterious inscriptions in the Memnonia make mention of the vocal properties of the statue?

Men not belonging to the sacerdotal order would not presume to supply the silence of the priests. The usurpation of such a right was incompatible with the sentiment of religious veneration, if we may judge ancient by modern manners. The devotees might fill the temple of the saint, to whom they believed themselves indebted for some benefits, with their vows ; but to write on the statue itself, far from being a testimony of their gratitude, would be a sacrilegious profanation.

The Ptolemies introduced the worship of Saturn and of Serapis into Egypt without being able to obtain permission to erect temples in the interior of cities, either to one or the other.* But whether from policy or superstition, and far from carrying this attempt on the national faith, the Lagides† adopted both their worship and their traditions. The priests then remained, as formerly, the guardians of the images of the gods, and preserved them from the injury they might receive from indiscreet admiration. It was only under Augustus that the assumed miracles of Egypt were revealed to the disciples of a foreign religion, to whom they were then for the first time entirely subjected. The first travelers who visited Memnon abstained, nevertheless, from an act which the natives, too recently subdued, would have regarded as an outrage. The Greeks and the Romans thronging to the shores of the Nile, gradually familiarized the people with their propensity to recognize their own divinities in every country. They pretended to remember Memnon ; they had heard him, and among them inscriptions were as allowable to private individuals as to the priesthood. The inscriptions multiplied, sometimes owing to superstition, sometimes to the pleasure of confirming the existence of a peculiar phenomenon which might be doubted by those who were not themselves able to verify it. Vanity also played its part. No one could have been in Upper Egypt without boasting of having heard Memnon. These motives were gradually

---

* Macrob., *Saturn.*, lib. i., cap. 7.

† The Ptolemies were named Lagides, from the surname Lagus being imposed on the first of their race, owing to the following tradition connected with his birth. Arsinæ, the daughter of Meleager, having had a disgraceful intercourse with Philip of Macedon, was, in order to cover her disgrace, married to Lagus, a Macedonian of low birth, but opulent. Lagus, as soon as the child was born, exposed it in the woods, where, says the tradition, an eagle sheltered him under her wings and fed him with her prey. Lagus, having had this prodigy divulged to him, adopted the infant and called him Ptolemy, from an idea that, having been so miraculously preserved and nurtured, he would become a great and powerful man. The supposition became true ; for, after the death of Alexander, one of whose generals Ptolemy had been, at the general division of the Macedonian empire, the government of Egypt and Libya fell to the share of Ptolemy, who, after he had ascended the Egyptian throne, preferred the title of *Lagides* to every other appellation ; and it was transmitted to all his descendants anterior to the reign of Cleopatra.—ED.

weakened by the number of visitors. The difficulty of being raised sufficiently high to find a space for the reception of new inscriptions* caused this custom also to cease after the death of Severus and of Caracalla ; and other causes, independent of the duration of the miracle, may have contributed to the same effect. To presume a necessary connection between that duration and the date of the latest inscriptions is to suppose that every witness must have written on the colossus, and, consequently, that the number of witnesses was not greater than that of the names preserved in the seventy-two inscriptions collected by M. Letronne, which are inadmissible consequences, and proofs that the principle itself is erroneous.

History is silent respecting the restoration of the colossus, and, consequently, it does not indicate the date. The fact is established by the existence of the remains of the blocks placed upon the ancient base ; and it appears that Lucian and Philostratus were acquainted with it, as they express themselves to the effect that, in their times, the statue was entire. Let us only remark, that in admitting their testimony, we must not mutilate it ; the miraculous voice of the colossus is mentioned by both ; thus, contrary to M. Letronne's opinion, the apparent miracles must have continued after the restoration of the sacred image.

Lucian died in the reign of Marcus Aurelius, and Juvenal in that of Adrian ; the restoration of the statue, consequently, must be placed between these two epochs ; and it must have been the work of Adrian or of Antoninus.

This opinion M. Letronne will not admit to be correct, for, according to his theory, Severus must have been the author of the restoration, in order to make the silence of the god coincide with the date of the last inscriptions. But, however little weight we may attach to the testimony of Philostratus, it certainly refutes this hypothesis. In addressing a tale, or rather a legend, to a superstitious empress, would Philostratus have placed the restoration of the colossus, an act not only eminently religious, but executed by the reigning emperor, in the times of Domitian or of Titus ? Would the author of a work dedicated to Queen Anne of Austria have

---

* The height of the statue was about thirty feet; and on the legs of it only the inscriptions, in Latin and Greek, were engraven. Most of them belong to the period of the early Roman emperors. There is a copy of this statue in the British Museum, but it does not exceed nine feet six inches and a half in height. The head of the colossal Memnon, also in the British Museum, is not that of the vocal Memnon. There were, indeed, many colossal statues called Memnonian in Egypt, but only one celebrated vocal Memnon.—ED.

conducted a cotemporary of Francis I. or of Henry II. to the
celebrated procession of the vow of Louis XIII. !

In default of historical testimonies to the effect that the
restoration took place under Septimus Severus, or in the
absence of the hieroglyphical scrolls where it might be
registered, M. Letronne asserts that, in imitation of Spartian, the Emperor Severus avoided inscribing his name on
the monuments which he raised.   But this assertion seems
only applicable to Roman monuments.   M. Letronne himself instances certain Egyptian monuments on which Severus had inscribed his own and the names of his children.
It is not, therefore, probable that he would omit placing it
on the colossus restored by his care.

M. Letronne conjectures that the unlooked-for silence of
the restored Memnon was the motive which prevented the
dedication by an inscription of this act of piety and vanity.
This suggestion lays too much stress on the silence of Spar-,
tian,* Herodotus, and Diodorus respecting a fact so notorious
as the restoration of the colossus, especially in an account
of that prince's travels in Egypt, and his visit to the statue
of Memnon.   So strange a silence would astonish us much
more if the cessation of a prodigy so long admired had immediately succeeded the restoration of the statue.   Would
not these writers have spoken of it were it only as a fatal
presage !   It would have been so natural for superstition to
connect with it the rapid extinction of the race of Septimus
Severus !

In conclusion, I believe we may consider it as fully demonstrated, that if the vocal statue was overturned by an
earthquake (and not by the fury of Cambyses), it was not
the earthquake which Eusebius places as having occurred
in the year twenty-seven or twenty-four before our era ; and,
consequently, that M. Letronne's theory is raised upon a defective foundation.

Secondly. That the hypothesis of the restoration of the
statue having been effected by Severus is supported neither
by proofs nor by historical indication.

Thirdly. That it is not demonstrated that the statue of
Memnon became silent immediately after the commencement of the reign of Severus and Caracalla ; and if the period at which the assumed miracle commenced is unknown,
we are equally ignorant of the still more recent period at
which it ceased.

* Ælius Spartianus, a Latin historian ; but he is not esteemed either as
a historian or a biographer.—ED.

The cause of the prodigy remains in equal obscurity. M. Letronne, as we have seen, adopts the explanation founded on the expansion caused by the sudden change of temperature. To the objections we have already offered, we may add the following:

First. That this variation of temperature could not recur in a degree adequate to insure the sounds on several different occasions during the day, while it must be admitted that the voice of Memnon has been heard two and even three times at different periods of the same day.

Second. It appears to me a gratuitous supposition that the weight of the blocks that were placed on the base at the resoration of the colossus became the cause of its sudden sience. The immense blocks of granite, the creaking of which was heard at Carnac, supported masses of greater weight than the stones which must have served for the restoration of the colossus; and their almost spontaneous sounding is beyond a doubt. As a general fact, the imposition of even a considerable weight, though it may arrest the vibrations of a body at the moment when it is actually sounding, yet does not destroy the power of producing sound, but generally changes its quality. The change becomes less perceptible if the substance imposed forms one body with the original, and if it is of the same nature. Now, the blocks, vestiges of which are still to be seen, are of a stone identical with that of which the base of the statue is composed,* and they are almost equally sonorous.

Lastly, these blocks having been almost entirely overturned, and the colossus being nearly in the same state as at the period of its first mutilation, would it not have recovered the voice which, in its restoration, it had lost?

Was the apparent miracle, we may now inquire, produced by fraud? I conceive that it was the result of a deception. M. Letronne absolutely denies it. He concludes it impossible that a subterraneous passage or cavity should have been formed in the base of the statue several centuries after its erection. The objection supposes that the apparent miracle was not coeval with the erection of the statue; yet the attempt to prove this has failed. Why, adds M. Letronne, did not Memnon cause himself to be heard every time that he was visited? I reply, because to deny occasionally, or to defer the assumed miracle, excited a more lively curiosity, and struck superstition with deeper awe, and inspired a more

* *Moniteur*, Mardi, 9 Octobre, 1838, *Lettre de M. Nestor l'Hote à M. Letronne.*

profound respect than it would have done had it become familiar and of every-day occurrence.

At Naples, has not the pretended miracle of St. Januarius been frequently deferred in order to serve the passions, the caprice, or the interest of the priest?

Mr. Wilkinson, an English traveler, has recently discovered a sonorous stone situated under the knees of the colossus. Behind this he discovered a cavity, which he conceives to have been purposely made for the reception of the man whose function it was to strike the stone and perform the miracle. M. Nestor l'Hote, a French traveler, ascertained the existence of this harmonious stone under the knee of the statue.* It is of the same nature as the stone employed in its reconstruction, and produced, on percussion, a sound similar to that of melted metal. The cavity behind it is nothing more than an enormous fissure that rends the seat of the statue from top to bottom. We are authorized in concluding that it has not been made by design, and that the sonorous stone was only one of the materials employed in restoring it.

This fair conclusion, while it overthrows the hypothesis of Vandale, which we have already rejected, proves nothing in favor of M. Letronne. Many other modes of performing the pretended miracle might be found.†

If we inquire when the vocal properties of the statue ceased, we find the thread of history broken. In the midst of the disorders and dissensions that distracted the empire, even after the accession of Constantine, the annalists had few opportunities of reverting to an isolated prodigy, foreign to the new religion whose tenets then began to predominate. It was even with difficulty that the assumed miracle could be renewed, and it was destined shortly to cease altogether; as, by the succession of controversies arising between the Christians and the Polytheists, religious frauds were often brought to light, and when, at a later period, the dispersant pagan priests, reduced to indigence, and exposed to persecution, abandoned their temples and their images, all was thenceforward deprived of the veneration of the people.

As too often happens at the end of the most conscientious researches, we are constrained to acknowledge our igno-

* *Moniteur*, No. de Mardi, 9 Octobre, 1838, *Lettre de M. Nestor l'Hote à M. Letronne.*
† In whatever manner the sounds were produced, it is probable that, as the priests were aware of the sounds still heard at Carnac from the rocks on the east bank of the Nile, they would take advantage of that phenomenon to produce similar sounds from the colossal statue.—ED.

rance, being neither able to deny the existence of the as
sumed miracle, to fix its duration, nor to give such an ex
planation of it as would defy all objections.

The numerous examples of apparent miracles produced
by means of the science of acoustics authorize us to ascribe
this one to the skill of the priests, who never allowed a
singular fact to escape them without seizing on it and turning it to advantage. But of what nature was their intervention here? How shall we explain a fraud, varied in certain
cases to render the miracle more imposing, but generally
performed in one way, in the light of the sun, in the open
air, and in the midst of witnesses, who presented themselves
in crowds to observe its effect, and which, nevertheless, was
never discovered? This, the real question, remains yet to
be solved.

GENERAL INDEX.

Abaris, the son of Seuthes, ii., 107.
Abbagumba, or Erkoom, i., 92.
Abracadabra, a word employed to cure agues, i., 201.
Abraxas, i., 199.
Abunde, who was also called Hèra, i., 230.
Academy, St. Petersburgh, aerolites sent to, i., 48.
———— of Sciences at Paris, phenomenon vouched for by the, i., 48.
Achilles, the blows of, i., 52.
———— Tatius, i., 67.
————, inconsistency of the spirit of, i., 264.
Achro, sacrifices made to the god, i., 107.
Acosta, Joseph, miracle mentioned by, i., 276.
Adam, Peak of, at Ceylon, i., 56.
Adonis, the river of, and blood of, i., 53.
Æetes, her reputation preserved as an invincible magician, i., 142.
Ælian supposed a casual phenomenon to be constant, i., 63.
———— accused of having exaggerated, i., 61.
Aerolites sent to St. Petersburgh, i., 48.
————, falling of, frequent occurrence, i., 103.
————, nature of, i., 46.
————, sought for by the Kicahans, ii., 102.
Æsculapius invoked in his temple, i., 145.
———————, note on, worshiped as a deity, ii., 90.
Africa, a parasol imported into, i., 73.
Agamede, Theocritus's account of, i., 211.
————, what it signifies in the language of Homer, i., 141.
Agamemnon, dedicated a vessel of stone, i., 54.
Agaric of the olive tree, i., 63.

Agnus Dei, sent to the Emperor of Constantinople, i., 199.
Agrigentum, a rock near, i., 56.
Ainos of the Kourila Islands, i., 90.
Air rendered pestilential, ii., 133, 134
Alamoot, account of, ii., 27.
Albania, men described in, i., 89.
Albertus Magnus, account of, i., 250, 251.
Alchemy arose from ignorance of true science, i., 192.
Alexander the Great employed the Greek fire, ii., 195.
————————, death of, attributed to poison, ii., 114.
————————, cause of the destruction of his soldiers at Thebes, ii., 209.
————————, the flowing of a spring in the tent of, considered as a miracle, i., 102.
———————— excited to deadly anger by songs, ii., 73, 74.
Ali, a miracle ascribed to him, i., 122.
Alladas, Sylvius, imitated the noise of thunder, ii., 157.
Almanacs used to instruct the ignorant to read, i., 83.
Almond, the bitter, described, i., 69.
Alphourians or Haraforas of Borneo and the Malay Islands, i., 90.
Althæa Cannabina of Linnæus, i., 62.
Amalekites inured to magic, i., 118.
Amanita Muscaria is the Muchamore, ii., 19, 20.
Ambliopia, or double images, ii., 38.
Amethyst, a precious stone, i., 78.
————, figurative description of, i., 78.
Ammianus Marcellinus flourished in the reign of Constantine, Julian, and Valens, ii., 164.
————————————, his account of the failure to rebuild the Temple of Jerusalem, ii., 199.
Ammon, Jupiter, account of the temple of, i., 233.
Amulet, definition of the term, i., 198.
Anamarana, ii., 29.
Anaxilaus of Larissa, i., 278.

Orphic mysteries, i., 184.

Osages, magicians among the, i., 150.

Oscellatoria rubescens, what was caused by the development of, i., 99.

Ossian, a comparison of his son's sword to flame, ii., 179.

Oupnek'-hat, passage of, ii., 172.

Oxus, wells dug in the vicinity of the, i., 102.

Pachymerus, assertion of, i., 300.

Pactolus, wonderful stone found in the, i., 248.

Paracelsus, note on, ii., 97.

Paragreles, ii., 148.

Paragrandines, security against hail, ii., 148.

Pausanias, his initiation, ii., 39, 40.

Paw, ii., 135.

Pegna, Francis, who, ii., 32.

Pelops, accessory to the death of Œnomaus, ii., 159, 160.

Pentheus, note on, ii., 38, 39.

Perfumes, use of, by the ancients, ii., 36.

Perkinism, account of, ii., 82.

Persian Greeks listened eagerly to the magi, i., 209, 210.

Persians, exulted in being able to drink much without suffering intoxication, i., 68.

Peter, the River of St., i., 72.

Petersburgh, St., pretended miracle at, i., 282.

Petronius Arbiter, his romance, ii., 9.

Phantasmagoria, now only restored, not invented, i., 268.

————, account of that brought out in London, i., 268, 209.

————, the instruments which formed, i., 269.

Pharachites, i., 150.

Phosphorus, how used by the ancients, ii., 183.

————, Bologna, ii., 177, 178.

————, Baldwin's, ii., 178.

————, the ancients acquainted with, ii., 182.

Phrygia, where Diana rewards the love of Endymion, i., 53.

————, Rome borrowed the fable of Anchurus from, i., 87.

Physical science, for the most part, can explain the sorcery of Thaumaturgy, i., 41.

Physics, natural, employed by magicians, ii., 147.

Pietramala, the fires of, in Tuscany, i., 97.

Pigeons, carrier, i., 315.

———— dung, burned the Church of Pisa, ii., 180.

Pigmies described by Ctesias, i., 90.

————, supposition of the ancients concerning them, i., 91.

Pisa, Church of, how set on fire, ii., 180.

Pliny discusses proper methods for preventing a return of the plague, ii., 138.

Pliny and Ælian accused of having exaggerated, i., 61.

———— names three plants endowed with magical properties, i., 62.

Poisons, Hindoo, named Powst, ii., 119.

————, trial by, ii., 123.

Polo, Marco, i., 89.

Polycritus, the ghost of, i., 252.

Polyphemus conquered by Ulysses, i., 54.

Polypi, dimensions of the, exaggerated, i., 61.

Polytheism, miracles of, exposed by the Christian religion, i., 169.

————, legends of, transformed into moral allegories, i., 215.

Pontiffs, the Roman, in their rites made use of words known only to themselves, i., 177.

Porphyrogenitus, Constantine, advice to his son, ii., 193.

———— used the Greek fire, ii., 194.

Porphyry, account of, i., 134.

————, his refutation of Chaeremon, i., 134.

Porsenna, story of, explained, ii., 156.

Posthumus, Dictator, victory gained by him, i., 57.

Potamantis, a plant, ii., 17.

Powder, offensive, ii., 135.

Prayers, miracle attributed by the Christians to the efficacy of, i., 103.

Priest, title inseparable with physician and sorcerer among the Nadoëssia, &c., ii., 94.

Priests of Phrygia and Syria threw open their sanctuaries, i., 210.

Proclus, a physician, ii., 36.

Prodigy, every thing so in the eyes of the ignorant, i., 42.

Protesilaus, the wife of, i., 266.

Proteus, account of, i., 275.

Psammenites, King of Egypt, cause of the death of, i., 71.

312

GENERAL INDEX.

THE END.

www.ingramcontent.com/pod-product-compliance
Lightning Source LLC
Chambersburg PA
CBHW031357270326
41929CB00010BA/1212